How to Get a Job in Publishing

A Really Practical Guide to Careers
in Books and Magazines

Alison Baverstock
Susannah Bowen
Steve Carey

A & C BLACK • LONDON

First published in Great Britain 2008
A & C Black Publishers Ltd
38 Soho Square, London W1D 3HB
www.acblack.com

A CIP record for this book is available from the British Library.

ISBN: 9-780-7136-8503-9

This book is produced using paper that is made from wood grown
in managed, sustainable forests. It is natural, renewable and
recyclable. The logging and manufacturing processes conform to
the environmental regulations of the country of origin.

Design by Fiona Pike, Pike Design, Winchester
Typeset by RefineCatch Ltd, Bungay, Suffolk
Printed in the United Kingdom by Cox and Wyman

y, which transformed the frumpy, dumpy
es in the early 90s, the other was called
n an 8-page fashion story called 'Here
' and upset a few vicars.
hich I loved, became a stylist of food and
hich I was hopeless, and then a commis-

haps, in the prospects for magazine jour-
her you work on a small trade magazine or
that today you can switch between maga-
h relative ease, giving you a much broader
aining and Fleet Street sneered at the soft,
s. This and the Internet have really opened
alist and somewhat limiting field.
dia, the magazine industry is more competi-
thors make clear, you have to be smart and
d and very determined to get to the top. And
– or even a slow one – is your main aim, it
lsewhere.
azine journalism is really what you want to do,
art. Get involved with your college paper. Blag
fashion shows and write a report, review an
ite an impassioned feature on global warming.
ess.
myth-debunking style of this book. Read it. Get
good luck.

Contents

Forewords

On books, by Richard Charkin, Bloomsbury Publishing

The title of this book begs a question. Why should anyone want a job in publishing? By and large it's a poorly-paid industry, not very profitable, arguably in a slow or no-growth market sector, and with many significant threats to its future prosperity and even survival. And yet and yet ... Every year the Macmillan graduate recruit scheme is oversubscribed a hundredfold; response rates to job advertisements are excellent; I receive any number of e-mails from would-be members
of our industry.

The reasons for this enthusiasm are neither consistent nor clear but these are the reasons I enjoy this business and have rarely regretted the series of events that led me to it.

1. I like the people. My database of publishing contacts is well over three thousand and there are only half a dozen people in it I would rather not meet again. The rest have been stimulating, decent, hard-working and fun.
2. I like the product. Books and magazines can be good, bad or indifferent and we've all been involved in all three categories but, however badly something sells or however badly it is reviewed every book (oh, maybe there are a few exceptions) has a redeeming feature and some intrinsic value. Compare that with, for instance, a poor-selling and badly-designed mobile phone.
3. I like the process. Publishing is not easy. Every product is different and needs individual care and attention. Prices are low. Supply chains are long. Egos can be huge. Everything is more

4. Th
   act
   Thi
   to k

When I s
of who yo
different
based on
when recru

This bool
may even di
genuinely wa
read this fro
lover presum
This is the *Wis*

On magazine
former Editor

Whenever one
Traveller, Good H
still get a little th
ping. Even after m
is something abou
that makes my hear

I've worked hard
tea and typing (badly
then of *SHE*, and mo
Style. I did stints on
going strong) and *Con*
magazines, both now

One was called *Having A Bab*
image of pregnancy magazi
Wedding Day, in which I ra
Comes The Pregnant Bride

I trained as a sub editor,
homes features, a job at w
sioning and features edito

The biggest change, pe
nalists – regardless of whe
a big consumer glossy – i
zines and newspapers wit
canvas than when I was t
mushy world of magazin
up what was once a spec

Like every field of me
tive than ever. As the au
sharp to get in, dedicate
if making a quick stash
would be wise to look

But if you know mag
it's never too early to s
a seat at the London
Almódvar movie, or w
Show you mean busir

I like the practical,
your CV sorted. And

Introduction

Over our years (many) in magazine and book publishing, each of us has heard thousands of times:

'I've always wanted to work in publishing. How did you get started?'

So we thought it was time there was a resource to guide people. And, given that no-one else had written it, we thought we'd get in there!

We've all been job applicants, employers and freelancers, in many different kinds of publishing. We've learned the hard way and we'd like to pass on the smart tips we've worked out between us over the years. We hope this book helps you in your search for your perfect job.

It's commonly said that the world is moving ever faster — and this book really was created 24/7. Around the time Alison clocked off for the day in the UK, Susannah and Steve started work in Australia. As well as being colleagues, the three of us are friends and have managed to remain so, with no fallings-out over artistic differences or editorial style (so far). The international perspective we offer (dare we use a current bit of publishing jargon and say 'boundarylessness'?) is particularly valuable these days; publishers worldwide are facing the same issues and we hope that this book will help you find a job, wherever you want to work.

We will spare you the Oscar-style tears, but there are a number of thank yous to be made. We consulted widely, and are grateful to all the following people. Some others made candid comments and preferred to remain anonymous.

Guy Allen; Amy Blower; Sarah Cassie; Richard Charkin; Averill Chase; Jane Cholmonley; Suzanne Collier; Tim Coronel; Christie Davies; Suzie Dooré; Anthony Forbes Watson; Helen Fraser; Patrick Gallagher; Travis Godfredson; Stephen Hancocks; Greg Ingham; Kristy Jacobs; Ruth Jelley; Andy Jones; Nicholas Jones; Stuart Jones;

Su Jones; Linda Kelsey; Anna Kiernan; Jenny Lee; Emma Lee-Potter; Rachel McDiarmid; Robert McKay; Natalie Meylan; Rose Michael; Margaret Mills; Julia Moffatt; Martin Neild; Charles Nettleton; Rob Pegley; Teresa Ponchard; Bridget Shine; Liz Small; Peter Smith; Sarah Townsend; Jeremy Trevathan; Paul Watt; Andrew Wilkins and Louise Wirz.

All job titles and affiliations of the people we've quoted in the book were correct at the time of writing.

Finally we would like to thank our publishers A & C Black, in particular Lisa Carden, who commissioned the work and who always sounds so cheerful; our agent Jenny Brown; and our families for ongoing support, endless listening and the provision of hot meals while we were busy writing.

Alison Baverstock, Surrey
Susannah Bowen, Melbourne
Steve Carey, Melbourne
January 2008

Part 1: Publishing
— *what's it all about?*

Chapter One
Why publishing and why you?

It took me a long time to get my first job in publishing, but someone (a publisher) said to me, 'Everyone who really wants to get in does, so just persist', which I did – and it worked.

(HELEN FRASER, MANAGING DIRECTOR, PENGUIN UK)

Since you're reading this, chances are you are seriously considering a career in publishing. Tell someone that this is your ambition and they're likely to tell you, 'But of course it's practically impossible to get into publishing, you know'. Whether or not this is true (and we explore this in more detail later), a lot of people give up before they even try. This book assumes a more robust attitude on your part: that you want to find out how the industry works, and what kind of people thrive within it, before deciding whether publishing is for you – and then if it is for you, this book will help you get the job that you want.

Why this book got written

We wrote this book to do two things: to help you decide whether you really want to work in publishing, and to help you get the job you want.

There are three of us, based in the UK and Australia – so you get three guides for the price of one! We all love the industry, have enjoyed working within it for more years than we care to remember, and want to show you why publishing makes a brilliant career. Between us we've worked in a variety of publishing houses in many different countries, and on a vast range of published products, from magazines, books and newspapers to CDs and websites, and we have consulted a wide range of people while writing this book. So what you're about to read is broad- and internationally-based, and applies across all types of publishing and cultural settings.

What this book is not

Buying this book doesn't guarantee you a job in publishing. In fact, however well you prepare, however often you read it from cover to cover, if you're not genuinely inspired by ideas, or able to take leaps of imagination and think about doing things differently from time to time, you won't enjoy working in the industry. Publishing is essentially an entrepreneurial profession; it needs people who are interested in ideas and willing to think about why and how the market will be prepared to purchase – and keep on doing so.

Publishing is a fantastic career. It's exciting, challenging and has given me the chance to interview amazing people all over the world. But it's definitely not for the faint-hearted. Working for newspapers and magazines involves long hours and being away from home – often for long spells and at very short notice. It can be highly stressful too. When I started working I was shocked to be asked to write a story in a few minutes flat in order to meet the deadline for the next edition. It was great experience though and gave me loads of material when I started writing novels. (EMMA LEE-POTTER, JOURNALIST AND NOVELIST, UK)

Having got that out of the way, here are ten good reasons to work in publishing. Read them and see whether it sounds like the industry for you.

Ten great things about working in publishing
1. You get to work with stuff you like

Magazine people love magazines. Book people love books. And, while you can admit that you love magazines when you're going for a magazine job, you should never, ever under any circumstances overdwell on your love for books when you're going for a book job (more on this later), although a genuine passion for the medium is a great starting point for any potential employee.

Of course, in the world of magazines it can be the subject matter that attracts and drives you. For the men – and they are almost all men – who work on car magazines, for example, what could be better? (Apart from the salary, that is.)

I can remember the format of almost every book I have enjoyed; I like their feel, their smell and heaviness – and I feel slightly panicky if I suddenly realise that I have time available and nothing to read. I can still remember spending my very first book token, and using it for a boxed set of Paddington Bear books. I read Hardy's *Tess of the D'Urbervilles* as a homesick sixteen-year-old, exiled to France on an exchange, and was utterly engrossed. I never throw my books away, but regard them as the most important kind of decoration – indeed the first thing I do on visiting someone's home is to look at the books on display. (ALISON)

Reading was just about all I did as a young teenager. I worked in my dad's fruit and veg shop, and he'd find a shop full of customers, with me engrossed in reading the newspaper we used to wrap stuff in. (STEVE)

Since I learned to read and write it's been the thing I do. I read while I make the bed, brush my teeth, make dinner, watch TV . . . Once I had to take a sick day from work because I couldn't seem to stop reading a novel I was hooked on (not a particularly good one, either). I'm not complete without a book, magazine or newspaper in hand. I've never been so thrilled as when I realised that by working in publishing I could spend my life legitimately surrounded by printed matter. (SUSANNAH)

To all three of us it's a huge bonus to be able to work with a product we value and respect so much. Perhaps if you work with toothpaste, hamburgers, hernias or legal contracts you can get as passionate about them as we do about magazines and books. It's just that . . . we don't see it, frankly.

2. You get to work with stuff that matters
Books stand for something, and magazines exert real influence within the industry or special interest group they serve. Most aspiring

politicians (and incidentally, eventual dictators) at some stage package their ideas between two covers rather than rely on dissemination through articles in the press or media interviews. Books displayed in the home or office have a representational value.

> The power of the printed word to me is still glamorous and magical. You put a magazine together, and then a couple of weeks later you go into the local newsagent and there it is on the shelf – wow! (STEVE)

> My father's tatty collection of 1950s' Penguins and Pelicans were a statement of his interest in ideas and a rejection of the burgeoning consumerism around him; to him they represented a more idealistic world, and ambition. I can remember clearly how as a first-year university student I self-consciously lay about the house reading Erica Jong's *Fear of Flying* during a claustrophobic family Christmas. (ALISON)

3. You get to participate in your culture

There is always more material seeking a publisher than there is space to print or bookseller space to stock it, so what finally does get published has made it through rounds and rounds of analysis and meetings. It follows that what appears tends to be the most interesting, most researched, most innovative, the most quoted, or the product of the hottest trends. This is fascinating. Publishers tend to know who are the movers and shakers in society, business, government, the charitable sector and the media; whose star is rising and whose is falling, and that is interesting information. Feeling 'current' is a satisfying reason in itself for doing what you do.

4. You're making something you're proud of – and can hold

> I feel lucky to still be working in publishing. I think it is a fast-moving industry, led by technology, full of very clever boffins and wacky

People love books and magazines – the written word on paper. An increasing number of books are now available as e-downloads, and there are as many e-book readers out there as there are MP3 players, but people still buy books and magazines – for reading in bed, in the bath, at the beach.

One of publishing's parallel industries is music – creativity harnessed and distributed on a mass scale. Music purchasing has completely changed in the last few years, from vinyl to CDs to downloads and iPods. But no-one yet has invented anything better than words on paper.

Michael Twyman, Professor of Typography and Graphic Communication at Reading University, came up with the concept of the 'eternal format'; a product that achieves a basic shape which is then tweaked and experimented with, but essentially stays the same for ever. The sandwich, the flush lavatory and the Post-It are examples. The basic codex is another.

New publishing formats come and go all the time, but they all approximate to the look and feel of the basic codex, because that is what people understand how to use, and it hasn't yet been bettered.

5. You get to meet amazing people

Publishing offers endless opportunities to meet interesting people – and this is not just confined to those working within the glitzy world of celebrity publishing but also people who are making a difference in the world, whatever they write about. Moreover, the general knowledge you pick up along the way tends to make you a real asset on a quiz team!

One of Alison's early jobs was with Macmillan's medical, scientific and technical division. Here she came across a group of doctors whose hospital received the UK's first AIDS patients, and hence were involved from the very start in firstly trying to identify, and later treat, the condition. Similarly she worked with researchers at the Royal Marsden Hospital who have since completed pioneering work in cancer treatment.

There is no other career where you can pick up a little knowledge on so many different things, and meet people from pop stars to politicians, from poets to princesses.

(MARTIN NEILD, MANAGING DIRECTOR, HODDER HEADLINE, UK)

6. You get to work with great people

A frequent comment by those who leave the publishing industry is that they miss the people. A television producer Alison met recently, through involvement on a series about books, commented afterwards on how much nicer publishing people are than television people. As with any industry, ruthlessness, naked ambition and internal politics are in evidence, and there are inevitable fallings-in and -out, but in general publishers are cooperators; eager to do a good job and get the product out on time and on budget. It's a congenial world to work in.

Although I no longer work full-time in publishing because I have family commitments and am also now developing a second career as a writer, I can honestly say that the ten years I spent in the industry as an employee were wonderful. The money isn't fantastic, but for me editing particularly was an enormously enjoyable and satisfying job, and one which I still miss. The friends I made in that time have become friends for life. As long as you are realistic about your aims and prepared to work hard, it is a brilliant industry to be in. (JULIA MOFFATT, FREELANCE EDITOR AND WRITER)

> I'm still tooling around doing bugger all except writing for various people I've met in the industry over the years. It's bloody great. (PETER SMITH)

Susannah sometimes jokes that she entered publishing because she has a literature degree and didn't want to be a teacher, so what other career options were there? Publishing is in fact full of people with literature and arts degrees, and who are interested in ideas and popular culture. We have all swapped recipes, gone on marches and had many long boozy lunches with publishing colleagues – people we enjoy spending time with.

Some take this a stage further. There are many publishing romances and relationships. And management issues of how partners working for rival organisations share information at home have in general been handled in a civilised fashion, without – as far as we are aware – any high-profile legal cases.

Others form liaisons on a more temporary basis, and there is a famous joke about the Frankfurt Book Fair which confirms this. The Frankfurt exhibition site plays host throughout the year to a series of industries; so while books dominate in early October, the week before it may be electronics and the week after machine tools. The joke is that during Book Week however, all the local prostitutes leave town because there is no need for their services – as the publishers all sleep with each other.

There is a wider point here: you should be very careful what you say; relationships are widely spread, and sympathies endure long after they are over. People in the industry tend to job-hop within publishing, rather than industry-hop, and you never know whom you are talking to.

Two adages Susannah had instilled in her by early career mentors: 'Don't dip your pen in company ink' (by someone who had!); and 'Never make an enemy in publishing'.[1]

---

[1] *Susannah broke one of these rules and kept the other (not telling)*

7. You get a flexible, long-term career

Publishing makes a very good choice for those who want a flexible career, and perhaps not to be office-based all their lives. Publishing companies are often run on the basis of slight understaffing, and there is a tradition of relying on external services and opinions (cheaper than employing them in house, full-time). It follows that you can carry on feeling useful long after you left. There are various roles that combine well with having a family, or living an itinerant lifestyle, and the industry is not as obsessed with youth as others. There is a wide understanding that you get better at publishing as more happens to you – as you have more empathy with a wider group of markets. Other industries tend to assume a much greater 'cult of presentness', which means that if you are not there you can't be part of it. It's much harder to be a freelance merchant banker than it is to be a freelance publisher.

What is more, the skills and competencies you acquire during a career in publishing are useful in a wide variety of voluntary and paid employments such as writing and editing newsletters, publicity and public relations, and managing other sorts of publications. Your experience will also give you a less socially-acceptable legacy – a life-long obsession with detail; you will be unable to read a menu in a restaurant or a programme at an event without spotting typographical errors – typos for short – or examining the production standards.

8. People think what you do is glamorous and exciting

Here's an interesting party game. How do different professions get greeted when they say what they do on social occasions?

If you're a dentist and mention that fact at a party, people tend to respond by telling you they don't like dentists. Doctors get pestered by people who want an instant diagnosis for a pain in the knee that has been troubling them but which they are too idle to investigate by making an appointment with their own doctor. Teachers get told they have long holidays; ministers of religion that it must be good to only have to work one day of the week.

Tell someone at a party that you work in publishing, and they will not wait for you to explain that it's selling high-priced monographs to academics in Japan – they immediately conjure up a mental image of you lunching with Salman Rushdie and scanning the morning post for potential bestsellers. 'That must be fascinating,' is the inevitable first response. The only downside is that the listener then tends to tell you all about the book they have in them!

The second response is often 'How did you get that job?' – make sure you refer them to this book!

9. You don't get looked down on as someone who's in it just for the money

Some wag once said, to make a small fortune in publishing, it's best to start with a big fortune.

> To stick it out in publishing you really need to love books. It's not just about reading the books, either. You need to be able to appreciate the audience and the market into which the books will be sold, and understand how and why books are sold. If you don't have a passion for the book industry, then you will only become disenchanted with the low pay and hard work.
>
> (RUTH JELLEY, COMMUNICATIONS OFFICER, SWINBURNE INTERNATIONAL)

Publishing has become vastly more professional in recent years, and salaries have risen in line with improved efficiency. Even so, it is still a very uncertain way to make your fortune. Profit margins are slim, and salaries in publishing tend to be lower than might be secured by your talents and inclinations in other professions. If you sincerely want to be rich, become a merchant banker or a lawyer. That said, most creative industries (journalism, arts marketing, working for a wine merchant) generally pay in the lower salary brackets. And many think the interesting work and congenial colleagues make up for it – *Bridget Jones's Diary* was set in a publishing house, not a pharmaceutical company.

10. You get your reading cheap

In what other industry could you buy loads of magazines and claim it as research? Working within publishing, of whatever kind, offers you the chance to buy products from other publishers at trade discount (usually at least a third off), and reading the trade press each week gives you many more ideas of what to read than you may have had before. You will probably find yourself reading more.

This can have its downside. Family and friends are often quick to find out if you can get something off for them, too, and an awareness of your special buying status does tend to mean that any books you give as presents are assumed to be discounted items, even if – as often happens to us – you pay full price through bookshops because you're not organised enough to get them ahead of time through the trade. (Susannah once swapped the latest 'in' cookbook with a dentist friend – for a filling.)

What kind of person does best in publishing?

Later sections of this book talk about the particular mental – and sometimes physical – attributes you'll need to succeed in specific parts of publishing. For now, let's talk about two main, and connected, requirements: you need to be insatiably **curious**, and **excited by new ideas**. The first gives you the material to work with; the second gives you the passion to do something with that material. Do you fit the bill?

Are you insatiably curious?

To succeed in publishing you need to be curious. Nosy might be a better word – or, even better, the Australian term: you need to be a stickybeak. You are fascinated by new markets: how and why customers buy and use their product, and why those who don't buy from them have not been tempted. You can spot trends and get excited by new marketing methods, production facilities, selling locations. You can imagine yourself subjecting your friends and family to a wide range of product ideas, and you can listen rather than just impose your own ideas or solutions.

In the magazine world, a good graphic designer is constantly absorbing trends and fashions, while a good journalist or editor is able to see a story where the rest of us see none. A new magazine idea can come from anywhere, and from anyone. All it takes is someone who is passionate about something, and believes there are others who share that passion.

Are you excited by the new?

To succeed in publishing, in any medium, you're going to have to excel at distinguishing between passing trends (which may still be profitable publishing opportunities, if you move quickly); lasting trends (more profitable, because they are enduring); and 'busted flushes' (over and no longer worth investing in).

You have to be able to spot leads – good ideas buried within unpromising submissions – and be guided by your instincts to look further. You need to combine enthusiasm with realism, be able to persuade others to follow you, but be open-minded enough to listen to negative feedback and make the right decision.

Publishing is fascinated with 'the ones that got away', ideas that were presented to a number of publishing houses but whose merits were only spotted by one, and relatively late in the day. Harry Potter, for instance, was turned down many other – and more famous – houses before being taken on by Bloomsbury. And William Golding's *Lord of the Flies* did the rounds many times before being picked up by Faber.

Based on this, there is a large and growing strand of publishing that copies what already exists. Many houses bring out their own versions of good sellers, or package their books to look like what has already been successful; witness the stream of *Da Vinci Code* look-alikes, or the different genres of fiction that can be judged on cover appearance without needing to read the blurb.

Copying can yield profits, and all creative industries work like this – artists copy each other, and journalists are more likely to believe each other (what they see in other media) than their publicity contacts. But really good publishers can spot a good idea that is fresh and turn it into something others want to own/read/access. Once an idea is up and running it can look like it was always appealing; an effective publisher can spot something in very unpromising material.

For example, Piatkus Books spotted a story on the slush pile from someone who had felt she had lived before. They engaged a ghost writer, retold the story, and the book is now the best-documented example of a previous life.[2] In other words, they were able to look beyond the poorly-drafted first manuscript to spot an idea that others would be interested in hearing more about. And the editor at Faber noticed that the first chapter of the manuscript of *Lord of the Flies* was yellow and worn, but the rest of it was untouched. She started with Chapter 2 – and discovered a classic. The book was published without the off-putting first chapter, and has gone on to sell millions.

So you think you fit the bill?

OK, you're a stickybeak and you can smell what's in the air before others do. So apart from these two nose-related qualities, what else do you need? You need to be:

Current. You're well informed and up to date. Certainly, around your subject matter you know *everything* that's going on.

Well organised. You need attention to detail, and a good memory for hanging on to what is where. Note that this doesn't need to be true of your off-duty self – just so long as you can find everything when you're at work.

[2] *Jenny Cockell,* Yesterday's Children: The Extraordinary Search for My Past Life, *1993*

Tactful. You'll be working with creatives: indeed, you may be one yourself. Any creative worth their salt will be passionate, and often that means neurotic and paranoid, about their own product, and they won't give a damn about commercial constraints or anything else that gets between them and their vision. Some writers are sweeties, and easy to deal with; some are the kind of people you could cheerfully strangle. Can you encourage the genius but work around the associated difficult personality?

> Provided your writing is good you can be as difficult as you like, but be consistent. I like to know where I am.
>
> (ANDREW FRANKLIN, MANAGING DIRECTOR, PROFILE BOOKS, ADDRESSING THE SOCIETY OF AUTHORS, UK)

Good under pressure. Publishing has an insatiable appetite for new product. So while juggling lots of new ideas is stimulating, you'll find you don't have nearly enough time or resources, and for what you're doing to be profitable it has to be out before it's anything like as good as you want it to be. So if you are a perfectionist who hates compromise and feels bitter disappointment if something is anything less than 100% perfect, publishing could kill you.

Actually this may be a little harsh. Publishers want things to be as good as they can be – the question really is, how good can they be *and* still justify their existence by making money? The debate rages on.

Thick-skinned. Everyone you know will want to be published. If you're writing for a magazine, they'll tell you exactly what needs to be done better and differently, including scathing criticism of your own work. If you have the power to commission you'll be besieged by talentless people who won't take no for an answer. If you're in marketing, you'll slave away for hours on a brochure, proofread it endlessly, proudly receive ten boxes of it, only to have ten people point out a typo on page 8.

Not overly sensitive. You'll do work for which you don't get the credit. How does that feel? Imagine, for example, you work for a magazine company and come up with a great idea for a new magazine. But the publisher decides you don't have the experience to edit it, and you see your vision distorted and, from your point of view, bastardised and prostituted. Or perhaps, even worse, your vision is taken on by someone else and turned into a glorious success, for which you get minimal credit. It can happen, and if such an experience would turn you bitter and twisted – rather than inspiring you to come up with another idea, and another, until you get to be in that chair – then think hard about potentially exposing yourself to such treatment.

There are a few things to be aware of that could otherwise take a while to work out: a) Publishing, and general publishing in particular, is tribal and inward-looking, so either be happy to play the game or work out how you can turn your lack of these attributes to your advantage; b) The book's been around for a long time and growth is sluggish, which means that you have to combine geniality with high levels of competitiveness with your colleagues to flourish; c) Publishing is about people, not books; d) Change jobs every three to five years without fail; e) Seek out the visionaries and make the effort to work for the best people – avoid drones and retreads.

(ANTHONY FORBES WATSON, FORMER MANAGING DIRECTOR OF PENGUIN UK)

Associate with knowledgeable, interesting, creative and professional people – you learn a lot and gain more job and professional satisfaction along the way. (RACHAEL MCDIARMID, JAMES BENNETT)

Conclusion

So, how does publishing sound to you now? We hope we've tested some of your assumptions and perhaps made you think about how well suited you are to it as a career.

However, it's important to remember that hardly anyone – and certainly not any of us – is completely suited in every respect to conquer the world of publishing.

Still, while researching and writing this book we became convinced that, whatever country you are working in, or kind of product you are working on, publishing requires the same personal and professional attributes. And since, increasingly, publishing is itself international, that's a good thing. If you can make it here, you'll make it anywhere.

More reading

Eberts and Gisler, *Careers for Bookworms and Other Literary Types*, Higher Education, 2002

Lines, *Careers in Publishing and Bookselling*, Kogan Page, 1994

Monti, *Career Opportunities in Magazine Publishing*, Independent Publishers Group, 2000

Aprhys, *Careers in Publishing and Bookselling*, Hale and Iremonger, 1997

Chapter Two
Where is publishing heading?

If you're serious about a career in publishing – and presumably you are, or you wouldn't be reading this – naturally you want to understand the industry and the issues it faces. Having an enthusiasm for books and/or magazines is good, but not nearly good enough.[1] To impress someone considering giving you a job, you need them to know you know this is a business, not just a nice place to work or somewhere to indulge your love of reading at someone else's expense.

Never say, 'I want to be in publishing because I love books.' Of course that is important but you need to make it very clear that you understand publishing is a profit-oriented business like any other, but its appeal is that it is a unique blend of the cultural and the commercial.

(MARTIN NEILD, MANAGING DIRECTOR, HODDER HEADLINE, UK)

It is very easy to be clouded by the romance of publishing – creative books, beautiful words, celebrity authors, swanky launches and writers' festivals – and forget that, for most companies, publishing is a business, and as such the need to make money will usually prevail over all other factors. My advice to those who are keen to enter publishing is to investigate and consider the commercial aspects and, in a sense, the realities of the industry.

(KEIRAN ROGERS, MARKETING MANAGER, HARDIE GRANT, AUSTRALIA)

---

[1] *As a general point, by the way, it's wise when you're at an interview for a book publisher to let your love of books be taken for granted. Funnily enough, the opposite is true of magazines: if you're at a magazine job interview go all out to show just how well you know your magazines*

This chapter runs through trends those within the industry are grappling with at the moment. If you find they're not the kind of thing you want to think further about, and certainly not devote your life to, then publishing is probably not for you.

If, on the other hand, the following prompts you to think you have things to say and experiences to contribute, then publishing could be just the job for you. And having something to say on each of these issues comes in very handy when the questions come thick and fast at interviews!

So, here are a dozen burning issues raging round publishing right now.

1. Is print dead?

Publishing comes from *making public*: publishers put information and entertainment into whatever format folk find it convenient to buy and use. And there have never been so many formats to choose between – the good old-fashioned book, of course, the magazine, the DVD, the CD, online delivery, TV, film . . . This is the 'Age of Also'[2]; there's no one way to present anything. The most useful attitude with which to approach all this is one of *flexible curiosity*.

Put yourself in the shoes of a publisher with a hot new property. Maybe it works best as a book – or perhaps it's a DVD or a website, a magazine or delivered online? So whereas once upon a time a passion for the printed word may have counted for something, today anyone looking at a career in publishing needs to think first of the market, and then work backwards to understand what medium or, more likely, which media best serve that market and therefore make most money for the publisher, so you can start over and do it all again.

Here's a question for you: *what is reading anyway?* You can hear people say they have 'read' something when what they mean is 'listened

---

[2] *John Merrion, Chief Executive of Merriam-Webster Inc, the US's leading dictionary publishers, speaking at the 4th International Conference of the Book, Boston, USA, October 2006.*

to it on a CD in the car', or even seen the movie. How do you 'read' a magazine? Does a quick flick count as reading, or do you need to spend a specific amount of time or read a certain proportion of it? Clearly not. And how do you quantify whether someone's 'read' a website? Our terminology is remarkably primitive.

2. Last man standing?

There's a major rush towards consolidation – of publishers, retailers, information providers and, arguably, even of authors. Bigger firms gobble up smaller ones to achieve economies of scale – not only because the prices of books and magazines are stable (or falling) and customers have masses of other options on which to spend their money, but also because companies are under increasing pressure from their shareholders to deliver bigger and bigger profits, and publishing is hardly the most profitable of industries. If you can't satisfy your shareholders with organic growth – and in a flat market that's tough to do – then the only other route is to grow by eating smaller publishers. Of course, whether this actually always results in greater profits is another question altogether . . .

And just as publishers are consolidating into fewer and fewer, bigger and bigger players, so there's another form of consolidation going on with information providers, too. Firms such as Google want to be a single port of call for customers, whatever they want. The emphasis here is more on speed of delivery for viable alternatives, rather than specific access to precisely what was requested in the first place.

Even author brands are being consolidated, with books marketed increasingly as *a particular type* of publication – recognisable by the lettering on the front (raised/foil/matt laminate), the size and format, and the cover and design. And this is true throughout the world.

3. Spirit of independence: alive and well?

But while consolidation is real and having a major impact on the world of publishing, that's not the whole story. The strong stubborn streak of independence that's always existed in publishing is still there, fighting to survive.

Here's why. The bigger the firm, the more it's vulnerable to thickening of the arteries, so that decisions take longer and longer to make and creativity loses out to bureaucracy.

Creative people (or 'creatives') find this infuriating and, given that the industry has always attracted people who are both optimistic and free-thinking, there is no shortage of independent publishing firms, or those setting up to become independents. It is within these firms that ideas often develop, new talent grows – and new publishing trends first flourish. To their intense frustration, independents often find themselves used as market research, seeing their ideas and writers swiped by companies much better resourced to do their own product development.

Where do you stand? Which end of the market would you like to be in? On the one hand, big firms offer the satisfaction of a 'name', which is nice at parties, and arguably more job security (though beware management restructuring). On the other hand, you can find yourself pretty much isolated from how the industry works as a whole.

Working for a small publisher, however, offers you the chance to learn about everything, to be much more closely involved with the successes and failures – and possibly the chance to work on your own personal passion. But then again, you'll be starved for resources, and may well find that your big successes just get ripped right off by the big boys without a please or a thank you.

4. Cash or quality?
Shareholders invest their money in a company because they believe they'll make a profit. As much as they want to produce high-quality products, if forced to choose between quality (which is expensive) and high profits, they're likely to choose the latter. Wouldn't you?

Lucky indeed is the firm that can satisfy its shareholders just through producing more and better versions of what it's already doing. Often a more aggressive approach is required, which can mean only one of three things: increased revenue, fewer costs, or a combination. Gobbling up the smaller fry certainly helps. So does cutting corners in quality, making your people do more on less (and declining editorial standards in publishing are becoming something of a hobby horse when books are reviewed). And so, too, does making deals with the devil, selling your soul and sacrificing long-cherished notions of editorial independence and integrity. So X can't write, is even more obnoxious than he's boring and has an ego bigger than Donald Trump? Who cares, so long as his book (written, of course, by someone else entirely) sells by the truckload?

Not only does this kind of thinking lead rapidly to self-loathing and cynicism, it also leads to moral hazards. Yes, moral hazards. We talk about this more later, but for now spend a minute thinking about these two examples, one from magazine publishing and one from books:

- Why not review that dreadful boat in *Boats, Blokes, Birds and Booze Monthly* when the manufacturer is your biggest advertiser?
- Why not get your celebrity chef to use a particular brand of cooking implements in his latest cheeky-chappy recipe book?

The decision you take on one of these is relatively harmless, whichever way you go. The decision you take on the other could make or break your career. Good luck . . .

5. Is this the Age of Celebrity?

Reality TV shows relentlessly feed our growing, and international, addiction to the famous, and as an industry, publishing is a dealer too. Every day there are more and more celebrity magazines and biographies, and we are just as besotted by the private lives of footballers as of royal families. What is more, we don't just want to read about these people, we also want to interact with them, through their websites and when they make public appearances.

Book publishing houses have benefited hugely from the rise of festivals, literary and other, which offer the public the chance to 'touch the hem' of those they want to know more about – and get their copy of a signed memoir. But whereas it's easy to scoff at yet another celebrity autobiography, spotting those for whom the public has a genuine appetite is a skilled job. The stakes are high and so are the risks – many of those commissioned lose money, while the few that succeed can sell tons. It's also a very unpredictable area of operation – celebrities are notoriously wayward, and their antics, or the press taking a sudden dislike to them, spell ruin for the publisher who has invested in their life story at the wrong time.

In 2006, HarperCollins announced publication of the autobiography of OJ Simpson, who was found guilty in a civil court of the 1994 murder of his wife and her friend Ronald Goldman. As it happened, this caused howls of outrage, the idea was very publicly dropped and shortly afterwards the publisher, Judith Regan, was sacked.

That's an example of getting it wrong, and in retrospect it does look horribly tacky and distasteful. But perhaps the publisher in this case was just a couple of years too early?[3] Or maybe this really was one of those rare cases where someone achieved what is often said to be impossible: underestimating the taste of the public?

6. Is the author part of the marketing department?

The role of the author is evolving rapidly. Twenty years ago the author typically wrote the book, and then pretty much left it to the publishing house to market it. Today the author must take part in the promotion of the book, not just its writing.

Some authors hate this, grumpily blaming the rise of celebrity publishing and a media more interested in gossip than good writing. There is a suspicion among writers that an author's marketability

[3] *In fact, the book was taken up for publication after all, after the Goldman family took Simpson to court and were awarded publication rights.*

(including their general attractiveness) has a disproportionate influence over whether or not they get published. (The naivety of this makes us smile. There are thousands of authors to choose between. Given two authors, one easy on the eye, talkative, outgoing and enthusiastic, and the other smelly, spotty and surly, which one would *you* go with?)

But for authors who do take the plunge and get involved with their readers and the marketing, public interest can bring a whole new sense of empowerment – and perhaps a recognition that they hold more cards in the publisher-author relationship than they realised. Many move from merely contributing to the publicity process, when asked, to playing an active role in shaping how the public sees them. As the hugely popular novelist Jodi Picoult, who is completely ignored by the reviewing press and yet regularly at the top of bestseller lists, commented: 'You can't just be an author, you have to be your own cheerleader.' Of course, an author *could* succeed without helping their book along – but they're choosing to do it with one hand tied behind their back.

7. Who owns the content?
Have you spotted the way this argument about the role of the author is going? Suddenly the author can be so much more than 'just' the writer – he or she can actually be the owner of the book, and even its publisher.

One place this debate is raging hottest is in the universities, which are setting up copyright departments to manage the intellectual property (or 'IP' as it's usually referred to) created by the individuals working for them. Academics are fighting back, arguing that they should own it themselves.

Meanwhile, their colleagues in the university marketing department are keen to fund media-friendly research that attracts newspaper coverage and promotes the university as a whole, at the expense of the 'dry' stuff. Academics don't like that much either, feeling that it's a restriction of their intellectual freedom.

What's common to both examples is that the authors are flexing their muscles, putting their power to the test.

The key issue here is *disintermediarisation*, a fundamental change in the delivery process, and it raises many crucial questions. Will authors exploit this development for their own agenda? Will they, for example, dictate the number of languages their material must be available in at the time of publication, or perhaps insist on the production of a low-price edition for markets too poor to buy?

The impact on publisher costs, and income, could be huge. The future publisher needs to be vigilant, and clear about the role they play in shaping a product for a market – and in particular to dispel the myth, popular among authors (who say it with an airy wave of the hand), that all they do is 'press a few buttons'.

8. What's the future of textbook publishing?

Nowhere is this change in the publishing landscape having more impact than in the world of textbooks. The changes are big enough to threaten their very existence.

You'd have thought that the boom in the numbers of students everywhere – the so-called *massification* of higher education – would drive the demand for textbooks, wouldn't you? Yet the vastly increased numbers have reduced the intimacy of the teaching experience (it's hard to know everyone's name in a huge class) and meant that the teacher's insistence on a particular textbook counts for less. And since students now are much more likely to be self-funding, and see themselves as consumers rather than merely absorbers of what is on offer, they're getting ever more demanding, and less and less likely to buy a textbook unless they're convinced it's necessary.

One direction that is picking up momentum is the creation of a Web-based course-specific resource, rather than expecting the students to find what they need themselves. So for some courses the book price or just the course entry price now includes an accompanying 'learning cartridge' of resources, some Web-based, some print, and often from a variety of different sources, and the whole thing attractively packaged and *available* (and hence more likely to get used).

Suddenly, you don't need a textbook. Suddenly, publishers who specialise in textbooks can't afford to eat. That's one way it could pan out, certainly. So, worldwide, academic publishers are scrambling to understand these trends, the impact they'll have on their business – and what they can do to find a business model that makes sense.

9. Booktalk

Ever since media producers realised that books and authors make for popular – and cheap – airtime, there's been a boom in booktalk on the air (the 'Richard & Judy' and 'Oprah' book clubs being the most obvious examples). And this doesn't just make cheap TV either: it drives sales. In fact, recent research indicated that *one in eight* books sold in the UK is the result of a Richard & Judy recommendation!

TV is just the most obvious aspect of all this. Literary festivals are booming and there are many initiatives to get whole communities talking about books. Chicago aimed to get the whole city reading *To Kill A Mockingbird,* and there are widespread schemes for freshmen at US universities to read the same book and discuss it as part of the initiation process. In Australia the government-supported 'Books Alive!' project promoting 'Great Reads' goes from strength to strength each year. All these create opportunities for promoting reading and selling books, and publishers have to be up to date with what's going on – and push hard to make sure it's *their* titles that get included.

10. How do you get to today's consumer?

Modern consumers are impatient, short of time, and know their rights. They want access to products they choose wherever they find it convenient to buy, and whenever that feeling strikes. Publishers need to think about how to make this happen, and a reliance on advertising or even featuring on the book review pages in the Sunday supplements and bookshops' stocking guides is not enough.

If you're a publisher, there are many different ways for you to reach your potential customer, such as through leaflets, through networking, through social sites on the Web, through e-mail campaigns and through cross-promotions with magazines and TV, to name just a few.

As tomorrow's publisher, you need to know how to exploit all these opportunities to make your next sale. Don't worry: for now, you just need to be aware that such opportunities exist!

11. Always judge a book by its cover

It's tempting to think that what really matters is what is between the covers, but instant decisions to buy or discard are based on how something looks and feels. As Oscar Wilde so wisely observed more than a century ago, you should *always* judge a book by its cover.

In fact, you already do. As a consumer you consider hundreds, perhaps thousands, of invitations to buy every single day. In a single trip to a bookshop or a newsagent you evaluate dozens and dozens of potential purchases in the blink of an eye. How can you make these judgements so fast? By how they look – by their cover, more often than not.

And publishers are often not even lucky enough to be appealing directly to their potential customer. For those selling *through* a market, for example to children or through academics to students, the game is to appeal to a parent or academic, who can be very quick to dismiss presentation as 'patronising' or 'not for them'.

One of the hardest things of all is to develop an eye that is not your own, so that you just *know* something will work for the market, even if you think it sucks. You don't have to like something yourself to have a view that it will appeal to its potential readers.

12. Publishing isn't marketing-led. It *is* marketing

When we all first got into publishing, about 450 years ago, commissioning editors (or publishers) ruled. It was publishers who found authors, publishers who commissioned titles they wanted, and publishers who told their colleagues what they had decided (usually from their offices on the prime floors of the building – a fitting metaphor). Today most firms are driven by marketing and sales people: what sells drives what is commissioned.

Debate rages about whether this means the quality of what is being produced is lowered, and whether, in the process, poorer titles are commissioned simply because the market has a taste for that. Do 'better books' get less profile, and marketing spend, than they deserve?

This is an issue on which everyone within the company you work for will have a strong view, and you need to approach it with caution. You also need to work out your own position on this. Just how important is it to you to work on titles you believe in and feel proud of? Can you sleep at night if you're actually part of the machine that is lowering standards in publishing? Or are you hard-headed about all this, and recognise that if you don't do it, someone else will? Perhaps you think readers should and will make up their own minds, and if they want what you're offering, then that's up to them?

Conclusion

So, there you are: 12 things for you to think about. If the answers are obvious to you, then we've not done a good enough job of explaining them, because these are all issues that are consuming publishers the world over. They don't know the answers, so there's no reason you'll be expected to. But at least knowing that there are questions will give you a head start.

Chapter Three
About book publishing

We wrote this book to help you get your dream job in publishing. And that innocent term 'publishing' covers a vast array of very different types of product – magazines, books, journals, e-publishing – for very different buyers in very different markets looking for very different things.

This chapter looks at those differences, and asks you some tough questions about whether you've got what it takes to be successful in each of those markets. And that's important, because to publish in a particular field you have to really identify with your customers, with their needs and wants; with your authors; and with the market itself. This is no place for dabblers!

> Publishers need to be part of the target community they seek to serve, not just a distant supplier. (ROBERT MCKAY, DIRECTOR CCH INFORMATION UK)

Different jobs for different kinds of people – what suits your style best?

It is important to keep reminding yourself that your first job and the first market you work in is highly unlikely to be the one you spend your whole career in. So, settling for expert status in just one small corner of publishing isn't the best move, since it limits your future potential. It makes much more sense to move around now, while you're early in your career and change is still a possibility. Otherwise you could find it's too late and you're stuck for good.

> It gets harder, as you become more senior, to move from one part of the industry to another, and particularly into trade publishing from another sector. It's very helpful to move from one area to another in your

So, in this chapter we're going to look at 'the big three' – trade publishing, schools publishing and higher education publishing. (You may be mildly surprised that it's worthwhile splitting schools and higher ed: we're coming to that.)

There are other markets – hundreds of others, in fact – but by taking a systematic look at these three you'll soon develop your own ability to analyse any market in similar fashion.

In each case we'll look at:

- **What's going on?** What's being published?
- **Who's the customer?** (This is more complicated than you'd think, actually) and
- **What does it take to get ahead ... ?** What it takes for you to succeed in this market

Trade publishing

This is a general term for products sold through bookshops – the 'trade' refers to the outlet through which titles reach the buying public (although, increasingly, consumers see online shopping as part of the same thing).

By the way, did you notice the use of the word 'products' back there? You may find it off-putting (we do), with its implication that books are like widgets, doobries or any other manufactured item. And that's just the point: they are. To be in publishing at all you have to drop (or at the very least be careful about) the sentimentality and the romantic swooning: this is business, and if you get it wrong you lose money for the company you're working for and pretty soon you're out on the street wondering what happened.

Besides, as we discuss elsewhere in this book (in Chapter 6 on e-publishing, for example), any publisher planning to be around for a few years is publishing in a multitude of digital formats, while continuing to publish the good old-fashioned book.

What's going on?

Trade publishing covers a huge range of different types of product, from mass-market to literary fiction, from biographies and 'how to' books to children's titles for reading on their own, to picture books for babies and everything in between. In effect, it's everything *except* everything else.

Trade sales matter to publishers because they are as close to cash in the bank as publishing gets – and that's not very. On the downside, publishers have to pay out a year or more before they see any sales revenue – to authors, copy editors, designers, printers and so on. On the upside, titles ordered ('subscribed')[1] ahead of publication by bookstores stand a strong chance of generating cash. The publisher knows with a fair degree of certainty that the titles selected will be displayed once the book is published – and so will be ready to meet the demand they plan (hope) to orchestrate at the same time.

Trade sales are the bread and butter of publishing, and publishers try to make big sales in this way to support more speculative ventures – investment in writers who are just starting out, perhaps, or the luring of an author to their list from another publisher (costly in the short term), or the setting up of a new imprint, or buying up another publisher.

And don't, by the way, think that publishers invest in new authors out of a sense of duty or public-spiritedness. They're doing it because today's brash new author is tomorrow's bread and butter. Imagine if you'd signed up JK Rowling or Stephen King. Not only would you be

---

[1] *Or 'subbed', short for 'subscribed', meaning the bookstore agrees they will stock to a certain level once the title is published*

walking about with a grin from ear to ear, you'd also have a massive cash float to go out and try and find the *next* blockbuster author.

Who's the customer?

That sounds like a daft question. *Of course* the customer is the person in the shop who's just picked up that book, carried it over to the counter and is about to fork out their hard-earned cash – as you've done for this book, and we thank you for it.

But hang on a second. There are in fact *two* customers for every book, and while their interests overlap, they are by no means identical. The book-buying punter is one of those customers, for sure. But the other is . . .

The book retailer/buyer

If you, the publisher, don't persuade the bookshop to stock your book, you'll never get the chance to wow your potential customer with that flash jacket and beautifully crafted blurb.

In fact, for trade titles the most important person in the whole world is the book buyer or retailer – the person who makes the vital decision whether their shop(s) will have your book on their shelf. Or not.

How do they make this decision? How do you persuade them to carry your title? Funnily enough, they're actually not so much concerned with the quality of the book, the intricacies of its plot or even its literary merit. All they want to know is this: *will it sell?* So you've got to persuade them to believe in your book's commercial worth. You've got to convince them that it will get enough support, through marketing and publicity, for the book-buying public to actually know it exists.

Remember, too, that the bookseller has very limited space and budget, and has to choose from the offerings of every publisher out there, not just you. Either they get a very acute sense of what jumps off the shelves in their shop, or they go out of business. They work to incredibly tight margins (perhaps a couple of per cent profitability), and that makes them very, very good indeed at spotting the good stuff. Publishers dismiss booksellers as tired cynical old dodderers who have no drive and won't take a risk to save their lives. In fact, the opposite is true: it's their lives, or at least their livelihoods, that quite literally depend upon them taking as few risks as possible.

Get yourself into a bookshop today. Look around at what's selling. Read the bestseller lists in the media avidly. Follow the emergence of new subjects as they take up more and more space in the shops. A while back, for example, the Western made a somewhat surprising revival, and you'd have to conclude from the shelves that your average punter was a creative writer with a deep interest in punctuation, worries about the environment and an obsession with bizarre and obscure trivia. There's money to be made from jumping on the bandwagon, which is why so many publishers do just that. There's even more money to be made from being there first.

My other tip is that industry experience – such as having worked in a good bookshop or volunteered for work at a writers' festival – can be more impressive than academic qualifications. It is all very well to have a degree in literature and to say how much you love books, but having worked in a bookshop actually demonstrates your passion.

(JESSICA, AUSTRALIA)

The customer

And so we come to the book buyer, the person who actually keeps this whole three-ring circus going by flexing the plastic.

Publishers have always relied on a steady bunch of regular book buyers – most of the books bought are sold to those who are frequent purchasers. These people buy wherever they see books available (in supermarkets and garage forecourts as well as in bookshops). On the back of this (or perhaps because of it) comes the accusation that publishers are happier commissioning titles they themselves like reading, for sale to their friends, which they can then discuss together. But even if this is true, this core market is getting older and, unlike previous generations, today's youngsters have lots of other calls on their time than the joy of reading a book:

> Today's under-30s – who ought to be tomorrow's hardcore book buyers – live out their lives on the playing-card screens of mobile phones, preferring to interact online with the social networks of MySpace, Flickr and Facebook. Inveterate multi-taskers, they listen to their iPods and text their friends while watching television with laptops, not books, on their knees. (MICHAEL HOLDSWORTH, *THE LONDON BOOK FAIR DAILY*, 18 APRIL 2007)

Finding new markets

Today the search is on for new markets of readers who can be persuaded to buy, and to widen the generational appeal of titles. So the trade publisher is not just trying to sell the latest batch of wares, but also to promote the habit of reading and book buying – in the hope that a new generation of buyer will arise to fund the industry in future.

Similarly, publishers are undertaking initiatives to widen participation within the industry, because without a broad range of ethnic backgrounds and lifestyles represented, we have little chance of producing the kind of books these groups want to read.

The other complication for the trade publisher is the difficulty – some might say the *impossibility* – of predicting the tastes of book buyers. Authors often speculate about what is going to be the next big thing in publishing, but some of the recent successes have been very surprising. Recent runaway successes have included a book on punctuation (*Eats, Shoots and Leaves* by Lynne Truss) and a novel for young adults about autism (*The Curious Incident of the Dog in the Night-time* by Mark Haddon). If you can honestly say you could have predicted the massive success of either of these titles, then (a) you deserve a big slap on the back for being so clever, and (b) why didn't you tell us about it? We could have made millions.

A recent competition to find a new writer on the UK TV show *Richard and Judy* offered publication as the prize. It duly produced a winner . . . and in fact the publishers sponsoring the competition considered the shortlist so strong that they decided to offer all five runners-up a contract, too. Guess which one of the six titles published was the runaway bestseller? It wasn't the 'winner', but one of the runners-up! The moral of the story is that picking winners is virtually impossible.

What does it take to get ahead in trade publishing?

In a word: curiosity. In two words: insatiable curiosity. In three words: absolutely insatiable curiosity. You need to be that unusual kind of person who spots trends and fashions way before anyone else sees them coming. In short, you have a keen nose for the spirit of the times.

What are people reading on buses, by the swimming pool on holiday? What books are the media getting all excited about? What are your friends talking about? For children's titles, watch what they choose themselves, given a completely free choice (preferably with the parent waiting outside the shop rather than helping them make their selection – which will undoubtedly influence what is taken to the cashier). Sometimes you'll find it is the jacket blurb that attracts attention, sometimes the cover blurb, at others personal recommendation. An effective trade publisher needs to be constantly curious about why people make particular choices and what they are interested in.

Ten Ways to See If You Have the Right Stuff to be a Good Trade Publisher

1. When did you last go into a bookshop? Or look through the book selection in a supermarket? How many books are for sale in your local garage? If you were looking for something specific, how long did you browse for after you had found it?
2. As well as looking at other products on offer, did you look at who else was shopping? If so, what time of day was it, and were

they the type of customers you would expect? Anyone who surprised you by being there?

3. When you are out shopping for groceries and waiting in the queue to pay, do you habitually look into other people's trollies to see what they are buying? Does this prompt a daydream about what kind of lives they lead?

4. What is your partner/best friend/parent reading now?

5. When you use public transport (and you should[2]), what's the book you see being read most?

6. When you drive, do you listen to talk radio and commercial/popular stations to find out what people are talking about?

7. Do second-hand book stalls at your local fundraising sale (and you need to be there too) tell you anything about which titles people bought but no longer want to live with? Why is this? Which non-book stalls are the most popular?

8. How much do you interact with popular media: news programmes that are targeted at different groups during the day, quiz and magazine programmes, chat shows and children's media?

9. What about newspapers – do you read a wide range or stick to those that confirm your own opinions?

10. How do you find out things that you consider news?

You can tell of course what the 'right' answers to these questions are. It's not something you can fake, and although you can sharpen your instincts and work on them, if they're not there in the first place you can't grow them.

---

[2] *This isn't a moral point – well, actually it is – but more importantly it's a commercial one. The more you hang around with people who could be your customers, the more you'll know about what they want*

The Seven Habits of Highly Effective Trade Publishers[3]

1. **Spot movers and shakers,** who are not necessarily writing books at the moment. Publishers often have to find not only the idea, but also have to spot the potential writer – and the person they settle on may not even be thinking of writing a book. Ideas for people to commission may come from almost anywhere: you may hear them on the radio, or spot something else they have written. If you notice a magazine article that generates a lot of hotly argued letters, for example, you could well be looking at a book in the making.

2. **Organise.** A strong ability to remember names, contact details – and where you noted them.

3. **Sharpen your research skills** – to explore and explain the trends you spot and the hunches you develop.

4. **Empathise.** Develop a genuine interest in other people and an ability to relate to them – the kind of interpersonal skills that encourage people to talk to you.

5. **Question everything** – and ask open-ended questions (the kind that encourage the other party to talk *to* you rather than just listen).

6. **Ditch the arrogance.** A willingness to listen to what other people are interested in and hence might want to read/read about rather than an assumption that everyone should be reading the books you enjoy/consider life-changing.

7. **Be bold** when explaining your preferences to your colleagues and able to persuade them around to your point of view. Balancing this one and (6) is every bit as difficult as you'd imagine.

---

[3] *We're paraphrasing here and below the famous business bestseller* The Seven Habits of Highly Effective People, *by Stephen Covey*

Schools publishing

Imagine a school without textbooks. You can't – well, we can't either. So, right away you have a ready-made market. Even better, in the developed world, education is compulsory, so not only is there a ready-made market, there's a massive one.[4] Throw in a need to keep revising these textbooks to stay up to date with new knowledge and educational trends (or, the cynical would argue, a need to keep updating these textbooks so that the publishers can make millions) and you can see why schools publishing is such big business.

What's going on?

Lots. Schools publishers produce resources for schools and teachers:

- Courses and textbooks
- Assessment and diagnostic materials
- Resources on educational theory, practice and implementation strategy for teachers
- Computer software, DVDs, audiotapes and much more

Unlike trade publishing, where publishers need to make decisions about what they think people might be interested in, educational publishing is very curriculum-focused – so topics and approaches are often predefined, and the variation between books competing for the same audience is much more narrow. So, while there's a lot to love about this market, it's also extremely competitive and cut-throat. This is no market for the faint-hearted.

Who's the customer?

Just as with trade publishing where you have to convince not only the end-user but the book buyer, so too with educational publishing you have to consider not only the kids who'll be using the books, but

[4] *In the UK, that is. In Australia, with multiple state educational curricula, schools publishers have more (and more fragmented, and smaller) markets to serve*

their teachers, their parents and, quite possibly, the government (in the shape of the Education Department), too.

Teachers are a group of people that are easy to identify and reach through marketing. They can be identified by where they work, and by the look of tension and frustration on their faces. You can reach them very easily with an e-mailing list.

Attitudinally, too, they can be grouped. There have been huge changes in the management of teaching in schools and colleges and most of these changes are in operation internationally. These have included more rigorous checking of what is being delivered through the curriculum, how it is taught – with strict parameters specifying what happens when – and an additional range of measures to cover what teachers can and can't do in the course of their professional lives. As a result, they are time-pressured, on the receiving end of many newly-developed government initiatives (not all of which have been, how shall we say, fully thought out), and frequently suspect that those advocating and implementing change do not understand the day-to-day realities of being in a classroom.

If only it were that easy. In fact, selling resources to schools is a horrendously complicated issue, as so many people tend to be involved in buying decisions. Teachers are natural collaborators and, while it may be the classroom teacher who wishes to use materials by a different publisher, the decision will have to be discussed with the head of department, the head teacher/principal, agreed with those who also teach from time to time, and it will usually be the school administrator who places the order. And all that is assuming, of course, that you've already got past the local education department.

What does it take to get ahead in schools publishing?

- It sounds obvious, but you really do, quite genuinely, have to be **interested in education**, and preferably even like teachers. A background as a teacher is immensely useful, of course, but not essential. What is essential is an understanding that teaching is a profession evolving all the time; an attitude that it will have changed little since you were last in full-time education (whether as pupil or teacher) is definitely not helpful.

- An understanding that **teaching is a profession** and that the best resources are developed through a clear grasp of teaching dilemmas and practicalities.
- An ability to **isolate important initiatives** from surrounding discussion. Proposed and even announced changes get shelved, while others get the green light and become immensely important. If you are able to predict which is which, you'll save yourself lots of time and your company lots of false starts (which means money).

The Seven Habits of Highly Effective Schools Publishers

1. **Befriend teachers.** Bribe or breed children of school age you can talk to – and do so on a regular basis. You absolutely *have* to be swimming in this water to succeed.
2. **Spread those contacts** as widely as possible; you need an awareness of lots of different educational delivery mechanisms, not just those you have chosen/experienced yourself.
3. **Think laterally.** A book may not be the most logical format. How will your material be used in the classroom? What kind of additional support materials do teachers need in order to get the most out of your material?
4. **Develop an eye for detail,** and in particular an ability to master educational buzzwords (and spot which ones are falling out of use or sound dated). Educationalists thrive on jargon and to be taken seriously you need to be able to get it right, too.
5. **Fight your corner.** If you work for an educational division that is part of a larger organisation, your in-house reputation may be dull/worthy; it's easy to brand educational publishing as less sexy than trade publishing. And, frankly, it is. But educational markets are here to stay, teachers will always need resources, and by coming up with the right materials you have access to

future generations, at the time of their maximum openness to receiving marketing messages. Educational publishers of the world, stand up and be counted!

6. **Be a political animal.** With more and more educational initiatives driven by central government, within financial/political objectives and spending plans, educational publishers need to be vigilant and good at spotting the long-term consequences of what is being proposed. They need to be effective negotiators, who can represent the industry position and the educational consequences – without attracting accusations of pure devotion to their own profits.

7. **Acquire good communication skills.** Teachers feel patronised by the rest of society, and they feel this way because they are, in fact, patronised by the rest of society. Stupidly, many people assume teachers only work during the school day and get long holidays. You must be joking. With all the monitoring strategies in place these days, teaching is immensely labour-intensive; lesson preparation and marking extend far beyond the school day. This leaves them little time or patience for fluffy, vague or ill-considered communication. You have to sell hard and fast just to get their attention, let alone win their business.

Higher education publishing

Those teaching at universities and colleges need teaching resources, too, to reinforce the material delivered through lectures, and to support independent learning, assignments and preparation for exams.

What's going on?

This market needs:

- **Textbooks** to support courses
- **Upper level academic titles** for more detailed exploration of specific topics, and increasingly
- **Summary and revision guides** to help prepare for exams (and which are often bought as a short cut instead of textbooks)

To support all these materials, the market has developed a vast array of additional items that offer 'added value' – websites (different ones for students and academics); resources for the lecturer, such as crib sheets that help them teach the textbook, and question banks that save them having to make up their own exam questions; free downloadable resources; competitions to enter for cash prizes/ enhancement of the organisation's reputation; suggestions for assignments and accompanying marking guidelines.

This market is heavily and increasingly into online delivery. Academics were one of the first professions to access information via e-mail (they all got free early access through their universities), and their learning resource centres (what used to be called libraries) make as much information as possible available online through searchable resources, because that is how students like to access it.

Who's the customer?

Lecturers expect free copies of textbooks, on the grounds that they can recommend them to those who are taking their classes. Class sizes are getting bigger all the time, and in theory their recommendation should result in a sizeable order. In practice, however, students are very short of money; they have to fund their studies and lifestyles, and most emerge with substantial debts. Book buying can be very low down their priority list.

The most 'wired-up' generation there is, students have got used to Amazon-style search and delivery speed for other commodities they need, and expect the same standards from libraries and publishers. In fact, such is the demand for specific information, and so great the concern that students are accessing material which is correct as well as quickly available, that many universities are moving to the production of a standard 'cartridge' for courses, culling chapters from a variety of different publications (with permission from the various original publishers).

Given the various pressures on them, many students are also seemingly just trying to get through – and there is less inclination to read well or widely around a subject. With vastly increased class sizes, and more assessment through group-based assignments, individual contributions can be hidden. Librarians seek to stock what their users want, and don't want to tie up capital in resources no-one uses.

For printed products produced for this market, it is vital that they both look appealing and are sensitively priced as students will find every reason *not* to buy them (while expenditure on phones and beer is essential, of course).

What does it take to get ahead in higher education publishing?

- **An understanding of the nitty-gritty details** of how teaching in your allocated subject area works, and what makes good resources – whether it's sociology, biology, economics or physics; whether you're interested and have technical knowledge of the subjects or not. A degree[5] counts for a lot here, not least because it means you've got a great understanding of how academic institutions function, and also because you've seen enough of academics to realise that for all their vagueness and blather, underneath it all, they're nearly as human as the rest of us.
- **An understanding of the new delivery patterns** for academic learning. You'll hear the older people talking about the 'good old days' and mixing up their jargon in most amusing fashion. That's where they're looking to you, as someone who 'gets' all this stuff.
- **A nose for opportunities** in this furiously evolving market, such as courses that are growing in popularity; delivery mechanisms that suit your existing product range – for instance, cross-curricular materials that meet the needs of several courses. The truth of the matter is, no-one knows where all this is going, and if you can develop even a better-than-average instinct for reading the runes, you'll rapidly develop a reputation as a guru.

[5] *Not necessarily in the subjects you publish in, by the way – any old degree does the trick*

- A genuine interest in **delivery mechanisms** (books, magazines or websites), supported learning environments and the student mentality.

The Nine Habits of Highly Effective Higher Education Publishers

On top of the seven highly effective habits of schools publishers (*see above*), you'll need another couple of tools in your kit box:

8. **'Instant expert' skills.** Given the specific nature of higher education, few publishers find themselves working on an area they know or understand. So you need to establish your credentials pretty well instantly. In your favour, it's true that a model of academic delivery can be adapted from one discipline to another. Following on from that, you need to be actively interested in the resources you are marketing, and the people you are selling to. It will probably not occur to academics that someone not qualified in the subject could possibly be employed, so the best advice is to keep your mouth shut until you feel you can say something useful.

How did I get my first job in publishing? I wrote to all the publishers I could find in the *Writers' and Artists' Yearbook*, asking for a job. I think I got two replies, one at Fontana, and was interviewed by Mark Collins, which I didn't get, and one as Science editor at George Harrap and Co, which I did. £1,200 per annum, looking after anything to do with science – schools, universities and general. I suspect I got the job because I was the only candidate with a degree in science – or perhaps the only candidate.

(RICHARD CHARKIN, BLOOMSBURY PUBLISHING)

9. **Be a good mixer.** Academics can be quite isolated; the profession these days is fiercely competitive and there are huge bureaucratic responsibilities to juggle as well as teaching and

> researching. And having a good research record is vital; both their department's and their own research funding depend on it.

Worse, they're often in direct competition with their colleagues, which certainly doesn't help. The result can be an unhappy working environment – and one from which you as a publisher can provide a very welcome relief. In fact, you'll need to develop some pretty sharp techniques for getting away from them without causing offence. It is rumoured that several higher education publishers have in fact been found dead of starvation in the offices of academics, who were still chuntering away oblivious.

Conclusion

In this chapter we've looked at just three areas of publishing – trade, schools and higher education, in case you weren't paying attention. There are, of course, many, many more. Wherever you find a bunch of like-minded consumers hanging out together, whether in a physical or virtual space, you'll find publishing companies anticipating and serving their needs. Sometimes they're subsets of bigger firms, and sometimes they are highly specific niche firms with a very limited area of operation. So, to take just three examples from among hundreds, there are publishers making entire businesses out of servicing:

- The business community
  - legal commentary for lawyers
  - advice on the latest financial regulations and how to present the information that is required for accountants
- Doctors and dentists
  - illustrated manuals on how to carry out the latest procedures
  - 'how to' guides on running a practice
- University academics, with their need for highly complex and theoretical materials – often provided by specialist university presses

Pretty much everything we've said in this chapter is relevant to whatever group you're publishing for. The bottom line? You must be fascinated by what fascinates them, and desperately obsessed with coming up with new ways to serve their needs now and in the future. Above all, you need to be flexible, to listen to their buying signals rather than impose your own. That show-stopping, epoch-defining, last-word-in-completeness book you had in mind may in fact be most usefully published for them as an e-newsletter with supporting website!

More reading

Clark, *Inside Book Publishing*, Routledge, 2000

Independent Publishers Committee, *An Introduction to Australian Book Publishing*, 2005

Chapter Four
About journal publishing

Journal publishing is a far less well known part of publishing than any we looked at in the previous chapter. Yet, arguably, it's at least as important. In fact, without it, whole areas of academic discipline – from medical and scientific research to philosophy and literary theory – would grind to a halt.

Publishers who produce journals perform a vital function in the academic world. They are responsible for bringing together and making available the best academic research, so that scholars can make known their own findings and discover what else is going on in their field. So specialised and so important is journal publishing that we've dedicated a whole chapter to it.

It's a curious beast, your journal – half book and half magazine. It's also dramatically challenged by the forces of economics: there are too many journals and too few readers; the cost of producing them is too high; technology, in the form of electronic publishing, is rapidly swamping the traditional 'dead wood' (paper) model.

What's going on?

Periodicals are generally published regularly on a subscription basis payable in advance, and are despatched directly by the publisher to the subscriber (even if the sale is made through a third-party subscription agent). A **serial** is usually published at irregular intervals (once a year or less frequently), is invoiced at the time of publication and is warehoused like a book by the supplier before sale. The term 'journals' is commonly used to refer to both.

Being published in peer-reviewed journals is an essential part of the system of progression for academic and scientific careers. The journals serve as the bush telegraph for innovations, ideas, the reporting of important research and the charting of both individual and organisational effectiveness.

Individuals, or teams working together, submit their work as an article (which is still referred to as a 'paper') for possible publication, and these are read for quality and relevance to the journal for which they have been proposed, and then a decision is made on which to include within the next edition. The overall journal editor may then write a foreword to the selection made, drawing the reader's attention to specific items of interest, or suggesting that the debate be continued in a particular direction. Sometimes a complete edition of a journal may consist of the proceedings of a conference, with all those who presented a paper asked to contribute to the journal that formally records what happened, perhaps with the addition of the edited questions and answers at the end of sessions.

- Some journals are started and managed by publishers.
- Some are run by publishers on behalf of professional societies and organisations.
- Some societies run their own journals, and while this means they keep any associated profits (from subscriptions and advertising), managing a journal is an immensely time-consuming process and arguably better organised by those who are experts and handle a range of other titles (ie professional publishers). Such society-run journals can make an attractive takeover option for publishers looking to expand, and a great option for people wanting to get a foothold in publishing – getting a job there may not be as competitive, and you can get some excellent experience before moving on. (Best not mention that's your plan in the job interview!)

Journals may be produced electronically or in printed format, sometimes both. Long term, it looks virtually inevitable that the printed journal will become extinct – not only because it is so much more expensive to produce and because readers are so scarce, but also because an electronically published journal can be accessed by scholars throughout the world without needing to take a trip to the library. Still, strong preferences for print within some markets (notably the communities involved in law and taxation) mean this will probably be a long time coming.

Who are the customers?

Customers for journals are, in the main, professionals involved in the relevant discipline, academics and libraries, although as the resources themselves become more expensive, the likelihood of individuals having their own subscription is diminishing. It is much more likely that they will subscribe through their corporation or library and be able to access it from their desk.

This creates a sticky issue. Journal publishers increasingly bundle together different journals as part of an offer price to organisations and libraries, and while this represents a considerable saving on the cost of subscribing to individual titles, it also means they end up paying for, and managing, lots of material they didn't want. Budgets are limited, and there is increasing resentment against what are perceived to be exploitative publishers.

Deep down, many librarians assume that they are financially supporting the academic reward system. Academics who publish papers gain research points (and hence funding) for their institutions, and promotion for themselves; founding or editing a journal offers similar profile advantages. And nor is each paper necessarily completely different from everything else that appears; in recent years the 'salami effect' of reporting research has been widely commented on: slicing the reporting of research thinly and publishing in a variety of different journals so that the number of publications goes up (and points win prizes). Librarians end up funding this out of ever-diminishing budgets. This is a very real concern when resources are already over-stretched – and a major problem for journal publishing.

What does it take to get ahead in journal publishing?

- **Instant expertise.** Journal publishing staff need to know about the areas covered by their publications. However, given that a far higher number of arts students than scientists come into publishing, it is unlikely that those allocated to the journal division will have a specialist understanding of the titles they work on. Even so, it's vital that you at least *try* to look as if you do. It probably will not occur to the market to think you are not involved. This means that if you go to meetings you must talk knowledgeably, spotting areas of the subject that might form a journal of their own.

> I had a friend keen to get into publishing. She started out as a consultant editor for a small medical journal – the only employee, working three days a week. The specialist topic of this journal was, ahem, sexually transmitted diseases. When I rang her at work, she would answer with a chirpy 'Hello, Venereology?' (SUSANNAH)

This makes journals an excellent place to get started in publishing if you've completed a science or business degree or have experience in those areas. It's a great opportunity for you to use your specialist expertise and knowledge to launch yourself and then slowly wiggle your career across to the (in your view) far sexier areas of trade publishing that really float your boat. Or indeed, find that you love science journal publishing so much that you're there to stay!

- **Commitment.** Subscriptions can be long term (on average seven years) and staff who give their time to a journal on a voluntary basis (the editor may receive an honorarium, but most of the board will only receive expenses) want to see the same faces from the publishing house – they like continuity in their contacts. A longer-term perspective is also enhanced by the increased understanding that journal publishers build up of their market. Whereas most forms of publishing tend to be one-offs, with a journal campaign you get the chance to feed what you learnt from one campaign into the next. And being able to demonstrate your increasing effectiveness in penetrating a market offers the chance to measure your profit: rates of pay are in general higher in journals than in other areas of book publishing, and are perhaps on a par with salaries in magazines (which is not entirely surprising, since they are magazines, of a specialist kind).

A word on timeliness

Journals publish to a strict and immovable timetable: the dates by which articles must be approved, changes submitted and signed off are all advertised long in advance, and you must be outstanding at both encouraging others to stick to them, and keeping within them yourself. When you are more familiar with the area for which you are publishing you need to look further ahead, spotting the opportunities for special issues, anniversary issues, or those timed to coincide with conferences.

There is a range of meetings at which contributors, editors and others involved (often those trying to sell to the market) get together, most usually at the annual conference. The journal's publishers need to be there too.

The Seven Habits of Highly Effective Journal Publishers

1. **Network** like crazy, and remember the names and faces of those you meet at conferences. (Chapter 13 is about networking: swallow it whole.) In particular, work on your memory. A good memory, backed up by meticulous record-keeping, will reap dividends – so you know, for example, which approach to which society producing which journal did or did not work. If you get into the habit of making notes and take the trouble to remember names and faces, you'll go far.
2. **Think strategically, act tactically.** You need to understand and think hard about the market you're operating in, your

publishing house's stake within it and the role the journal(s) you are working on perform. The key to journal publishing is opportunism, the ability to build upon your presence within the market to launch more journals and/or make your existing ones more and more a part of the subject rather than a feeder to it. The ability to spot new publishing opportunities, or new commercial opportunities within existing ones, is fairly rare, and consequently very valuable.

3. **Be a political animal.** Because of its high degree of specialisation, journal publishing attracts contributions from both geniuses and self-promoting also-rans, and the ability to spot the difference is critical. All professions have their rising (or aspiring) stars who cultivate eccentricities to get noticed (bow ties, being late for everything/entering with style, unusual jewellery or clothes, voting Tory), and the publisher's job is to distinguish the genuinely talented from the attention-seekers.

4. Develop a **ferocious eye for detail.** You're dealing with immensely complicated and technical material, which you probably don't even begin to understand. Getting it 100% right is hard, thankless work – no-one's ever going to congratulate you on getting a fiendishly complex mathematical formula right, for example, however many you clock up. Get one wrong, however, and you'll never hear the last of it.

5. **Have a thick skin,** for the above reason.

6. **Be tactful.** Those who are submitting papers are in general not paid for their contributions; they have to juggle the time to write them with their other personal and work responsibilities. Coaxing out the material you are expecting, by the agreed deadline, requires tact, diplomacy and the patience of a saint.

7. Finally, **commercial nous.** An understanding of financial realities and the ability to read a balance sheet are useful to journal publishers, who must remain conscious of their usefulness to the publisher they are part of. You need to be

ever mindful of the benefits your journals operation offers to the publishing house's overall profitability – many journal programmes form a huge and enduring part of the house's overall income. Even more useful, it is in general a stable and recurring income, as subscribers are more likely to continue taking the journal as long as it is professionally useful to them – or until their librarian suggests it's no longer economically viable to subscribe.

Conclusion

Like any area of publishing, journal publishing is not for everyone. However, it's been the springboard for many a successful and profitable publishing career. It pays pretty well. You're dealing with people passionate about their subject who genuinely need the information you're publishing. For those who do it, journal publishing can be every bit as rewarding and intellectually stimulating as any other area of publishing.

Chapter Five
About magazine publishing

If your ideas about life on a magazine come from *Ugly Betty*, *The Devil Wears Prada* or *Just Shoot Me*, think again. Just as in every American movie people seem to be able to afford multi-million-dollar houses and drive hulking great SUVs despite being on the minimum wage, so it is with *Just Shoot Me*. A huge staff and hardly any work is hardly representative of the real world.

Yes, the very biggest magazines *do* have substantial resources and, yes, there are even one or two superstar editors with giant budgets and bigger egos. But to imagine that's Magazine World as a whole is as misconceived as to imagine that life for *everyone* in the music biz is like Beyoncé's, or every footballer's life is like David Beckham's. There is, as his fans like to insist, only one David Beckham.

And in fact it's pretty obvious when you think about it why *The Devil Wears Prada* isn't a representation of reality – it's not trying to be. Its purpose is to entertain and amaze: it's not a documentary. (Actually, while we're at it, even a documentary wouldn't tell you what day-to-day, boring, humdrum reality is like, for the fairly basic, boring, humdrum reason that no-one would watch it except the people involved and their mums.)

So, what *is* life in Magazine World like? Here are five truths. They're mostly based on the editorial side of things, because that's where magazines are most distinctive – advertising sales, on the other hand, is pretty much like sales in any other area.

1. It's a money-making venture

This is Number One for a reason: we can't stress it enough. First and foremost, magazines are there to make money for their owners. For some people, this discovery is just like biting lustily into an apple and finding, not even a maggot – but half a one. The disgust and disillusionment is palpable. The fortunate ones, perhaps like you, find this out by being told about it long before they ever get to experience it for themselves.

Yet even as this book was being put together, one of the world's richest men, Paul Getty, was looking for a buyer for *Wisden* and *Cricket Monthly*. In Australia, the brave two-year-old, left-leaning online magazine *New Matilda* was being sold for a dollar. Admittedly it was being bought as a rich man's enthusiasm, but your authors wonder how long he'll be content to watch his money dribbling away in hundreds of thousands. If he can't see the day his new toy will start to pay its own way, he's likely to tire of it pretty fast.

You won't be compromising, or at least not in the way you're probably expecting (see item 4 below), which is an understandably common misconception. But you will certainly be required to contribute towards making the magazine you're working on profitable – and that means understanding the needs of your advertisers as much as those of your readers. Doing so while maintaining your integrity takes some skill, political savvy and the ability to tell the difference between a battle and a war. Anyway, more about that later. Short version? If being in business (and working on a magazine is being in business) makes you queasy, best look elsewhere: you won't like it. You really, *really* won't like it and had best head off in a different direction, rather than find out the hard way. Magazines are not for you.

2. It's fantastic, fantastic fun

OK, can we talk? Has everyone who thought magazines were about something More Noble Than Money flounced off in pious, self-satisfied disgust? Good. Because just as true as that is this: working on a magazine can be every bit as creative, exhilarating, exciting and just sheer bloody *fun* as you can imagine – and maybe more. The sheer excitement of seeing *your* story on the newsagent's shelves never goes away. In fact, you'll be delighted to discover, the pleasure gets deeper, though perhaps quieter.

If you're genuinely thrilled by seeing your words in print (as we are), if you're bursting with enthusiasm for your subject matter (as we are), and if you're overflowing with passion for communicating that enthusiasm – then you've found your base: welcome to Magazine World! You've found home. Why? Because:

- Magazines are **interactive** – what good magazine doesn't have a vibrant, scintillating 'letters' (even though most are sent by e-mail these days) page? There's an intimacy about magazines between author and reader that books simply cannot match. It's a dialogue, not a monologue.
- Magazines are **responsive** – there's a lag (perhaps about six months or so) while the readers catch up with what you're doing. But if you have something they want, and you're serving it up to them, they'll let you know about it in their droves and suddenly you have a raging success on your hands. Admittedly the opposite is true, too: they'll vote with their feet, right out of the newsagent's.
- Magazines are **fast** – what you write today can be on the shelves, beautifully packaged and illustrated, in a matter of weeks, while you can still remember how you felt when you wrote it, and your editor will get letters or e-mails within days. You can float ideas, get them adopted and get them implemented in a gratifyingly short time.

3. It's fast-moving

Steve started his first job on magazines in September and was an editor by the following July and a publisher within another 24 months. If he can do it, so can you. He was fortunate in working for a particularly fast-growing, vibrant business – but such stories are by no means unprecedented. You can make your mark fast in Magazine World, not least because the product cycle itself is so fast

A magazine can go from thought to newsstand in a matter of months – and, admittedly, go from newsstand to history even faster.

Every year there are thousands of magazines launched around the place, and every year it gets cheaper and easier to do.

In fact, you should think about launching your own magazine. Seriously, why not? Not now, perhaps, but down the road it's certainly an opportunity. Great magazine genius Felix Dennis, one of the most successful and weirdest of proprietors, often told his employees that if they were any bloody good they'd be off doing their own bloody thing instead of bloody working for him. (He may not have said 'bloody'.) Put that thought in there somewhere and carry it around. If you don't do it, then sure as anything one or more of your colleagues and co-workers will, and almost certainly they'll be less talented and smart than you. So, why them and not you?

4. Magazines are like family

We're a social species and work best as a group, and a magazine resembles a group of friends or, perhaps, a family (ie lots of rows and no sex). A typical magazine has an editor, who looks after the whole thing, and an art editor or art director, who puts together the look. Pretty much they're like mum and dad, and pretty much, working on a magazine is like being one of the kids. At first you're a baby, and everyone looks after you and shows you round. Then you're the teenager, with an urgent desire to make your own impression on the world. Then you outgrow the magazine, and fall out with mum and dad, and leave home – or find a way of staying without everyone killing each other.

Whether this is a dysfunctional family or a harmonious one depends to a large extent on the editor's ability to get everyone to pull together. If you're very lucky you'll have an editor who is teacher, mentor, protector and boss. If you're very unlucky, you may find you have an editor who is a small-minded tyrant who hates to share glory or do work, who has as much loyalty as a cockroach and will sacrifice you without a moment's regret if it suits. Most editors, of course, fall somewhere between the two extremes.

It's not rare for the happiness in your working day to be determined by your boss. But here, in Magazine World, you're part of a small, tight team and your boss has a particularly powerful influence on your career, at least while you're on *this* particular magazine. If it's a good experience, savour and celebrate it; if it's not, grit your teeth and remind yourself it's not forever. It'll just feel like it.

Among my duties were acting as a receptionist, dealing with the switchboard and picture files, and delivering complimentary copies around Fleet Street on Thursday mornings, before the magazine formally came out on Fridays. I also typed up handwritten contributions. Quite often my job was simply to keep people at bay, as the all-women editorial staff were really quite eccentric, sometimes even hanging out their underwear on a little line in the corner – after pre-publication all-nighters, I suppose. They were all on edge at such times and I often got shouted at, and suffered greatly from all the smoke in the air. But soon I was having to pitch in and help with the subbing and do mock-ups for the little booklets brought out by the magazine. I saw a younger member of the team leave to work on the fashion pages of a big daily, and realised that this was a way into journalism at a more exciting level, and it was obviously a valuable experience for publishing too.

(DR JACKIE BANERJEE, ON HER FIRST JOB WHILE WORKING ON MAGAZINES – SHE EVENTUALLY OPTED FOR A CAREER AS AN ACADEMIC)

5. Editorial integrity makes good sense

Your proprietor or, more likely, editor, calls you into his magnificently opulent office and lights a cigar. 'Look sonny/darling,' he'll drawl, scratching himself in a most unseemly manner, 'The Nitwits Company is our biggest advertiser, and we don't want to go upsetting them, now do we? So perhaps we can give them a good review and not say anything about that camera they make that keeps exploding and blinding people. Am I right? You know I am. Now run along and let's not have to have another chat later. Close the door on your way out.'

Well, perhaps. If anyone really ran their magazine like that, readers would sniff it a mile off pretty quick and drop the mag shortly thereafter. Life isn't quite like that.

Instead, here's a real-life scenario. A very, very big car advertiser books a whole heap of advertising in a publisher's magazines – and, much more importantly, across the publisher's TV channel, which is in fact where 90% of the money is spent. As part of the deal, the advertiser demands lots of things (like slots in the breaks of the biggest shows), and, oh yes, nearly forgot, right down the bottom, almost as an afterthought, it demands a front cover for its next launch on one of the publisher's car magazines.

Now it's not as if this manufacturer's latest launch isn't one of the biggest of the year, and in fact it has a reputation as a maker of pretty good cars. So why did the editor feel compelled to resign? Think about it for a few minutes – we'll come back to this later.

Editorial integrity in magazines is often more subtle than that in newspapers and on TV news, where it's pretty obvious what you should do. If a newspaper proprietor you're working for doesn't want you to report that the leader of his favourite political party beats her children with a heavy rolling pin, you can easily see the threat to the public's right to know. Whether you pan the latest toaster that is advertised in the same edition of the magazine you're working on, however, is less a moral issue than a *commercial* one.

What do we mean? Well, short term you'll make more money if you bury the bad news and don't trash your advertisers' products, because your advertisers won't flounce off in disgust and will continue to advertise. Over time, however, your readers will start to notice how you're a massive fan of everything that Nitwits & Sons makes, while at home they've a pile of melted toasters and kettles that make the water taste funny. Once the word gets around you're a prostitute, it's very hard to get your good reputation back. So longer term, your magazine will suffer and your proprietor will find himself buying cheaper cigars.

Here are three little questions that you may like to think about now, rather than when they crop up at work . . .

a) Suppose you're working on a gossip mag and your proprietor's daughter appears topless on the beach. Do you use the pic?
b) You said no? Good on you. Try this. Suppose you're working on a lads' mag and you have the choice between two bikini pictures: one of Girl A, and another of Girl B. Girl A is married to the son of your proprietor's biggest enemy. Does this influence your choice?
c) You said no, because you're better than that. Now, you find out that Girl B is married to the son of the proprietor. Does this influence your choice?

(By the way, your first and natural reaction may well be to say that you wouldn't work on a lads' mag anyway, and certainly not one that prints photos of young women topless on the beach. Would you, though, work for a company that profited from such grubby activity? If not, you'll soon find your scope for potential employers is greatly reduced: most of them have their grubby department.)

Issues of editorial integrity are difficult, and can be tangled. Work hard to do the right thing, think hard about the choices you're asked to make – and don't be too quick to condemn others until you've stood up for yourself and refused to do something you believe to be wrong. A principle is not a principle until it's cost you something.

The Mystery of the Resigning Editor

So, why did our car magazine editor feel he had to resign? (See above.) Two reasons, in fact: one commercial, immediate and largely irrelevant; and one longer-term – and also commercial, and hugely, massively relevant.

The short-term reason is that the car in question was perfectly fine for its market, but that market was not the one the magazine in question serves. Putting a safe, value-for-money family car on the front of a boy-racer magazine is commercial suicide. Magazines are highly sensitive to what's on the cover, which can make a massive difference to sales.

(The chick equivalent, by the way, is putting a model entirely dressed in Marks & Spencer or (in Australia) Sussan on the cover of *Vogue*.)

The second, longer-term reason is that once the word gets round that your front cover is up for sale, it's going to become next to impossible to make your own decision as to what goes on it. If the competitor to the company mentioned here knows you've done it once, it's pretty hard to refuse when they come knocking.

Once you're for sale, you can never again make a stand on principle. That's really why our editor resigned, and would have done even if the car in question *had* been suitable for his readership.

Jobs on magazines

While it's unfashionable these days to talk about hierarchies, the fact of the matter is that you'll find yourself a good way down the pecking order in your first job.

Bear in mind, though, that there are no hard and fast rules on getting jobs in publishing, and this is particularly true of magazine publishing. 'Sometimes it does come down to whether you as the employer have a gut feeling about an applicant, whether they have a GSOH (good sense of humour) . . . anything really,' says Andy Jones, Director of feedBack Media & PR and much-experienced magazine journo and editor. Sometimes the most bizarre route can result in a job, as this cracker from Greg Ingham illustrates:

My first job was as a staff writer on a now defunct TV listings mag called *TV Choice*. I hung around for five moons in their unmanned reception, waiting for a job interview. Phone rang: it was a splenetic Peter Dulay, from *Candid Camera*, complaining that the BBC had stolen one of his sketches for *The Late, Late Breakfast Show*. I pretended to be a journalist, quizzed him, got some great quotes and then rang Michael Hurll at the BBC (I'd remembered his name from seeing TV credits; deeply, deeply sad, I know). Hurll rudely rebutted or rebuffed or refuted or whatever it is that you do, and I got some even better quotes from Dulay when I told him what Hurll'd said. I then wrote all this up and so had a real, live, almost interesting story ready by the time I was eventually interviewed. Mag went bust six weeks later, mind. Moral? You can have too much planning, you know.

(GREG INGHAM, CHIEF EXECUTIVE,
MEDIACLASH AND FORMER CHIEF EXECUTIVE OF FUTURE PLC, AUSTRALIA)

The term for this is chutzpah – or, perhaps better, balls. Magazine World is no place for shrinking violets, and a ridiculously cheeky swagger will often do the trick (either that or get you thrown out).

However, there is one absolute golden rule for every job in magazines, or indeed any job in publishing – with the exception of sales:

I can't overstate how important and obvious it is to be good at English. The number of job applications I have dealt with and CVs I have seen with bad English is appalling. I don't even bother looking at qualifications if there's a typo on the CV. (ANDY JONES, DIRECTOR, FEEDBACK MEDIA & PR, UK)

So here are the five traditional routes into magazine publishing . . .

1. Editorial

Your first job in magazine publishing might be as **editorial assistant,** which means running errands, helping out, filing and generally doing the jobs no-one else wants to. Do them exceptionally well, stay cheerful and keep telling yourself that one day you'll be in a position to be nicer to the editorial assistant than this lot are, and you may find that you get yourself a role as a **staff writer**, writing the bits no-one else wants to. Do them exceptionally well, stay cheerful and keep telling yourself that one day you'll be in a position to be nicer to the staff writer than this lot are (does this sound familiar?), and you may make it as a departmental **editor**. Here's where things get interesting, and where you get some clout to manage your own area of the magazine, and we'll come back to this in a minute.

Naturally to succeed as a writer on, say, a photography magazine then you'll need to be passionate about the subject matter yourself. So take a look at yourself and work out what you have to offer the market. However, if you 'quite like' music, that really doesn't qualify you for a job on *Q* magazine: you need to know what track Vanilla Ice was ripping off on *Ice Ice Baby* (*Under Pressure* by David Bowie and Queen), Justin Timberlake's middle name (Randall), how many Billboard number one hits Michael Jackson's had (13 – we're not expecting this information to get outdated), who originally recorded Toploader's *Dancing in the Moonlight* (King Harvest), what amp Jimmy Hendrix used (Marshall) and about a billion other bits of knowledge.

2. Editorial production

Alternatively you may find that you enter Magazine World on the **editorial production** side of things, dealing with copy-editing and the transmission of the manuscript from receipt onto page. (That's how Steve started, working on a computer magazine basically as a filter to stop too much geekish being left untranslated.) Although this may seem less creative than being a writer, it leaves you with a surprising degree of responsibility and the opportunity to really contribute to the magazine.

Your department gets to write the captions, the crossheads (the mini-headlines in the story), the introductions and the headlines themselves. Work up a good reputation in this area and you can quickly get noticed. (Steve's favourite from his computer magazine days was a letter from a reader complaining about what was on the cover disk: 'Now is the Whinger of Our Discontent'.)

Arguably you *don't* need to be an expert to work in production, though opinion is divided on this. (Some feel you need to be able to verify all the facts as they come speeding through; others that you need to make sure the magazine doesn't end up appealing to a smaller and smaller subset of über-experts like the writers themselves.)

3. Design

A third option is the design stream, the **graphic design** department. (Department might be putting it a bit strong, since on many magazines it's a grand total of two or even just one.) Yet again in your first role your title may well have the word 'assistant' in it, and from there it's just a case of putting strychnine in your boss's tea and working your way up to the lofty position of **art editor** or **art director**.

4. Sales

A fourth option is on the advertising or commercial side. Here you'll find opportunities for **advertising sales,** getting out there and selling advertising space in the magazine. We talk elsewhere in this book about whether this is the right kind of gig for you (see Chapter 7). If you're entrepreneurial, outgoing, something of a lone wolf rather than a team player, terrible at paperwork and generally a bit of a geezer then advertising sales may well be your thing.

A word of warning: *do not* try to try to use selling advertising as a way to get into editorial: it won't work. Yes, it's definitely possible, but it's such a bad bet you'd be better off getting an editorial job – *any* editorial job – and work your way up that way. (The same is true in the opposite direction, by the way.)

5. Magazine production

The fifth and final option is **magazine production,** the logistical department who are responsible for ensuring that the adverts sold by the advertising team make it into the magazine, and that the editorial on page 73 doesn't turn up on page 37. Again, it is rare though not unprecedented for someone to get into a magazine this way and then make their way across to editorial, and it's probably not a good way to try and do it.

So, that's a brief summary of the various ways you can infiltrate the closed world of magazines. *How* you do that is what this book is all about. Part III will show you how to start making your wish a reality.

More reading

Morrish, *Magazine Editing: How to Develop and Manage a Successful Publication*, Routledge 2003

McKay, *The Magazines Handbook*, Routledge 2003

Chapter Six
About e-publishing

Most people overestimate the impact of technology in the short term –
and underestimate it in the long term.   (ARTHUR C. CLARKE)[1]

It's a sign of the times that there's a chapter dedicated to e-publishing in a book about careers in publishing. A few years ago we probably wouldn't have needed one. And pretty soon it will seem odd to talk about it in a separate context, as if it were not just as much a part of publishing as anything else.

But that's what it is, a sign of the very extraordinary times we live in, the dawn of the digital age. E-publishing is just one corner of it, of course, and yet in its way e-publishing is as revolutionary as the invention of the car, the plane or – going back a couple of thousand years – the book itself.

Before we get into this, here's why it matters to you. The best and the brightest young talent (that's you) are up to date with what's happening electronically. And in fact if you are faced with a choice between two jobs, one 'old school' and one in e-publishing, *pick the latter*. Why? Think of publishing as a see-saw, and digital delivery is on the way up as physical delivery is on the way down. Go where the action is. You wouldn't want to be making horse carriages when round the corner there's a bloke making cars.

Let's take a more appropriate and dramatic image. Though you can't see it, a fault line runs right underneath your feet. The occasional rumble and mini-earthquake have knocked a few books off your shelves. Many people slept through and missed the whole thing.

---

[1] *Actually it's not at all obvious who said this first. Maybe it was Bill Gates? If you know, do contact us via the publisher*

However, the experts are in absolute agreement that these little rumbles are pre-echoes, signs that soon – and even the experts don't know exactly when, they just know it will be soon – the Big One is about to hit, and the landscape will change forever. You won't know the place.

In the process, entire massive publishing houses and even whole districts of physical print publishing (such as, arguably, academic journals, higher education textbooks, travel books, encyclopaedias, hefty dictionaries and atlases) will be swept away forever, to be replaced by a new horizon. Some jobs (and the people who do them) will be swallowed up, to join typists, milkmen, horse-drawn carriage builders, typesetters and telephone exchange operators in the history books, while others that we can't even yet imagine will emerge.

And, while it's probable that books, magazines and newspapers are here to stay, at least for a while longer, it's absolutely certain that their time as the *only* way to deliver content is at an end.

Even so, when they think of publishing, most people still continue to think of books, magazines and newspapers – in other words, bits of tree squashed flat and driven around the country in a truck.

In one sense they're quite right to do so, because, despite all the hype, very little book publishing is actually done online, compared to what most of us might still think of as 'the real thing', magazines still continue to pack the newsstand, and not too many people are happy to pay real money for their online news.

To illustrate, in the US e-books still represent less than three-quarters of 1% of the US$25 billion publishing market.

To judge from these signs, then, this is all a big fuss over nothing. But make no mistake, online publishing is not only well and truly here to stay, it's only going to get more important, even if it's taking rather longer than many people thought. And here's why. Because, despite what some say, it's not the reluctance of readers to read online and electronically that's holding things back. In fact, it's the twin difficulty of finding a workable business model and a reader-friendly technology that's preventing us going full pelt for an electronic future.

In short, you can't get people to pay as much as they will for a book or magazine or even a newspaper for its electronically delivered equivalent; and even if you could, you can't give it to them in as elegant a form as its physical counterpart.

It's the business of the three Bs – bed, bath and beach: find a way of providing people with a good electronic read in those three leisure locations, and you have an official licence to print money on a grand, and perhaps even unprecedented, scale.

Here are three indicators that the digital earthquake really is about to happen, if it hasn't actually started already:

- The chief executive of Bloomsbury, Nigel Newton, recently predicted that 50% of all fiction sales in 2016 will be digital – half! Even if he's wildly out, that's still a massive shift in the mode of delivery.
- In the UK, Random House and HarperCollins are digitising 25,000 titles.
- The Chinese government has announced that it will supply all its 165 million students with e-readers.

Think about your own habits for a second. It's probable that you're one of the Digerati, a Millennial (born in 1980 or since), who's grown up interacting with your media, be it videogames, Facebook, MySpace, YouTube, instant messaging, text messaging, your iPod . . . You're used to scanning things fast and being in charge. You get much of your information online, be it news (if you're even interested in news – chances are, you're not), reviews or what's on.

If you're a student you know all about Web-based course management systems. You may well access lectures and other materials via MP3. And you know what? Academic publishers and campus booksellers are *absolutely petrified*. They have no idea – or rather, they have

100 ideas and no clue – how to address these issues effectively, and simply cannot see what tomorrow's business model is. Yet.

Newspaper publishers have rushed online to deliver news . . . Actually, let's start that again. Newspaper publishers have rushed online to deliver *eyeballs* (yours) to advertisers, and in the process discovered that once you've taught people to expect stuff for free, it's mighty hard to re-educate them to pay for it. So while newspaper sales continue to decline like a bike tyre with a slow puncture, the very publishers of those newspapers are busily engaged in teaching their readers to get for free what they used to pay for!

Finally, books. Even if you still only need to sell a few hundred electronically to have a bestseller on your hands, don't think for a moment that the publishers aren't taking it seriously. In fact, they're spending millions and millions on digitising everything they can. (They're doing it in India, which is a whole other story.) And they're also ensuring that they buy the electronic rights to whatever properties they buy these days (including the one you're holding in your hands right now).

So publishers worldwide are ready, poised and eager to take your cash for online delivery. All it takes is a decent e-reader and a workable business model. The sorts of issue they are struggling with are: How much would *you* pay for the electronic edition of a book? Would you pay the same as you'd pay for the paperback? The costs of circulating an e-book are substantially lower than printing the book version. How much is convenience worth?

Still, it's only a matter of time before the technical and commercial issues get sorted out – just as the technical and commercial issues relating to the delivery of online music were sorted out by Apple – and when they are, look out for seismic shifts in publishing that are every bit as dramatic as in the music market. When it happens, you want to be part of it.

So there it is. Books and magazines aren't going away, but they no longer have the place to themselves. Information that can be more efficiently published and consumed online will be so, and books and magazines will keep what's left, whatever that is. That's why we say, if you can get an e-publishing gig, take it.

But e-publishing is so much more than replacing one form of publishing with another. It has created thousands of opportunities that never even existed before. Just a few years ago, for example, hardly any business had a website or could see a need to get one. (By the way, an utterly fascinating way to spend a few minutes is to look at how websites you know have developed over the years, using the wonderful Wayback Machine, **www.archive.org/index** and its 85 *billion* archived Web pages. You can see what Apple's website looked like a decade ago, or Wikipedia the day it started, on 28 August 2001.)

What do we mean by e-publishing?

It helps to think for a second about what e-publishing actually is. Because it can mean one (or more) of three (or more) things:

- **Selling** online. For example, a publisher's website and a publisher selling books through Amazon or other online booksellers
- **Promoting** through the use of digital information – for example, e-mail marketing to customers and potential customers
- **Delivering** digital content – publishing a product electronically, to be read through an e-reader, or online

And outside of what publishers themselves are doing there's a whole worldwide Web of online authoring and production. For instance, Steve used to work in marketing for a big corporate law firm, and any decent-sized firm in the professional services area (lawyers, accountants, consultants, advertising agencies) worth its salt these days produces a ton of reading material ('marketing collateral' in the jargon) for its clients and prospects.

Here are just a few of the many positions and career paths with an online twist:

- **Copywriter** – there are jobs for Web copywriters, sometimes called digital copywriters or technical copywriters.

- **MarComms** (Marketing and Communications) positions, from junior assistant through to marketing manager right the way through to a director on the company board.
- **Production and Publications**, pulling content and design together and making the whole thing happen.
- **Editing** – although the delivery mechanism and the way content is put together have changed, the traditional role of an editor at the helm exists just as it always has.
- **Graphic design** – a whole industry has sprung up creating websites.
- **Web-delivered information services** such as searching, online directory listings and other interactive electronic services have thrown up new jobs and careers that simply did not exist a decade ago.
- **Advertising** in particular has warmly embraced all things digital, expanding beyond print and broadcast ads into viral advertising, websites, advergames, the creation of rich media banners, ambient digital content and a thousand and one other ways to attract the attention of the time-poor and media-savvy consumer. In fact, UK online advertising spend now counts for more than 10% of the entire advertising market (globally the figure's about 6%), being worth more than £2 billion. It's worth more than national newspaper advertising, and in early 2007 overtook radio in revenue terms. Opportunities here include wordsmithing (copywriters who become editors who become creative directors) and crayon-wielding (graphic designers who become studio managers who become creative directors), online advertising account and traffic management (the traffic in this case being the mechanical handling of the advertising material itself, rather than looking after the company car park).

Conclusion

As someone once said, in a somewhat different context, this is not the end for e-publishing. It's not even the beginning of the end. It is, however, perhaps the end of the beginning, in the sense that there is no longer any doubt whatsoever that we're living in the future. And this future-present is moving so fast that even to start a paragraph about it condemns you to be out of date by the time you finish it. It's for those reasons that it's so exciting and enticing. You don't have to be an über-geek to be part of it, though if you find the life of an accountant, with its stability and solidity, even secretly just a little bit attractive then this is not the place for you. If, however, you love change and uncertainty and the thrills and spills of driving at 150 miles an hour blindfold in heavy traffic, then you've found your spiritual home (it's on wheels, naturally).

So, to repeat: faced with two attractive job offers, one of which has an 'e-' attached to it, take that one. It'll be a wild ride.

More reading
Anything we put in here will be out of date by the day you read this.

Part 11: About you

Chapter Seven
What kind of person are you?

Most men lead lives of quiet desperation and go to the grave with their song still in them. (HENRY DAVID THOREAU (1817–1862), US PHILOSOPHER)

Many (too many: maybe even most) people hate what they're doing. They hate their job and they *really* hate their boss. Yet many (too many: maybe even most) of them never do anything about it, other than complain in the pub and bore everybody to death, again. Cue deep sighs and raised eyes all round.

If you think that's not nearly good enough for you, the best way to avoid this is to make sure you head off in the right direction to start with.

So this chapter is something of an honesty session. It's where you get to take a good, hard look at yourself in the mirror and work out what you love and what you're good at.

It's hardly a surprise that these two things – what you enjoy and what you excel at – usually overlap. It's probably something to do with the fact that your aptitudes shape your skills and experience. Some people, in this corner over here, are fascinated by mechanical things right from the moment they can see, and that means they love to spend time taking things to bits and putting them back together again, apart from a mysterious very small spring. Meanwhile, over there you'll find some people who just love language, and reading, and books. That's them, with their noses in a book right now. If you fancy a good belly laugh, get them to swap places with the taker-apart mob over in this corner.

In effect, that's what happens to a lot of people at work. It's not them, and it's not the job: it's the combination. Find a square hole for the square peg and suddenly what used to be a crushing bore is now the most fun you can have with your clothes on.

The reality is, if you don't find out what you love doing and make a point of doing it, no-one will make you leave and go and find out what you were put onto this earth to do with your life. And ploughing on with a job that you can manage, but which you find soul-destroying, is hardly the route to happiness.

So before you go any further, give some hard thought to what you love to do – and the key words here are *you* and *love*.

You, because too many people (perhaps nearly all people) live out their lives doing what their Mum and Dad want them to do, or what they think will impress people, or what they stumble into, and never, or perhaps only too late, put themselves first. If not now, when? Someone has to do that job you'd secretly love to be doing: why not you?

And *love*, because between, 'Yeah, wouldn't mind doing that I s'pose', 'I could see myself doing that', and 'I will not be happy until I'm doing that: that is what I exist to do, so get out of my way', there's all the difference in the world.

Who are you?

So if we're right, and how you're made up determines what you enjoy, and what you enjoy determines what you're going to be really good at, then how do you decide what's the right kind of job for you?

Try this. For each of the ten questions, circle the answer in the column that best matches your own response. There's no simple pattern here, so don't expect that all your answers will be in the same column. In some cases two columns have the same answer: circle both.

	A. I'm... 'A talker, absolutely'	**B. I'm...** 'A bit of both'	**C. I'm...** 'Mainly a reader'	**D. I'm...** 'A reader, absolutely'
1. Are you more of a talker or a reader?				
2. Do you get easily embarrassed – for example, when buying condoms, or (if you're male) buying tampons?	'What's the big deal?'	'What, again? Oh, OK'	'I'll buy online'	'Someone else can do that, thanks'
3. Are you good at meeting people?	'I have a hundred thousand mates'	'I don't mind getting out there'	'A quiet drink in a crowded place for me, thanks'	'I have my mates – don't need any more'
4. Do your friends rely on you to be the one to organise everything?	'I can be organised when I need to be'	'Oh yes, yes indeed'	'Sometimes'	'Oh yes, yes indeed'
5. Are you good at jokes?	'Did you hear the one about ...?'	'When I can remember them'	'When I can remember them'	'They're a poor excuse for a conversation'
6. Are you creative?	'Not too in love with precious arty stuff'	'Absolutely!'	'Yes, I'd say so'	'Moderately'

(continued)

	A. I'm ...	**B. I'm ...**	**C. I'm ...**	**D. I'm ...**
7. Do you take people at face value?	'Absolutely not! I believe they are lying until I find out otherwise'	'There are good and bad people out there. Who are you thinking of? Introduce me, and I'll let you know'	'There are good and bad people out there. Who are you thinking of? Introduce me, and I'll let you know'	'Absolutely – I believe people are telling the truth until proven otherwise'
8. Are you a ruthless careerist?	'Yes. Isn't everyone?'	'Careerist maybe, ruthless no'	'No. Would I be, working for this pittance?'	'No. Would I be, working for this pittance?'
9. Do you want to be rich?	'Yes. Doesn't everyone?'	'Wouldn't say no'	'I'm not a materialist'	'I'm not a materialist'
10. Is it very important to you to drive the right car, if not now then some day?	'I can see it in my mind right now'	'Not my highest priority'	'The right car is one that starts on cold mornings'	'No. I have more serious things to think about'

WARNING: The following contains gross generalisations, and may lead to elevated blood pressure and fainting. To counteract, take a pinch of salt and a reality check. *Of course* there are exceptions to all of these rules (including this one), and if you seriously think a five-minute questionnaire is going to sort out your career dilemma, then you should probably not risk exposing yourself to the next page or two. It's just a bit of help, is all, and can't be much more, even if it is based on a lot of self-reflection, experience and observation.

Mostly As? You're the classic SALES BEAST

As a sales person you're competitive, driven and career-minded. You're also . . .

- **A talker and banterer**, the life and soul of the party
- **Great at putting people at ease** and at chatting up and flirting (some editorial people are too, of course)
- **Shameless and thick-skinned** – you need it, too: most of your life is spent being rejected. Don't fool yourself about this one. You can toughen up, but only if you're not sensitive to start with
- **An inveterate haggler**, driven by the bargain
- **A master joke-teller** and spinner of tall tales
- **A cynic**, with no illusions about anyone's motives
- **Clear about why your boss values you**, and it's not for personal reasons
- **Target- and bonus- and performance-related pay-driven**
- **Competitive and status-driven**. That's why you're attracted to a career that measures success by revenue and clearly visible wins/losses

On the downside?

You're likely to find detail and paperwork and process less than exciting. You may think of it as a necessary evil at best, and just plain evil and not necessary most of the time.

Mostly Bs? You're the creative MARKETEER

You're a people person, creative and bubbly. You're highly organised and a just a teensy weensy bit bossy. You're also . . .

- **A lover of words**, a reader, a talker and a chatterer
- **A diplomat**, the public face of the company. But unlike Sales people, you're not completely brazen. You never forget that the product, not you, is the star
- **Detail-driven**, with a keen eye for deadlines and how to hit them

- **An ideas person**, constantly working on strategies to promote, position and push your product. You want brochures, you want better blurbs, you want the best for your authors and their books

On the downside?

You're likely to be frustrated at the budgets you have to work with. They're laughable (and not in a good way). Plus, you're on display all the time and while you won't get any credit for most of what you do, the first little typo is apparently obvious to everyone, your boss included.

Mostly Cs? You're the creative PUBLISHING GURU

You're the engine of the whole thing. Without you your Sales Department has nothing to sell and your Marketing Team has nothing to market. You're also . . .

- **A lover of words and reading**
- **Deadline-driven and you love the challenge of pressure**
- **A sceptic**. You're not cynical exactly, but you're not naïve enough to think that things are going to improve that much
- **In love with what you do** – that's why you do it, despite the terrible pay and the slight career prospects

On the downside?

For some ridiculous reason, publishing is still perceived as glamorous and sexy, and so jobs are in high demand, which makes it harder to get on, and means you're expected to work for laughably small amounts of money. An ability to live on fresh air is definitely an advantage.

Mostly Ds? You're the indispensable COPY EDITOR

You stand between the human, fallible author and the critic and the hyper-critical reader. If you weren't so good at what you do, your manuscripts wood be jiberlish. You're also . . .

- **The organised one** – if there are tickets to buy or a trip to arrange, it always comes down to you. You'll set out the timetable and make sure everyone's where they're supposed to be
- **Detail- and deadline-driven**
- **Fond of a good argument and even a bit of a devil's advocate**. You like to thrash things out by discussing and debating. But generally you're . . .
- **Quiet, too**. You're not necessarily always the most social of creatures – you know who you like and they're who you want to spend time with

And the downside?

Well, the world isn't always as neat and tidy as you'd like, and neither are the people you work with. You can no more understand how they can live like this, than they can comprehend why your CDs *must* go back *exactly* where they came from, thank-you-very-much-is-it-really-too-much-to-ask?

Conclusion

Most of us don't fit one of these boxes precisely, and we're not suggesting that because you circled six in one column you should rush off and get a sales job and dismiss all thought of doing anything else. Of course not. Your authors illustrate the point nicely. Steve is hardly a detail kind of a guy (Column D), but that's what he started off doing, working as a copy and production editor on a computer magazine. Susannah scores highly on detail, but of the three of us she's the one who's spent longest in sales roles.

But even so, you may find it helpful to start thinking about what your skills and, more importantly, your aptitudes are, and use that knowledge to explore what kind of thing you want to be doing.

> It's important in publishing to be yourself. Publishing is such an intuitive industry that you really need to be open and honest and yourself.
>
> (STARR JAMIESON, SALES COORDINATOR, WALKER BOOKS AUSTRALIA)

Chapter Eight
Getting ready for your job in publishing

An undergraduate degree is the basic start point for any career in book publishing, and this chapter discusses the options open to you.

Which course should you take? Where? What do you do once you have graduated? Are you better off getting into a job as early as possible? Or would you benefit from getting some more letters after your name, perhaps with a publishing/journalism-specific MA? Such courses usually offer internships, and of course you can also try to get some work experience without embarking on a course. But are these useful opportunities leading to full-time jobs, or are you just being used as cheap labour (or perhaps both)? So many questions. This chapter explores your best choices.

A word of advice

It's a great idea to ask around, but treat the advice you're given by friends and acquaintances with caution and even scepticism – and this applies even if they're already in publishing and doing the job you'd love. If Daniel went to university and did a journalism degree, then you can bet your bottom dollar that's the route Daniel will commend to you – and if Louise didn't, then she'll tell you not to waste your time. Making a decision based on a sample of one is not wise. By all means ask. But treat the answers with caution.

Higher education: university education

An undergraduate degree may be the stated starting point, and you should be aware that some publishing staff will be more interested in *where* you went to (and how it overlaps with what they did themselves) rather than *what* you studied. What discipline you study tends not to get prescribed. You may already be clear about this – and if you have already graduated then it's obviously in the past and not worth fretting over now. But if this is still ahead of you, the basic issue is how specific do you want your degree to be?

Seven Recommendations

1. **Go to the best university you can**

   This definitely counts. What is best, though? Some institutions (and you know which ones we mean) just have that reputation, deserved or not. Others excel in particular subjects and even courses. Either way, aim as high as you can: you'll be living with this on your CV for the rest of your career.

2. **Study what you're passionate about**

   Rather than what you think will be useful, work on something you're mad about. It may even be a talking point at interviews – at least, that's what Alison's degree in Fine Arts and Mediaeval History was! Many publishing people have literature degrees – it's much more common than having a business qualification.

3. **Keep your options open as long as you can**

   While you can change courses, the momentum of the system is always going to encourage you to continue with the one you began – and three or four years spent on something you are not entirely sure is for you sure is a big risk to take. Some universities offer you the chance to spend a taster year (or sometimes two for a four-year degree) trying things out, before committing yourself to what your final subject will be; others work in modules where you build up credits as you go along. These are good options for the undecided.

4. **Consider studying something with a wider applicability . . .**

   . . . especially if it's something that will sustain your interest. Most people working in publishing and in the media generally didn't start out with a burning desire to do exactly the position or even the career they now find themselves in. If you're lucky enough to know that your calling in life is to be the Sports Reporter on The *Toowoomba Chronicle* or the *Birmingham Post*, then studying journalism gives you a head start, because it's much easier that way to head in the direction you want. Most of us have a hankering to be in publishing, but may not know precisely what role will suit.

I started out as a trainee reporter for Mirror Group Newspapers in Devon – along with 11 other aspiring journalists, including Tony Blair's former spin doctor Alastair Campbell and his partner, Fiona Millar. We spent eight weeks studying shorthand, law, local government and writing techniques – then we were dispatched to weekly newspapers across Devon and Cornwall to be real reporters! My first responsibilities included covering golden weddings, council planning meetings and village fetes – not exactly glamorous!

(EMMA LEE-POTTER, JOURNALIST, AUTHOR AND FORMER PUBLISHER, UK)

5. **Alternatively, study to prepare yourself for employment**
   On the other hand, if you are unsure what to take, rather than studying a subject 'for the sake of it', why not look at something specifically designed to prepare you for your career? The rise of the vocational degree or training course has been recent, but is well documented. Even so, as we researched this book, the sheer variety of media, journalism and publishing courses on offer took us by surprise.

6. **Consider just how *practical* you want your course to be**
   If you take on a 'hard core' practical course and find that your interests take you in other directions, you might feel you've wasted valuable time and money. On the other hand, if you're by nature a practical person with little patience for what you would consider pointless intellectual hot air and theory, then finding yourself in an environment with no real industry connections and exposure will be frustrating.

7. You are a valuable asset to them, too

Finally, while you're considering your options, it's worth reminding yourself that the universities and colleges are after you, too. Without students there is no university. So treat their claims seriously, but not unsceptically. Consider whether what you're impressed by is the course itself . . . or the quality of the university's marketing department. You need to satisfy yourself that the sausage is as good as the sizzle. Equally, some universities still don't match the high quality of their courses with the quality of their marketing, so don't write them off just because they haven't got a flashy brochure or bang-up-to-date website.

Postgraduate degrees in book and magazine publishing

I studied English at Liverpool University and in my second year got stuck on the thorny question of what to do next. I didn't want to be a teacher like my dad, was too anxious to try journalism, and thought being a librarian would be dull. My ex-English teacher suggested publishing and I found out about a postgraduate course at the London College of Printing. It was four months, so not too long (though long enough when I could see my debts mounting), and three weeks after I'd finished I was lucky enough to get a job with Routledge as a production assistant.

(JULIA MOFFATT, FREELANCE EDITOR AND WRITER, UK)

Taking a postgraduate qualification is an increasingly popular route into publishing, and there are new courses springing up every year. What's happened has been a form of educational inflation. Once upon a time the traditional, and maybe even the best, route into getting a job in publishing was to take a secretarial course, put up with being someone's assistant for a year, and then you were on your way.

These days only the very senior staff have the luxury of their very own personal assistant, and you have to find some other way of differentiating your application from all the others. Hence the temptation to take a vocational Masters degree as a way of getting to the head of the pack.

We find those who arrive with a Publishing MA are well equipped for a starting job; they tend to hit the ground running. They are familiar with how things work; they understand the language of publishing and feel confident. Courses tend to equip them with a valuable bird's-eye view of the industry and I am sure the qualifications get them employed more quickly. Certainly an MA in Publishing shows motivation and commitment, and were we in the position of trying to choose between two identical candidates, one with one and one without, I am sure we would see the additional qualification as a benefit.

(HELEN FRASER, MANAGING DIRECTOR, PENGUIN UK)

Postgraduate courses are now available for magazine journalists, and some of the best newcomers I've employed have done just such courses.

(LINDA KELSEY, FORMER EDITOR OF *COSMOPOLITAN* AND *SHE*)

These days it's useful to have attended a course or courses on publishing, partly to gain the knowledge, and the piece of paper, but equally importantly to show the employer that you have a real commitment to the industry.

(PATRICK GALLAGHER, CHAIRMAN, ALLEN & UNWIN, AUSTRALIA)

And of course taking a postgraduate course gives you the chance to explore whether publishing is for you – and lots of useful skills to take elsewhere if you decide it is not. (In addition to publishing, graduates end up working in PR, internal communications, museums, arts marketing and many other jobs that need the same skill set.)

When I got my Postgraduate Diploma in Book Publishing at Oxford Polytechnic it gave me a detailed background to all aspects of book publishing, including the less 'fashionable' ones. I discovered that far

> from being cocktails and literary discussions deep into the night, publishing was a real business and that things like production, marketing and subsidiary rights were as vital to the whole process as the editorial considerations. In effect it was like doing work experience with a publishing company for a year with people who actually had the time and the inclination to explain to you what they did and why they did it. It meant when I got my first job in publishing I was up and running within a few weeks, confident in my knowledge of how the really complex business of publishing a book happens.
>
> (JEREMY TREVATHAM, PUBLISHING DIRECTOR, PAN MACMILLAN, UK)

Even so, you should bear in mind that the sudden availability of dozens of Publishing MA courses is market- rather than industry-driven. Taking one doesn't guarantee you a job in the business, and neither does the availability of all these courses imply that there are enough jobs for all the students taking them. What drives the courses is not the need for students with those degrees: on the contrary, it's the desire for students to have those degrees.

You should also consider how up to date the course you're considering really is. The media are[1] evolving at a very fast rate, and although some traditional skills will always be needed (editing, writing, production), the ways in which those skills are used tomorrow will certainly be very different from the way they're being taught today. Be wary of courses, lecturers or universities that strike you as not having woken up to this fact.

Here are half-a-dozen tough, smart questions to ask when you're being sold hard by a university. Ask them of every institution you're considering, and record the answers. Give each a score.

1. Are your lecturers full-time or part-time?

The ideal is lecturers who are also doers, and who are thus continually refreshing their knowledge; thus if the course is

[1] *If 'media are' sounds odd to you, see **media** in the glossary*

delivered by part-time staff who are active within the industry, it's probably a good sign. What you want are lecturers who are active in the market they teach. This means they'll be fully up to date with what is happening in publishing right now, rather than what went on in 1980.

2. **Who arranges work placements?**
   Some universities boast about their work placement programme as a key part of the course . . . and then leave you to organise it.

3. **What activities/facilities do you get access to?**
   Are there programmes of guest speakers to which students from across the faculty are invited? What about trips and opportunities to see relevant organisations?

4. **What is the employment history of previous students?**
   How many had a placement? What percentage of these opportunities turned into full-time jobs?

5. **Is there a buzz?**
   Do the staff you meet ask about you and your aspirations? Do they talk about the course and students with enthusiasm? Or do you, perhaps, get the distinct impression you're helping them make up the quota of students they are required to recruit?

6. **When was the course put together?**
   Long-established doesn't necessarily mean well-organised. Newer courses must necessarily have been put together more recently; older institutions may be trading on their reputation rather than the good experience they offer. Ask questions, and switch on your antennae.

If you have your heart set on working for a particular employer or type of publisher, of course don't assume that the best way in is to stay well away from them and spend years and years and piles of money studying. Some publishers, especially those in the magazine world, really don't see the value in postgraduate degrees. Nose around the section of the industry that you're keen on first, ask other employees how they got there, take the temperature of your (hopeful) employers to be. If the consensus is that an undergraduate degree and a bit of editing your student newspaper won't do the trick, and you quite fancy finding out more about the different roles in the industry through some more study, then a postgraduate degree might well be a great option.

But if your favoured section of the industry universally sneers at postgraduate degrees, and you feel happy with your skills and experience base, consider saving yourself some time and money and jumping straight in.

Work experience

For every publishing job there are so very many people. How are you going to make your CV stand out? One thing that certainly helps is to have made your mark already. Having been around magazines or books and got into print already shows you're serious.

What kind of work do you need to have behind you? That actually matters much less than the fact that you have *some*. Experience is vital, says Debbie Baron, who looks after cadet/starter job applications on the Melbourne *Herald Sun*. Each year she gets about 120 applications for just two to six positions. Being involved in street press, says Debbie, or your school or community newspaper is an excellent sign that you're really committed to journalism. (By the way, she also makes the pertinent point that, since you're applying to work at a business built on news, you'll want to ensure your knowledge of current affairs is bang up to date.)

Still in Australia, Jacqui Cheng at Fairfax Newspapers paints a similar picture – although, strictly speaking, there are no cadetships there, since you need a tertiary education to get in. With its business titles, *BRW* and the *Australian Financial Review*, there are certainly opportunities if you're from a business background. But in any case, you'd better be a news junkie. Fairfax attracts more than 800 applicants for about 20 positions, and once again it's a process of applying and, if you get that far, sitting an exam and then getting through the interviews.

'The exam's pretty tough,' says Julia Medew, one of 2005's trainee intake, 'it expects you to have a wide knowledge of current affairs, and it quickly weeds those out who don't'. Julia is a good example of what persistence can achieve. With so many people and so few opportunities, talent by itself simply isn't enough. Starting out as a 'copy kid' at 18 and then working in various departments in different roles while she did her Arts degree at Monash, she was able to build up her experience and contacts – so much so that, when she faced the editorial panel, she knew them all, including the editor-in-chief. And she had a stack of published stories to show, too.

When we spoke to her she was not long back from interviewing film stars at the AFI Awards – but this, she was keen to stress, was hardly typical. Her advice, not surprisingly, is that experience beats all. 'It's changed a lot in recent years, I think,' she says. 'An arts or a journalism degree is not enough by itself. You need work, work, work, whether it's on the local paper, on a website, on your university paper – *any* hands-on real-life experience in a workplace that means you're pumping out copy and having it published regularly.'

Here's the way to get ahead:

1. **Get involved as early as you can**
   If you're at school, edit the school magazine. If you're at uni, get involved in as much of the media activity (newspaper, radio, TV) as you can. Not only is this terrific experience – a deadline is a deadline, and a crisis a crisis! – it proves that you really are keen.

2. **Get a job in publishing, or as near to it as you can get, in your holidays and weekends**
   If it's not at all related, find out if you can bring in some publishing-related ideas. Would the firm like a staff newsletter or a blog for their website? If you're working in a shop on your days off from uni, make sure it's a newsagent or a bookshop, not the local bakery.

3. Make yourself available for as long as you can

Since it'll take you a while to pick up anything but the simplest job, it's unlikely that anyone is going to find it worth their while to train you if you're only going to be around for a week or two. If, though, you're able to commit to a month or longer, and you're ready, keen and cheap, then you become an attractive proposition.

Internships

Internships are the best way to see if you like publishing, meet the right people and find the right job for you. Not surprisingly, they're screamingly competitive.

Here are a couple of stories from people who got their break in publishing through internships:

I did work experience with Kogan Page and Bloomsbury, both arranged by my tutor from the MA programme. After I had finished, I left my CV with both firms and both subsequently came back to me when job opportunities occurred. I like to think it was because I made a good impression, but to be honest both firms admitted that when you need to find someone it tends to be a in a rush, and if you have already found an intern who meets your needs and you know fits in well, it saves huge amounts of time and money to opt for them. In fact the job I eventually took was with Wiley, and I am about to start as their rights and licensing coordinator.

(NATALIE MEYLAN, STUDENT ON THE 2006–7 PUBLISHING
MA PROGRAMME AT KINGSTON UNIVERSITY, UK)

My first job was at a small publishing house in Reading. I had just left university and was staying with my parents, so I wrote to any publishers I could find within easy commuting distance and offered myself for work experience. They originally took me on for a few days a week, inputting editorial corrections, then gave me more hours working on reception and running the post room. The best thing about it was probably the office subscription to *The Bookseller*, where I found the advert for my next job

How internships work

- **No-one pays you**
  If you're lucky, you may get expenses.
- **Most internships are at least two weeks**
  If you're lucky, you might get up to six months of full- or part-time work.
- **You get a desk and a mentor in the company to guide you**
  If you're lucky, you'll get some meaningful projects to work on. That gives you a taste for the job, and the company a chance to get work done which wouldn't happen otherwise.
- **You get the taste of the company**
  If you're lucky, managers find out how ace you are and get accustomed to seeing you around; and you're first on the spot when a paid role comes up.

What will you be doing?

Often companies get interns working on things they've wanted to do for ages but haven't had the resources. That can lead to some really juicy and interesting projects that might include, for example, researching potential new publishing markets, reviewing editorial systems and streamlining existing processes. You might cover a junior position during a recruitment freeze or maternity leave vacancy (and hopefully be offered the job yourself).

Don't leave this to chance, though. If you don't work on the manager to define a solid project for your time there, you can end up doing the filing and photocopying. You'll still get to know people and see if you like the company, but you won't get a chance to show off your ingenuity and brainpower. So do your best to structure the internship to suit you.

How to set it up and make it benefit you

For an internship to work for you, you need half-a-dozen things, which we talk about below. Most of all, though, before you go any further, you need *cash*. Since you're not going to get paid for your work, how are you going to keep body and soul together? Maybe you could be an intern for three days a week and work the other two, or work in the evenings/at weekends? Maybe you have supportive parents or partner, or funds saved up?

Find out about your entitlement to benefits and whether it is compromised by taking an internship – it may be that if it improves your long-term employability, and you are still available for paid work should it arise, your entitlement may not be reduced. Don't, for goodness sake, take our word for it. Get the story, in black and white (in writing), before you jump.

Here's how to do it:

1. **Outline your goals**
   Do you simply want to see if publishing is for you? To check out a company where you want to work? To try a few different areas of publishing? To make contacts? To get a job? Once you know what you want, you can make sure the internship is structured to maximise your chances of getting it.

2. **Work out where you want to go**
   Internships don't grow on trees. They do, however, grow on the lists in trade directories. Talk to friends and relatives. Research the Web (Google 'publishing internship' for a start). Try your university course/university careers service/writers' centre/ careers counsellor/association (such as for women in publishing or young publishers, etc). Make lists. Follow up leads. Become obsessed: this is going to take a lot of work.

3. **Get in touch!**
   If you know which department (marketing/editorial/production etc) you want to work in, start with the department manager – they're the person you'll be working for, so if they can't see the

opportunity, it's probably not going to work out. If you're looking for general experience or to work across a range of departments, the HR (Human Resources) manager or (in a small company) general manager will probably work best.

Large publishers work by divisions. So, for example, McGraw-Hill in the UK has School Education, Higher Education and Professional/Medical divisions. These divisions often have parallel roles, but the management structure only joins together at the top. So if you want to try the marketing department in three separate divisions, you'll probably need to do this organising three times over, or find an energetic HR person who will do it for you.

4. Make your approach by phone (not e-mail or letter)

Yes, we mean it. It increases your chances of success tenfold, for the very simple reason that it's very easy to tip a letter into the too-hard basket, and far harder to do the same with someone on the phone. It takes a bit of nerve to do this, but believe us, it pays off, big time.

Try something like this:

> I'm a graduate looking for a career in publishing, and I particularly want to complete a voluntary, unpaid internship position with your company. I wondered if we could meet to discuss how this might work, please?

Make it clear right from the start that you're proposing an unpaid internship, and that you're a university graduate (if you are) – you don't want them getting you confused with 16-year-old work experience candidates!

They may have a few questions for you on the phone, but if they are within travelling distance, trying to set up a meeting is always a good idea. (And if they're not in travelling distance, why do you want to work there?) If they pass you on to someone else such as HR, then pursue the lead with them. This is a good thing, by the way: you've just been referred, which means you already come carrying a little credibility.

Remember, too, that you're talking to someone who's almost certainly over worked and you're offering to work for free. There's a real chance this could go somewhere.

5. **Be creative**

The best internship is one that interests you, and if you suggest a project (based on your understanding of what they do), you're more likely to get it. You could suggest, for example, one of the following:

- **A new, growing area of publishing** that particularly interests you – and looking into who publishes within it, which books have been hits, who the top authors are, whether there is export potential – everything they might need to start publishing in that area?

- **A marketing project** such as a frequent buyer scheme, website/e-mail voucher campaign or bookshop window dressing competition . . . think of schemes you've seen that work well and how they might be adapted for your chosen publisher

- **Research** on how the firm's competitors are approaching their market and the image they are promoting in the process

  You're probably thinking that you're unlikely to hit the spot. And, frankly, you're right: you won't. But most potential employers will appreciate the time and effort you've put into researching their business – certainly we would.

6. **Make sure the company respects you and your skills**

You're working for free, but you're not worthless. Ideally, you're looking for a company/manager to:

- **Provide you with a proper workspace of your own,** including desk, phone, computer

- **Take the time to discover your interests and skills** and assign you to projects that use your expertise, as well as giving you opportunities to stretch yourself

- **Provide you with at least one mentor/manager** you can work with closely and who shows you where the loo and the kettle are
- **Treat you like a regular employee,** include you in departmental treats and pay for work-related expenses

Not surprisingly, we don't recommend handing over a list of these requirements before you start. Instead it's probably best to try to establish the answers to these questions in a general meeting, before you start (can you call in the week before to find out how things work; or perhaps they can put you in touch with someone else who has done work experience so you can chat about how it went?). The bottom line is that you are doing work for nothing, and if they don't treat you with respect, it's probably not somewhere you'd like to work anyway.

How good interns behave

You're trying to make a good impression so that you can get a job. So it's not surprising that mostly your behaviour should be as if you were already working there. Here's some pithy advice for interns and employees alike:

Take the time to know what you're talking about. There are few things worse than being told insightlessly about your mag/paper/site by some faux-knowledgeable character who has spent all of three google-nanoseconds researching you . . . Consume media, voraciously. And if you can't do it voraciously, do it vicariously: read the media pages of the nationals; read *The Week*; see how the same story can be treated differently by different papers.

(GREG INGHAM, CHIEF EXECUTIVE, MEDIACLASH AND FORMER CHIEF EXECUTIVE OF FUTURE PLC, UK)

Be cheerful, be low-maintenance, tackle anything, but ask for rewards when you really deserve them. In the meantime, learn the basics of the culture, the software, photography and sound. And – most importantly – learn how the business operates.

(GUY ALLEN, PUBLISHER OF GUIDOMEDIA.COM, AUSTRALIA)

Seven Top Dos and Don'ts For Being An Intern

1. DO treat this like a permanent job (and maybe it will become one). Remember, you're on show here. Always get to work on time, and call if you are running late. Dress like the other employees. Take the same amount of time as everyone else for lunch and breaks.

2. DO keep a positive attitude. Never, ever, ever let resentment at how they are getting your services for nothing get in the way of doing the job to the best of your abilities. Even if you feel this way, do not share your feelings with those you are working for – they work for the host company and that is where their first loyalty lies. Don't forget that they will view how you do the job in the context of how the previous intern performed.

3. DO be great! This sounds so obvious that it shouldn't even need saying. But it does, believe us it does. Be outstanding and you may well get asked back: be a pain and you won't. A mate of Steve's has this little gem stuck just below his monitor: 'Go the extra mile. It's much less crowded there.' So: be helpful, be thorough, be friendly and cheerful, be willing to do anything and everything that needs doing. Make yourself useful. Follow directions. And don't be afraid to say that you haven't understood what's been said to you. That's much better than struggling through for a while hoping you've got the hang of it, and then finding out that you haven't. All this can be hard when you feel like a spare wheel, or don't feel like you're getting much feedback. But don't give up, and don't let the smile fade.

4. DO make an effort to meet the key people – general manager, editorial, sales, marketing directors and managers, HR. If you're worried you might not be able to think of something to say, have a stock sentence up your sleeve in case you get introduced to someone important when you're not expecting it. 'I love the new campaign on . . .' or 'I've just been reading your new publication XXX' is fine. Avoid 'Rubbish weather'.

5. DO come up with useful and interesting ideas, and run them by your line manager before anyone else. They will get very suspicious if you start passing your bright ideas to the departmental head before they have heard of them.
6. DO, when you're leaving, thank anyone and everyone who helped organise the project (card/gift such as bottle of wine or book), and remind them you'd love to work with them again when something comes up. Call every few months while you are still job hunting too. Oh, and if you plan to list them on your CV as a reference (which you should), remember to ask permission.
7. DON'T get carried away at the pub or the office Christmas party. You've worked hard to create a solid image of professionalism, and a single slip of the tongue (as in a slip of the tongue into someone else's mouth) can undo all that work in five minutes.

If there is any opportunity to demonstrate your reliability, then take it. Publishing is about deadlines, so if you are able to show that you can do what you say you can, and in the time you promise, then you'll go far. I bumped into a script editor years after I had written some one-liners for his programme. Not thinking he would remember me, he clapped me on the back and asked how I'd been. 'You were our best contributor,' he said, 'every week, rain or shine we knew you'd come up with the goods. Brilliant reliability. Not that funny, mind you, but very reliable.' OK, you can't win them all.   (STEPHEN HANCOCKS, CO-OWNER, OUTLAW THEATRE LIMITED, UK)

I'd love to give sound advice to people wanting the exact route into publishing, but the way I got into it was quite haphazard. Having applied to any publishers who offered a graduate recruitment scheme on leaving university, and heard nothing, I was fortunate enough to get a fortnight's work experience placement with Ebury in the very department I am working in now. As luck would have it, an assistant post cropped up while I was there, and I was asked if I'd be interested. I had an interview when I returned from my summer holiday a few weeks later, and the job was mine.

The message is to never ever underestimate the usefulness of work experience. Even though it is inevitably mundane and only really consists of stuffing endless envelopes, battling endlessly with temperamental photocopiers, and endlessly feeling as if you're hassling people, it really does pay to try your hardest to be the ultimate example of that shiny new addition to the team that even they didn't realise they needed.

While you may feel completely redundant in the office, people are, more often than not, more grateful for your presence and assistance than you think, and I'm saying this having had experience from the other side now. Be the most efficient, dynamic and smiley person despite the rubbish jobs – and get them done too – and you will be noticed for it.

(SARAH TOWNSEND, PUBLICITY ASSISTANT, RANDOM HOUSE UK)

More reading

Lowe, *Networking All in One Desk Reference for Dummies*, Hungry Minds, 2005

Lindenfield, *Confident Networking for Career Success and Satisfaction*, Piatkus Books, 2005

Timperley, *Network Your Way to Success*, Piatkus Books, 2002

Peterson, *Peterson's Internships*, Petersons, 2005

Chapter Nine
What kind of publishing job is right for you?

It's a great start to be aware that you'd like a career in publishing – in fact, without that you're unlikely to get any further. By itself, however, it's not enough. To find the right job for you, you need to understand what kind of roles exist and what will suit your particular skills and attributes. You can do this the hard way, by finding out through experience what you're not good at – or you can read the next couple of pages. Having done the former ourselves, we recommend the latter.

> Everyone can teach you something – ask if you can shadow different people for a day to get an understanding of how actions in one department affect those in another.
>
> (SARAH CASSIE, MARCOMMS MANAGER, MCGRAW-HILL EUROPE)

Sales

The sales team is the driving force of any publishing organisation. In popular myth your typical sales person is money-driven, highly competitive and a lone wolf. In reality, your typical sales person is, in fact, money-driven, highly competitive and a lone wolf. So if you are money-driven, highly competitive and a lone wolf, then perhaps sales is for you.

Sales suits people who are:
1. Confident and assertive

You're up for knocking on a door and getting told 'Not now!' – and then knocking on the next door. And the next. And the next. And ringing for appointments, getting told 'Don't bother' … and going anyway.

2. Organised

You're together enough to manage a sales territory with 200 book-shop buyers or 500 advertisers or 2,000 teachers, to know who is who, what they want, to learn a bagful of product and remember what's different about each and why. (This isn't about memory, by the way – it really is organisation.) You have great relationships with key decision-makers. You network easily and effectively (see Chapter 13 on this).

Actually, even if you've not thought of yourself as particularly organised before, if you're driven enough by results and sales bonuses (ie cash), then you'll find you learn some tricks and gain a fabulous grasp of the required detail.

3. Self-sufficient

You could enjoy working alone for much of the day, driving around or out on campus/at schools or at the premises of your advertisers, and stick to the job when for all anyone knows you could be playing golf instead.[1]

4. Up for it

You love meeting new people, travelling to remote parts of your territory and to sales conferences. You get really quite strangely turned on hitting targets, being under ridiculous amounts of pressure and achieving against apparently impossible odds. When you hit target and your next target is shifted sharply upwards as a result, your response is not 'That's not fair!' but 'I'll show you buggers'.

Sound like you? Then read on. Next are a couple of characteristics that aren't exactly essential, and indeed don't always apply, but may mark you out as potential sales material:

[1] *Susannah managed a rep who did this once ... and 'once' is the key word. Don't be tempted: you will get caught and fired, and rightly so. It's theft of the money your employer is paying you to do your job*

5. Interested in a publishing career

Sales can be a great way to get to know the market and the business in detail, before moving up in the company. It's common for senior managers within publishing to go out and spend a day visiting with the reps, and you can get some good contacts in this way. In magazine publishing, publishers often, if not most often, come from a sales background: spending your time wheeling and dealing in cash is a great way to show you can hack it as a commercially-minded business manager. (But don't, however, make the mistake of getting into sales in a magazine company and thinking you'll get the chance to transfer to editorial later on. You won't.)

I was looking for a 'school hours only' job to do after my youngest child started school and responded to a position in the local paper. My first position in publishing was working as a commission sales rep selling books direct to primary schools. It was a great introduction to the world of publishing. I learnt how important it is to consider the target market when publishing books. While it was hard work lugging suitcases of books into schools during lunch hours, I was frequently surprised by how envious teachers were of my job. Most had a very romantic picture of book publishing. I always valued that experience later on – it was excellent training to start from the coalface and work my way up as a publisher.

(AVERILL CHASE, DIRECTOR, THE AUTHORS' AGENT, AUSTRALIA)

How did I get my first job in publishing? I wrote to lots of literary agents, thinking that this was the profession for me. They all replied saying, 'Don't be so stupid. You can't just become a literary agent. You need wider experience – the media, publishing or bookselling – first.' One sent me the ads page of that week's Bookseller with a job ad for a Fontana Sales Trainee circled. I applied and got the job. I was given a Ford Cortina with packs of Agatha Christie in the back and off I went.

(CHARLES NETTLETON, MANAGING DIRECTOR, WORKING PARTNERS TWO, UK)

6. Based in non-central locations

In some branches of publishing, reps can be based all over the country looking after the local area. If you want to get a start in publishing and want to live somewhere other than London/Oxford/Sydney/Melbourne/other cities, repping is a great career option. (Reps are based in the big cities as well, of course.)

In both magazines and books this may work to start with, by the way, but if you're interested in moving up the ladder, the odds are you'll need to move to a head office location to make your mark.

Sales jobs include:

- **Sales assistants**

  Support sales reps and managers with research, arranging appointments, organising sales tools. In a smaller company, marketing assistant roles might be combined as **sales and marketing assistant**. This might be a graduate-level job where people spend a year or so, or it can be a longer-term option for a non-graduate or someone who wants a less demanding job.

- **Field/territory sales reps/consultants**

  Sales reps tend to have a company car, phone and laptop, and be on the road at least four days a week, sometimes five, meeting customers and talking about product.

  In **magazine publishing**, reps sell advertising space to whoever is relevant for the magazines they are working on – furniture, make-up, tourism providers and so on. The most successful ones actually become part of industry themselves, or come from it in the first place – they drive the cars (if it's a car magazine), sail the boats (if it's a boat magazine), wear the designer clothes (if it's a fashion magazine) and generally live the life. That way, they're perceived as an ally to the advertiser, rather than a bloodsucking parasite – it's a handy advantage!

In **trade publishing** (fiction/non-fiction/scholarly/medical), reps meet with bookshop buyers and persuade them to take stock of new releases and top up on old ones, and perhaps chat about merchandising and promotional options. This is usually a speedy process – you might get literally a second or two per book before the bookshop buyer moves on – and you would visit key bookshops once a month, two months, or quarterly, depending on your product.

In **schools and higher education** repping, sales reps visit teachers and lecturers and persuade them to recommend ('adopt') OUR book, not THEIR book. Reps might zip through schools/ universities a few times each year, and also spend time in bookshops, making sure the books are available.

Some repping jobs can be quite physically demanding. Susannah once counted the flights of stairs she climbed in one day: 42, while carrying a large bag with manuals of book information and book samples.

Most rep jobs are graduate-entry, or graduate plus a few years' work experience, preferably in a relevant field. Schools publishers tend to hire ex-teachers to do the repping.

- **Inside/telesales reps**
Work from within the office, ringing up customers to promote products. **Telesales** works well in publishing when there's a big geographical distance between customers. This is a fun role for someone who doesn't want to be out and about as much, and for people who like working the phone. For everyone else, it's hell on earth. It's bad enough getting rejected or abused in person: somehow it's even worse on the phone.

- **Business development/senior sales reps**
Might have the most important customers, or might combine their territory-repping roles with sales training for other sales reps.

- **Sales managers**

Work with their reps to make sure the focus is right and to train them. **Sales managers** often travel a lot to spend days out calling with their reps. They also provide lots of input in the office to publishing direction and company strategy. Sales managers have almost always done a few years of repping themselves.

- **Sales director**

The boss at the top who ties it all together might have a number of regional sales managers working for them. Sometimes this role is combined with marketing director.

- **Rights sales**

This is a specialised field – selling foreign publication and translation rights. (The first is where someone takes your product and re-publishes it in their local market, possibly tweaking it a bit but still in English; the second is where you allow them to translate your product and publish in certain foreign language areas.)

This is becoming a hugely important area for publishers, as securing print deals for several languages/different editions at the same time (rather than just for one market) can make the difference between printing being viable and non-viable.

Great **rights sales** people combine sales skills with excellent cultural awareness and an eye for detail; you'll be working with publishing people all over the world, many with English as their second language, sometimes through translators. This role is mainly office-based with stints of international travel to your key contacts and to the major book fairs (Frankfurt in October, London in March, Bologna for children's books in April, Book Expo America in June). Increasingly though, international communications make time out of the office at book fairs the chance to confirm deals made in principle through electronic media.

In small companies this is handled by the **sales** or **publishing manager**; it's only large companies that have a special person doing just this job.

Marketing

Marketing is in many ways the public end of the company – your work and words are what come to mind when people think about your organisation.

There are two types of marketing in publishing companies (and indeed in most of the corporate world):

- **Where marketing drives communications**
  Marketing primarily looks after communications, fulfilling the strategy and drive that come out of editorial and sales departments. In this type of company, the marketing department creates direct mail, publicity, advertising, websites, sales tools and other MarComms (Marketing Communications) functions.

- **Where marketing drives strategy and product decisions, as well as communications**
  In this type of company the marketing department works closely with authors, trains the sales team and has lots of input into publishing decisions, as well as fulfilling the MarComms functions.

Either way, entry-level marketing roles tend to be about MarComms – making brochures, making media releases and making tea, usually in reverse order – but it's worth bearing in mind that a company where marketing is respected as a strategic function is likely to be a more dynamic and creative place to work if you're looking for a long-term career in this field.

Marketing suits people who are:

1. Creative and ideas-driven

What's a great new way to get everyone's attention about this new book? What's a different, innovative, effective way to reach this audience? What copy style and design look will suit this brochure? How do I get people to wander into a bookshop, wander past the 50,000 other books on shelf, pick up THIS book – and then walk it to the till?

2. Happy in a fast-paced, demanding role

Roll out a publicity campaign by tea-time please. As a **marketing executive**, you might be simultaneously creating a number of brochures for a direct mail shot, thinking about who to mail them to, letting the customer service and warehouse/inventory departments know that the campaign is about to go, talking to the designer about the latest corrections, liaising with the editor to make sure the copy is accurate, liaising with your manager to make sure the copy is stylish, innovative and hits your market, planning supporting point-of-sale material for bookshops, reassuring an author that you're doing a great job with their book, planning a price rise for your list, reviewing competitor materials and campaigns, updating your website, rewriting a bunch of book blurbs for your next catalogue, costing a new campaign idea, taking calls from reps about product information, preparing sales tools for your upcoming rep conference, commenting on proposed front cover designs, reviewing a pile of book proposals to give feedback to the editor, planning a bookshop visit with your rep in Stockholm, proofing your colleague's new catalogue, answering a phone call asking for a suggested book list for a bookshop campaign that they need this afternoon, trying to get in a bit of lunch, and failing to do so (again). So if you fancy a quiet life, best look elsewhere ...

3. Confident

Your work is often public, in the form of brochures, ads and campaigns that everyone can see, admire and critique, and boy can it get annoying when you create a huge campaign and the managing director notices the one thing you got wrong.

4. Interested in presentation, style and the written word
Good promotion is all about hitting the right notes in the words you use and the image you create. If you've ever found yourself browsing dictionaries or books on language, if you have a favourite font, if you enjoy words and language for what they evoke, this could be the right job for you.

Good marketers need an eye for what looks good to other people's eyes; not as much as actually doing the design, but the capability to explain to designers how you want something to look and to work with them on a design that matches your message. Don't panic if this bit sounds foreign – a lot of this is a learned skill and you pick up ideas on how good design works as you go along.

5. Good at detail
This is often overlooked. But think about it: you've got to copy edit a 72-page catalogue while managing a $400,000 budget with expenditure allocations across 12 key areas and 15 types of promotions.

Marketing jobs include:
- **Marketing assistant/coordinator**
  An entry-level graduate role, often involving support duties such as copying information, updating websites, events (conference and book fair) coordination, and perhaps some basic design. Many assistants work in this entry-level role for one or two years and then look to move up the chain. In a smaller company **marketing assistant** roles might be combined into **sales and marketing assistant**; in a larger company there will be a number of marketing assistants, each one working in a subject area (Literary Fiction, Secondary Schools and so on).

- **Marketing executive/product manager**

  Often graduate plus two or more years' work experience. These roles might include creating promotional plans for books, author or list support, copywriting, placing advertising, briefing sales reps, and creating campaigns in direct mail, e-mail, the Web or bookshops. Some **marketing executives** might also be specialists in job functions such as direct mail, e-marketing and the Web etc.

- **Publicist/publicity manager**

  A role found in large, trade-focused companies (in fact sometimes this area is so important it operates as a separate department alongside the marketing department). **Publicists** specialise in coordinating book and author press and public relations campaigns including media interviews, planning campaigns and writing press releases. Smaller or less trade-oriented companies often give this function to a marketing executive and hire freelance publicity when needed.

- **Research manager**

  Magazine publishing houses need to be able to muster a lot of data to show advertisers why they should choose their magazine rather than anyone else's; and they also need to understand who their readers are, what they do and what makes them tick. Enter the **research manager**, a cross between a maths geek (like the bloke nicknamed 'Database' in the Simpsons); a cultural anthropologist, studying the strange habits and behaviour of readers; and scriptwriter, helping shape a great story for the advertising department to sell. To get a flavour for what this role is like, listen to one talking about one of his magazines:

  As a researcher, you need to spend as much time on your readers' values as you do on the content. So, readers of [Australian souped-up

See? Travis is talking about his readers in a way that reveals he obviously knows them intimately, and sees them as a group that can be packaged together and sold to advertisers.

- **Marketing manager/director**
  In a small company, the **marketing manager** does all the work listed above ... and answers the phone, too. In a large company the marketing manager may have staff who look after the detail of product and campaigns, freeing them up to create campaigns and strategy and work with editors on publishing direction.

  In large companies the **marketing director** is the top banana, perhaps with a number of marketing managers reporting to them. They might be **sales and marketing director**, too.

Editorial

'Editorial' is a word that creates some confusion – the difference between **copy editors** and **commissioning editors** is pretty major! For simplicity, we've split this wide field into editorial (meaning **development** and **copy editors**, who work in producing the book) and commissioning/publishers (meaning **commissioning**, **acquisitions editors** and **publishers** – people who find authors to write the books): see below. There's some crossover, and some companies start you in one and promote you to the other, but some don't; so if you're keen on going into editorial, make sure you know which it is you want.

In some ways editorial is the engine room of publishing – the people who create the words that make the books and the magazines.

Editorial suits people who are:

1. More than a little anal

Or 'with a keen eye for detail and precision' might be a more polite way of putting that. Taking a piece of writing, moving words about, making it completely consistent in layout, structure and style, and loving it; that's editorial.

Ever submitted an essay or report and then lay awake at night worried that your bullet points had inconsistent punctuation? You're a born editor. (You're also a bit scary which, come to think of it, a lot of good editors are.)

Editing is not a vague open-to-interpretation kind of skill. It's a set of rules and principles; you're being trained as a professional editor with skills to do editing, to do mark-up, and there are fundamental skills in grammar and expression and feel for words that you need. To achieve a high editorial standard is hard – there are only a few people who are going to be good editors – I don't see that as something you can train a mass of people in, anyway. That might sound a bit elitist but you need a temperament, to be anal, all those things.

(MANAGING DIRECTOR OF A SMALL CONSUMER PUBLISHING HOUSE, AUSTRALIA)

2. Crazy about words and grammar

And not just on a micro-level in terms of where the comma goes. A surprising amount of editorial is structural, for which your ability to grasp the whole direction and style of the story/piece/entire book you're working on and to apply your best efforts to reshaping the material is invaluable. Did you lose track of the end of that sentence? If you did, editorial might not be for you!

3. Happiest in the back room

There's not much glory in editorial: best managed, your work is invisible to the untrained eye (because it's so harmonious). Only other editors are going to congratulate you on a beautifully (re)constructed sentence, and authors hate to have it pointed out to them how much you amended what they wrote; they just assume the seamless prose was theirs all along. In your career as an editor at some point you will almost certainly find yourself rewriting material to such an extent that you should really get a co-authoring credit, although of course you won't.

On the other hand, if you don't fancy the knocking-on-doors-getting-yourself-out-there-public-face-of-the-company that is sales and marketing, editorial could work out for you perfectly.

4. Clever, widely interested and tactful

You're working with authors, after all, who are also clever, and giving them feedback about what they've written, so you'll need to have a mind quick enough to understand the structure and argument. And that applies to books about physics, life cycle of the earthworm and tractor parts, as well as the latest Zadie Smith (depending on where you work).

And authors are generally bloody touchy about someone messing with their precious words, so you'll need buckets of tact.

Editorial jobs include:
- **Copy editor**

  Works with the author from manuscript in to book out, as the main point of contact. Has the sometimes dubious pleasure of reading the book word by word, looking for errors and inconsistencies, and going back and forth with the author over queries and new drafts of the manuscript. **Copy editors** may also do structural editing (see below) and prepare permission and artwork briefs.

  If this is what you want to do, on top of your BA you'll need specialist training – either in-house at a publishers, or (more commonly now) in a postgraduate editing course, and possibly then to get an entry-level job as an **editorial assistant** (see below).

- **Structural editor**

  This role usually occurs in trade/fiction publishers. **Structural editors** sort out the story – make sure things are in the best possible order before the manuscript goes off to be tidied up by the copy editor. Structural editors don't need the eye for detail that copy editing demands but do need to understand how the story works and how it could work better. After a while they often graduate on to become commissioning/acquisitions editors.

  It's worth noting that structural editors now also thrive in agencies offering their services directly to authors; helping them manage their material before it gets to the agent or publisher.

- **Development editor/project editor**

  This role is more common in educational/professional publishing. They take on a structural role, and sometimes work in partnership with a commissioning editor (see below). So the commissioning editor might sign up the author to write the book, and the **development editor** then works closely with the author while they do the writing, to make sure the book does exactly what the publishers want it to do. They may also be responsible for market research such as investigating areas for publishing a potential new list. They need editing skills, an eye for detail, and great structural understanding of what's needed – the lot really.

- **Proofreader**

  At the end of the process, someone has to do it – working through the page proofs. This is the absolutely very last no turning back final checking, looking for spelling, grammatical and typesetting errors, and probably spot-checking contents list, index and author's name (at least twice).

  Most **proofreaders** are now freelancers, with just a few left as employees of publishing houses.

- **Managing editor**

  Organises production and briefs copy editors. Depending on the size of the company, this job might run in combination with production manager (see 'Production', below).

- **Desk editor**

  This is an outdated term for a managing editor or copy editor.

Editor jobs come in two flavours: in-house and freelance. Most editors start out working in-house for a publisher and then at some point may choose to go freelance, working for themselves, once they have the experience and contacts (and guts or lifestyle requirements) to set up on their own.

Commissioning jobs

These are also often – confusingly – called editing or publishing jobs. They suit people who are:

1. Knowledgeable and in tune with society

Publishers are product development engineers, creating products for mass or specific audiences. So you need to provide what those audiences want, or the magazines will sit in the newsagents and the books won't get bought. Commissioning publishers need to be up to date with the latest trends, half a step behind the zeitgeist, to create the books and magazines people want to read.

2. Strategic thinkers

Magazine publishers are strategic thinkers, working out what the next big thing is going to be and getting a new magazine launched before anyone else is out of the starting blocks. You need to build a portfolio that blocks competitors without eating itself (ie one in which the magazines complement each other and don't steal advertising from one another).

Similarly, in book publishing, building a list can take years of careful planning – by the time you've figured out what you want to publish, found the author, signed them up, given them a year or two to write something and then got it out into bookshops – and done it again and again to create a list of books with a specific style and focus. And you need to do it all years in advance to figure out what will be the hot topics by the time it all publishes.

In both areas, a highly developed sense of strategy is essential.

3. Able to see the 'big picture'

For the reasons mentioned above, you need to be able to see the forest, not just the leaves. Few people can do this well, and even fewer in publishing. After all, if you've been in a job like editorial or sales where detail is king, it can be difficult to make the adjustment to a position where what really matters is not the comma, nor even the chapter (feature), nor even the book (magazine), but the range and the market. It's the difference between using a microscope and a telescope.

4. Political animals

You've got to be good at taking the credit and avoiding the blame. There's big money at the top end of any business, and no-one's going to step aside and offer you the floor: you've got to take it for yourself. Many of the best people in publishing are shrinking violets who never get to fulfil their potential because they just don't like the limelight. That's fine, but it does mean you never get to have the influence you could have.

Commissioning jobs include:

- **Editorial/publishing assistants**

  Assistants do the really bottom-end stuff; photocopying manuscripts, ringing authors to remind them of submission due dates, sending out questionnaires for feedback on proposals. This is a great entry point into the world of editorial and jobs can be very hard to come by. As you get more experienced you'll be given more responsibility and maybe even a small list to manage in combination with your assistant-level roles. In a trade house you might even be the one reading through the slush pile of unsolicited manuscripts to discover the next Harry Potter, and be promoted into a great commissioning editor role.

- **Commissioning/acquisitions editor**

This is the person who signs up authors to write books. There are a few different models for this.

In schools and higher education publishing, the **acquisitions editor** works on a list and identifies areas where they would like to publish a new title: 'We have two introduction to business books, but neither of them uses the approach that the most popular competitor does'. Having identified the market gap, the acquisitions editor works with their contacts (teachers, lecturers) to find the right person to create the book. Unsolicited manuscripts initiated by the author are rare (or rather, they are common, but rarely published).

In these two fields of publishing, publishers are often promoted out of the sales team; the on-the-ground experience of a few years out talking to the people who then become authors is invaluable.

Trade, professional and university press publishing tends to be a mix of identifying a market gap and seeking an author, working with previously successful authors and agents to secure their new projects, and working through prospective new authors to see what projects might work (much less common than you'd imagine). In these areas publishers often start as editorial assistants, and are known as **commissioning editors** (though not always).

There's more than one way to get to your dream job. If you want to be a commissioning editor, you don't necessarily have to start as an editorial assistant at your favourite publisher and work your way up. I started off in book clubs and then bookselling, getting an overview of all the publishers' lists and reading hundreds of new titles across all fiction genres. When I moved over into publishing proper, they wanted me for my commercial knowledge as well as any editorial skills I possess. I'd also spent years meeting people from all the publishing houses and had a very clear idea of which companies I would and wouldn't want to work for. (SUZIE DOORÉ, SENIOR EDITOR, HODDER & STOUGHTON, UK)

My entry into magazine publishing came via a less than usual route. I started as an apprentice bookbinder all those years ago. There are more than the usual ways to end up in publishing!

(STUART JONES, CIRCULATION MANAGER,
AUSTRALIAN CONSOLIDATED PRESS)

- **Publisher/publishing director**
  After a number of years as a successful commissioning or acquisitions editor, you might become a **publisher**. Sometimes this means getting more internal power in creating the list you want, the authors you want, creating a whole new area of publishing for the company; sometimes it means having a bunch of junior editors reporting to you while you plan the strategic direction and they fulfil it. Definitely no making cups of tea for others now.

Production

Production staff are often the cement of publishing companies. Intrinsic problem-solvers, they tend to break down difficult situations into component parts and then look at how to deal with each issue in turn. In addition to being good at their jobs, they are great people to talk to!

Production suits people who are:
1. Organised, competent and calm
If you can keep tabs on 200 different projects in varying stages of a long process, this is the job for you.

2. Collaborators

Production depends on people responsible for all the other stages in the chain doing their bit in time, and adjusting schedules and suppliers as problems arise. Effective production people can come up with solutions as the plot thickens, not just throw their hands in the air and think 'it's all awful'.

3. Makers and doers

Production people quite literally make the book, turning a massive great long Word document into something that sits in your bookshelf. They need to be up to date with current technology and future trends.

Production jobs include:

- **Production editor/production controller**

  Organises production and manufacturing – works with printers and typesetters and copy editors and proofreaders to get a book through the process. Sometimes this job comes under the editorial banner, too.

- **Production manager**

  Does what it sounds like – runs the department, making sure every project is where it should be. Might manage some projects personally as well as working with **production controllers** who handle most of them.

Technical jobs in production include:

- **Designers and illustrators**

  Often freelance but occasionally working as employees, these people make the books and covers look pretty.

- **Multimedia**

  Again often freelance, but sometimes employees – designing CDs, DVDs and websites. Most often occurs in educational/ professional publishing houses.

Other departments in publishing

There are other job opportunities within publishing too, of course, but many of these require skills that are transferable from other industries or professions, rather than being specific to publishing. For example:

- **Royalties, copyrights, contracts**
  Do some kind of highly technical thing to make sure authors do what they should and get paid what they should.

- **Stock control/inventory management**
  These hugely important people make sure the books are where they should be, in the quantity they should be available. On locally published books (ie ones that originate in the home market) they'll work closely with the production and publishing departments to organise reprints; on imported books they'll work with rights and marketing to make sure they're stocking the right quantities, where and when they are needed.

- **Business management**
  Accounting types who make sure the business is on the right side of the balance sheet.

- **Customer service**
  Handle direct customer orders and ensures efficient despatch; deal with subsequent contact with customers, complaints and praise. These staff are capturing essential first-hand information from customers of all sorts (individual and bookshop buyers); their feedback on how the ordering process feels to the customer can be invaluable. Often situated away from the main offices, their input all too often goes unacknowledged.

- **Warehouse**
  Look after the books. Often warehouses and offices are separated but if you're lucky, you'll work for publishers where the

warehouse is on the same site, and you'll be able to see huge piles of your books on racks, learn about how pick and pack of orders work, and dive through the box of damaged stock that's been returned to see if there's anything your mum would like. And hear and repeat amusing anecdotes about the warehouse bloke who drove a forklift into a pallet of books, lit a cigarette to calm his nerves and set off the sprinkler system.

- **Accounts and finance**
  They pay the bills and send out bills and chase cheques. They may also pay you.

- **Human resources (HR)**
  Help managers to hire, fire, train staff, create policies and manage the workplace.

Politics between the various departments

In general, publishing is a collaborative industry. Most organisations have a relatively flat management structure – in other words effective publishing relies on deals between different departments/individuals, rather than a hierarchical management structure where layers of management tell lower layers what to do. So an editor for a particular title will liaise with that title's production editor, marketing person and rights coordinator, and each staff member may subcontract to freelancers. Working relationships tend to be informal and people typically casually dressed (or downright scruffy). Susannah recalls a chap at a place she once worked who regularly used to come into the office in his pyjamas. You should however be aware that there may be long-standing tensions between various different departments; the coordination required to get a book out may not be quite as readily available as required.

Looking back, I wish I had understood more clearly the ideological divide that exists in many publishing houses between sales/marketing and publishing/editorial. It wasn't until after I had worked on both sides that I really appreciated the different concerns and viewpoints held by each.

(JESSICA, AUSTRALIA)

Senior staff are often ready and willing to give advice and mentoring to those who are starting out, and several firms offer such schemes, on a formal or informal basis. Publishing personnel often take part in industry-wide training schemes as part of a general attempt to train future publishers, whether or not they eventually end up working for *them*. There is a widespread and altruistic nurturing of younger members of the profession, which strikes those from other industries as remarkable.

My first job was for a direct marketing agency, but after 18 months I got a job with a publisher and it was announced in the moves section of *The Bookseller*. One of the first calls I got was from Liz Newland of Dent, a former client (and now competitor), who congratulated me and then told that if I ever wanted advice, I had only to ask. I can still remember what she said: 'There will be times when you don't know what to do, and don't wish to reveal this in-house. In which case, you are more than welcome to ring me.' I thought this extremely generous and her offer was hugely appreciated.

(ALISON)

I was fortunate to have a great mentor who trained me in so many aspects of the industry – local, international, professional bodies, ISBN agencies, bibliographic providers, competitors, trends, products and customers. The best advice he ever gave me was 'don't make an enemy in the trade'. This was probably the wisest advice you can give someone in the book and publishing industry.

On a general business level, he also passed on the 'never assume something, as to assume makes an ASS out of U-and-ME' and he stressed the importance of the customer, service and supply. My second mentor, a creative and dynamic woman with whom I worked for nine years, passed on her business and marketing knowledge, and continued to build on my enthusiasm and passion for the industry, the products and the customers.

(RACHAEL MCDIARMID, JAMES BENNETT, AUSTRALIA)

More reading

Gitomer, *The Sales Bible*, Wiley, 2003

Gitomer, *The 25 Habits of Highly Successful Salespeople*, Adams Media, 1997

Bettger, *How I Raised Myself from Failure to Success in Selling*, Simon and Schuster, 2004

Baverstock, *How to Market Books*, 4th edn, Kogan Page, 2008

Smith and Hiam, *Marketing for Dummies*, Wiley, 2006

Evans, *The Layers of Magazine Editing*, Columbia University Press, 2004

Frost, *Designing for Newspapers and Magazines*, Routledge, 2003

Owen, *Selling Rights*, Routledge, 2006

Jones and Benson, *Publishing Law*, Routledge, 2006

Part lll: How to get your job

Chapter Ten
Before you start . . .

Now's the bit where you pull it all together and actually get yourself that job. That job might be the job of your dreams, or the stepping stone towards the job of your dreams; not just any job, but one that you enjoy, that's rewarding and challenging, and puts you on the right career path for even more long-term success and rewards.

There are lots of ways to approach this. Some people jump head-long into recruitment agencies and interviews and work everything else out as they go along. Oddly enough, one of the hardest things about job hunting, from about your second job onwards, is not so much getting the job; instead, it's knowing whether it's the right job for you in terms of what you want and where you want to go. It's nerve-wracking to accept a job if you're not sure it's what you want, and even worse to start with a company and discover a few weeks or months in that it isn't right for you. There are some basic prep steps that can help you to avoid this.

One final thing before you get into it. Are you ready to get that job or are there other things you should do first, such as travel or more study? A lot of people find it hard to get off the full-time wagon and end up with their heads down for the next ten years – so if there's something else you want to pursue, now might be a good time.

On the other hand, don't pick up a course or travel or engage in some other form of time-filling just because you're worried you won't be able to get a job you like.

Susannah once knew a guy who spent six years 'working on his portfolio' to get work as a graphic designer before actually showing any of his work to anyone, and then another two more years of work before taking a job. Instead, we encourage you to give it a whirl and see what happens! If you're not sure if you're ready, one way of find-ing out is to give it a go – if you go through interviews and it feels wrong, or potential employers tell you that you need more skills or more study, you can always reconsider.

There are lots of ways to job hunt – what works for you will depend on your own motivation and work style:

- Most people **read through the job ads** on the day they come out, circle a few and send off CVs over the following weekend.
- Some people **treat it like a full-time job** – clock on in the morning, spend the day browsing the Internet, ringing contacts and tweaking CVs, clock off at the end of the afternoon.
- If you're really desperate for a job and you're flexible about which job and where, try making a rule whereby you **apply for, say, ten jobs each week**. If you have to hit a number week in, week out, it can make you look in places you wouldn't normally, and apply for roles you might not have considered otherwise. You never know what might come up.
- **Remember networking and getting proactive** – targeting companies you want to work for and approaching them, and letting everyone you can think of know you're job hunting and asking for their help (more on this in Chapter 13). Remember, too, that a high percentage of jobs never get advertised at all – they go to friends of employees, those who had provided CVs that were on file in the HR office, and so on.

OK, let's go get that job.

Getting started

The starting point is to think about which job you want and which job you can realistically get! There will be lots of advice on this in the rest of this book, but for now, let's start with what you are looking for.

You might enjoy making a list of essential/desirable attributes for your job. A great way of doing this is to think about attributes for your perfect job and how far you are prepared to compromise. So for example, if you want to be a marketing assistant at *Vogue*, you might consider being a marketing assistant at *Wheels* but not a sales rep at *Vogue*, or vice versa. If you know what the perfect job is, you're more likely to find it; and if not, it's good to know where you'll draw a line.

	Perfect	**Not quite perfect but a good stepping stone**
Type of publisher		
Location		
Salary and conditions		
Area of publishing		
Position		
Size of company		
Culture		
Opportunities		
Other		

Some things to think about:

1. Type of publisher – fiction, non-fiction, magazines, journals, educational, children's

What are you interested in? What do you enjoy? You spend a lot of time at work so you're going to enjoy it more, be more motivated, and be better at your job if you're working in an area you're interested in.

The first few jobs you take can set you on the path for the future – which can be good OR bad. It's often harder to change the area of publishing you work in once you've got a few years of experience behind you, so best if you can get it right from the start.

> After a few years in educational publishing, I wondered if I might enjoy fiction/trade publishing more. I looked into it and realised I had to choose between my current junior management role in educational publishing, or stepping back to an assistant/executive-level role in fiction, which meant

> a drop in pay and responsibility. I decided to sit tight, so I have never worked on the popular literature that I enjoy reading myself. If I were to start my career over again, I might hold out for a job in literary fiction, rather than beginning as a book rep for educational publishing and then following an educational publishing path.   (SUSANNAH)

Remember that areas of publishing which might not sound very glamorous on the surface can actually be fascinating. For all that Susannah has never done media interviews with Gordon Ramsay, she gained huge enjoyment out of working with textbooks and academic authors. There is also an argument that people shouldn't work on products they are too close to . . . the lit theory graduate may write fabulous book blurbs for sociology books but atrocious ones for lit theory books! (This also tells you a lot about why authors shouldn't write their own book blurbs, by the way.)

2. Does it have to be publishing?
Think about non-publishing companies which have publishing-esque jobs:

- **Newsagents and bookshops** are obvious places to work for getting to know the magazine and book trade
- **Editorial and marketing** work can be found in the corporate communication departments of universities, banks, law and large professional firms
- **Writing and design** is a key part of advertising
- **Charities and direct mail** companies create catalogues and other publications
- **Libraries and education** are good related professions
- **Government** sectors of all sizes have publishing divisions who pump out printed material and websites
- Also think about **publishing industry services** including training organisations, general organisations that promote reading, book information companies such as Bowker, publishing industry magazines, library suppliers, mailing houses and so on

All these are legitimate careers or great back door entry paths into publishing (see also Chapter 14).

> Although I always planned a career in publishing, my first job was for a direct marketing agency that specialised in the supply of mailing lists and campaigns to academic and educational publishers. It was an excellent place from which to review the publishing industry and to decide firstly what kind of firm I wanted to work for, and then which one. And when I applied for my first job, I already knew the person I would be working for.
>
> (ALISON)

3. Location: which city, and where in that city?

If you're in the UK and you're serious about a publishing career, most opportunities can be found in London or the M4/M40 to Oxford belt – with a smattering of companies in Edinburgh and the Home Counties. If you're in Australia, it's mainly Sydney, followed by Melbourne, and the other places a long way behind. Big companies can be flexible about location but usually not until you're in a senior role. Would the right job be important enough for you to relocate? Before you answer that, ask yourself:

- **If you have a partner, will he or she move?** Or be prepared for a long-distance relationship?
- What would it be like **living away from your parents and siblings** and the area you grew up in, if you went to a local university?
- How would you manage **building a new friendship circle**?

If you live in a small town or the country, the answer to whether or not you're prepared to move almost certainly has to be 'yes' – there are very few publishing opportunities in the country (though there are some, and this can actually be a career advantage to start off with – see below). So figuring out where you will live tells you where to hunt for jobs. Once you're got the city/region right, look at location of companies. Long commute? Short commute? Public transport versus driving? Note that many multinationals have small hub offices and sales reps who work from home. Again, this can be a good foot in the door, but you will find as you work up the career ladder that the location issues come up again; promotion opportunities are limited if you're the northern region rep based in Huddersfield, and the head office is in Chichester.

Another thing to consider about location is that sometimes it can work the other way; the pool of graduates prepared to work in publishing for less money and in a remote location can be smaller than those applying for work in a metropolis – and so you're more likely to get a job in the country/a remote area. In Australia, it's quite common for people who want to work in newspapers to move to a country town for a few years and get a start at a regional newspaper and then move back to the city with great experience. If this is something that might work for you, it's worth browsing regional job ads and thinking about local newspapers, newsletters and magazines, regional head offices with corporate communications, universities and colleges in regional areas with editing, design and writing work, and so on.

4. Salary

Well, no-one should go into publishing for the money. Let's say that again: no-one should go into publishing for the money! But you do need to know what you can expect, what's realistic and what's not, and whether you can live on it.

Broadly, bigger companies tend to pay slightly more; magazines tend to pay more than books; companies located in bigger cities tend to pay more than those in the regions.

Good ways to research what's reasonable include:

- **Ask your friends** – and making adjustments for industry, size of company, experience and training.
- **Google** general industry information and salary surveys. See if any have been carried out recently by your national professional association of publishers.

- **Talk to recruitment agents** – who may or may not tell you anything, and will tell you 'it all depends', but may also provide some level of helpful information.
- **Ask companies** when they interview you. See salary discussion below in the interview section. You'll find trends emerging which will help you figure out the rough going rate.

As well as salary, consider other conditions including:

- **Bonus/incentive schemes**
  Traditionally more common in sales roles and increasingly found in areas such as marketing, editorial and, in some progressive companies, right through the company. Schemes are performance-based and might be for just you, or you and the team you're part of. So if you do well against the target you're being measured on, you get a bit extra. A typical bonus might be a certain amount for every percentage point of sales over the team target, for example. Bonuses are worked out at end of the calendar or financial year. The best kind aren't capped – so if you or your team have a great year, you get a juicy reward! The key thing about bonuses is they're exactly conditional on performance; so one year you might earn an extra big stack on top of your salary, and the next, nothing. If a company is talking a lot about its bonus scheme, a good thing to ask is 'how many times in the last five years have bonuses been paid' – which is the same thing as asking how many times your group has hit its sales/performance targets.

- **Commission**
  Usually paid monthly to sales reps – also performance-based – and can replace part of the salary. So instead of being paid a certain set amount each year, a sales rep might get paid half that, plus monthly commissions worked out by how many sales are made. This can be a bit scary – if the economy goes down and no-one is buying, or the product you are trying to sell isn't good,

it's your take-home pay that suffers. On the other hand, the potential is there to earn loads of commission. Commission-only sales roles are unusual in book publishing.

(Note that terminology for bonuses and commissions can overlap – make sure you clarify exactly what you're prepared to take.)

- **Pension schemes/extra superannuation**
This can seem pretty distant if you're in your 20s, but extra pension is something you will appreciate one day. Some companies offer a matching scheme where if you put a bit in, they will too.

- **Holiday and sick leave allowances**
All companies must offer legal minimums; some companies include extra leave as part of generous working conditions. If they do, they're usually pretty proud of them and will highlight the good conditions for you.

- **Other benefits**
These include share schemes, health insurance schemes, flexible hours/working from home, crèche and family facilities, financial support/flexibility for study and so on – obviously some of these are things you'll look for if they're relevant for you.

In general, good conditions aren't something people consider when they're job hunting; maybe they should be. A company that invests in good conditions for staff will often have a happy work environment where you'll enjoy spending your time.

If you're graduating from university and this is your first full-time job, starting salaries can seem enormous, compared to student allowances/the pittance you've been managing on until now. This is almost certainly an illusion. Remember that once you're working full-time you'll have all kinds of extra costs like travel, business clothes, lunches and so on. You might also want to upgrade where you've been living/your evening haunts, buy a car, and so on.

On the other hand, if you're coming from another industry, especially something more business-y such as finance or insurance, starting salaries can seem very low.

5. Area of publishing/department

Where do you want to work? Sales, marketing, editorial, design or somewhere else? Would you rather work for the right company in the wrong job and hope to move over, or wait until the right job function comes along, even in a company you don't like the look of?

This really depends on the company and how sharp you can be about looking great in a job that you secretly see as a bit of a stop-gap. In many companies, once you're in, you can move around easily.

> I applied for anything which had 'Assistant' or 'Administration' in the title – it didn't matter what area or publishing house. Once you've got that proverbial foot in the door, moving around and up a company is that much easier.
>
> (MEREDITH REES, HIGHER EDUCATION DEVELOPMENT EDITOR, AUSTRALIA)

Be careful, though – it's often easier to move between sales and marketing and between editorial/production/publishing than it is to swap between those two sectors, especially in the magazine sector where sales is quite far away from editorial functions.

6. Position

This really depends on your level of experience and training, and what you're prepared to do. Most graduate/entry-level jobs will be called 'assistant', 'officer', 'executive' and involve a certain amount of standing by the fax machine, filling in at reception, sticking labels on books and other banal work. If you're moving into publishing from another industry and have some work experience behind you, you'll be looking for a role where you can use that experience as well as break yourself gently into the industry. Be reasonable; there is really no point deciding that you want your first job to be a commissioning editor or marketing manager, because it almost certainly won't happen without you serving a few years as associate editor/editorial assistant/marketing assistant first. This can work the other way too; employers will think you're a bit odd if you're applying for jobs that are clearly too junior for you. Balance is the key!

7. Big company/small company

Most large publishing houses are local divisions of multinational corporations, such as Penguin, Random House or McGraw-Hill. Broadly, in a large company (say, 30 or more staff), you're more likely to:

- **Work in one job area**, because the company is well resourced – so you might snare a role as one of eight editorial assistants, where you work with, say, the popular science editor with research and reviewing, and don't have too much to do with other subject areas or job functions
- **Get structured opportunity for promotion**
- **Get average or above-average (for the industry) rate of pay** and conditions and well-organised bonus schemes
- **Get involved in structured business planning**, decisions and practices

In smaller publishing houses you're more likely to:

- **Get wider experience** – so your job might be **sales, marketing and editorial assistant**, working across a variety of job functions
- **Get below-average salary**
- **Experience publishing at its most creative** – where books get published because of gut feel, ideology or government support

I got a job in Tokyo, working for an art/graphic design book publisher by answering a newspaper ad. I had already moved to Tokyo to live. I was the

8. Culture

This is a tough one, and hard to gauge before you get a job, and even
harder if you've not worked full-time before. People often know what
kind of culture they **don't** want to work in – stuffy, overly structured
and where new ideas are quashed.

What kind of culture might you feel comfortable in?

Ways the company might be described	Good points	Bad points
Innovative, creative, responsive	Energising environment with lots of great ideas	Young, energetic staff tend to move on – can be unsettling
Stable, experienced, knowledgeable	Lots for you to learn from experienced colleagues	Dull, lacking in creativity – *'We tried that eight years ago and it didn't work'*
Like a big family. *'We work hard and play hard – and we do it together'* (and we talk in clichés)	Strong group culture – supportive and fun	Are they supportive of difference? If you don't fit the culture you might not enjoy it

9. Opportunities

Do you want to progress quickly in your career? You might look for
a company that offers a formal advancement plan (more likely to
be a bigger company), or consider a less formal company where

advancement happens if you do a good job. Most companies will say they offer potential for career advancement but this is not always the case – see Chapter 16 for more on this.

> I started at Black Inc. in 2001 as a publishing assistant, doing editorial work, publicity, administration . . . you name it! Five years later I became managing director. You could say that I have grown up with the company.
>
> (SOPHY WILLIAMS, MANAGING DIRECTOR, BLACK, INC, AUSTRALIA)

If you have a particular career goal in mind, think about what type of company you should work for to help you achieve this.

> I started in publishing as a sales rep in Melbourne, Australia. I was always interested in working in the UK – so I made sure I worked for an international company and made myself known to the UK managers whenever the opportunity came up. In time I was able to step straight into a great job in the UK. I certainly wouldn't have been able to do this in a locally-owned company.
>
> (SUSANNAH)

A word of warning. If you're in a job at the moment, or have some experience though previous jobs/internships, be wary of over-simplifying based on your experiences which can make you sound over idealistic or just naive. Don't fall into the trap of 'I loved/hated that job in the large magazine publisher, so I need to find work with/ absolutely avoid another large magazine publisher.' Apart from avoiding presenting yourself as a negative person, it pays you to think about *why* you loved/hated the job; and as well as things like type of company, don't forget:

- What **kind** of work you were doing
- What your **boss** was like
- The **challenges** you had
- Opportunities for **promotion**, pay rises, travel, variation of role

- **Physical environment** – nice office space, ease of transport, proximity to shops etc
- What kind of **emotional space** you were in at the time

All of these factors influence how much you enjoy your current job.

OK, so now you've got some ideas about what you're looking for. Figuring out what job you want and where is the first step in your plan to getting your job in publishing.

More reading

www.bookcareers.com

www.careersonline.com.au

www.careersa-z.co.uk

www.prospects.ac.uk

http://jobstar.org/index.php

www.services.unimelb.edu.au/careers/student/index.html

Lees, *How to Get a Job You'll Love*, McGraw-Hill, 2006

Bolles, *What Color Is Your Parachute?*, Ten Speed Press, 2006

Chapter Eleven
How to create a stunning CV

This chapter is all about creating a great general CV that you can use as a basis for job hunting. Chapter 12 shows you how to write a job application letter and adapt your CV to the job you are applying for.

Your CV is your introduction. Done well, it makes your future employer (think positive!) go further and find out more about you. It's a display of the most appealing, interesting, relevant and attractive things about you – not every detail, just the key things that show you at your best.

If you were a shop, your CV would be your shop window, and getting an employer interested enough to invite you for interview is like enticing them to step inside.

> **Remember: your CV gets you the *interview*, the interview gets you the *job*.**

Your CV should:

- **Include key details**, representative of the rest of you:
  - your education
  - your experience
  - your skills

It should give just enough to show you could be the right person for the job, and it's worth interviewing you.

- **Have just the headlines**, not the whole story in excruciating detail. Too much info in a CV looks cluttered and can be hard to understand without context.

- **Look great**, ie:
  - easy on the eye
  - easy to find core information
  - attractive layout
  - free from grammatical and spelling typos

> It sounds very obvious, but an application letter full of typos for a publishing job is not a good start. (LIZ SMALL, PUBLISHING SCOTLAND)

Stick to these basic rules and you're well on the way to creating a great CV.

One thing to say about the mechanics of putting your CV together is that there are fairly standard templates around with small variations to choose from and show your individuality. This is good advice. CVs are emphatically *not* the place to get creative. You should stand out from the crowd through flawless language, spelling and grammar and by creating a superb piece of communication, especially in a words-driven industry such as publishing. Don't use multicoloured paper; don't demonstrate just how many typefaces your computer has; don't be 'different'.

There are hundreds of books on how to put together a CV, and even more opinions from agencies and friends who offer conflicting advice about how important it is to put employment first then education, or the other way around; about having really classy headers or keeping it simple; about layouts, colours and so on.

None of this matters. What *does* matter, however, are the following:

The Seven Golden Rules of CVs

1. **Be clear**, neatly laid out, and with a legible font – professional in appearance.
2. Show off your absolutely **flawless spelling and grammar** – and plain English language, too, not packed with jargon.
3. Contain all the **key information** and nothing more.

4. Be **three pages** at absolute most – two is better.
5. Give your **best reasons** for getting the job. Focus on what you know about the company and job and tweak your CV to fit.
6. Add **nothing** you don't want to be asked about. Omit school results, middle names that embarrass you, peculiar interests (maze designing, penguin baiting, you name it) . . . *If in doubt, leave it out.*
7. Be **safe, friendly and pleasant.** You want to come across as someone they might want to employ. Don't worry about looking bland; you can show your fascinating style and personality at interview. If you don't get that far, all the interestingness is for nothing.

Non-publishing jobs such as sales assistants in vacuum cleaner companies may attract 10 or 20 applications. Not surprisingly, perhaps, you're not competing against a high number of people. Many jobs in publishing, however, see 200 or more CVs land on the desk of the advertiser. The record we've heard of is 566 – for an editorial assistant job.

So how much attention does each CV and covering letter get? Well, it's measured in seconds, not minutes.

In magazine publishing, if we advertised for an editorial assistant we would get 300 or 400 applications. After a while I got clever about it and made it harder for employees to apply, by asking for a 1,000-word written piece on the role of contemporary magazines, or something like that. That used to cut it down to around 20 good applications.   (STEVE)

Rejoice when you find it hard to apply for a job: the higher the hurdle, the better, because the more people will give up and eliminate themselves before they get to the starting block. If a job ad is tough to apply for and needs you to do a bunch of work, it's really worth gritting your teeth and getting on with, as you're much more likely to be considered.

In general if you're competing against 200 other CVs, yours needs to be *easy* to flick through and the most relevant details must *jump up*.

Your CV is actually working on two levels:

1. It has to stand up to the quick glance through so that it gets put in the 'Yes' or 'Perhaps' pile
2. It will get a longer, detailed examination as recruiters decide whether to call you for interview

Getting through the first, quick-glance stage gets you from the full pile of 200, 300 or more CVs to a long list of perhaps 20, 30 or 50. Progressing from that long list to shortlist interview stage means you're in the last 5 or 10 CVs.

Alright, let's get started.

Layout, paper and appearance
Font

Pick something easy to read, preferably not Times New Roman since that's the default on Word and therefore what people without imagination use. If you can find out what their house font is, it's a good idea to use it back to them – you look like you fit in already!

Go with a serif or sans serif font. Serif fonts are those with little feet on the letters, traditionally easier to read, such as

- Georgia
- Garamond
- Palatino

Sans serif fonts are those without little feet, traditionally cleaner looking. Try

- Verdana
- Trebuchet MS
- Arial

Whatever font you prefer is fine, though check with your Honest Friend[1] that it's readable. There's a whole unconvincing debate about women liking sans serif and men liking serif (or was it vice versa?). Don't worry about that; just pick something readable that works for you.

Don't get into lots of different fonts for headings and body text, it just gets confusing and looks messy. If you do go for a different font for headings, make sure it's readable – we said this before but it's important.

EMMA WOODHOUSE	Stands out. Simple. Clear.
Emma Woodhouse	Looks classy but isn't easy to read.

Typefaces also become dated very quickly. So, for this reason, don't use Comic Sans MS. It's about as groovy as wearing a tie with Bart Simpson on it.

Paper

Plain white A4 is fine. You might go for a slightly thicker paper or creamier colour; nothing more complex than that though. Stapled is fine; don't use a paperclip (papers separate out) or bind (impossible to split pages out and photocopy – it also makes you look inflexible, as if the same CV has been over-manicured for impact; a CV should change with each application).

The entire CV should be just two or three pages; absolutely no more. We've never met a CV where it wasn't possible to chop out some irrelevant or unnecessary information. If you can't bear to trim anything, give it to your Honest Friend to help you cross bits out.

Some people like a title page with your name and contact details, before getting into the nitty-gritty on page two. If you're going to do

---

[1] *Honest Friend: an honest friend. See glossary*

this, we suggest also having something to grab the attention, such as a summary of your experience and what you're looking for, and your mission statement. The first page is obviously the first thing to get attention and a page with nothing but 'Emma Woodhouse' is a waste of that attention, when you could be driving home something about yourself.

CV
Emma Woodhouse

Address and tel details

Summary:

- A keen and bright graduate looking for a career in publishing
- Experience in sales, marketing and customer service
- BA (First Class) from Oxford Brookes University; MA in Publishing Studies, Kingston University

If you want to get straight into it with the body of the CV, that's fine too.

CV
Emma Woodhouse

Address and tel details

Summary:

- A keen and bright graduate looking for a career in publishing
- Experience in sales, marketing and customer service
- BA (First Class) from Oxford Brookes University; MA in Publishing Studies, Kingston University

Experience:
- And so on

Headings can be centred or aligned left. Body text should be aligned left. Right justify makes things stand out if you use it sparingly. Whatever style you choose, be consistent. Avoid justifying the full text; it's alienating.

Your name

Remember, put nothing on your CV you wouldn't be happy to discuss at interview. So don't include middle names or nicknames if they embarrass you. On the other hand, the details kindly donated by your parents may be just the things to attract initial interest:

> My first job in publishing was at André Deutsch. I was twenty-one, relatively new to London and didn't know how to use apostrophes. I got the job mainly because Tom Rosenthal (then Chairman of Deutsch) is a huge fan of James Joyce and my name is Anna Livia Plurabelle – the 'floozy in the jacuzzi' in *Finnegans Wake*. It also helped that I lived on Deronda Road – another literary reference.
>
> (ANNA KIERNAN, COURSE DIRECTOR, MA IN PUBLISHING, KINGSTON UNIVERSITY, UK)

However, if you have a gender non-specific name, or your daily-use name is a nickname that's not intuitive, you might like to explain yourself. It's not a legal document, so your name doesn't need to be what's on your birth certificate – it should be whatever you like to be known as.

Emma Woodhouse	Good – simple and clear
Emma Isobel Woodhouse	Middle name isn't necessary
Emma Isobel Woodhouse (Isobel)	Use Isobel Woodhouse
Darcy Brown	Not that it should matter, but recruiters like to know if you're male or female – so they can start to build a mental picture of you. So offer 'Mr Darcy Brown' or 'Ms Darcy Brown'

Mei Gui Cheong (Dawn)	People get confused about names in unfamiliar
Dawn Cheong	languages, so if you use an Anglo name, definitely
	say so, putting it in brackets and perhaps not
	listing your original name (what's the point if
	you don't use it anyway?). Be aware that if you
	have a non-Anglo name, recruiters may assume
	you aren't fluent in English, which (depending on
	the job you're applying for) may be enough to put
	you straight into the 'no' pile. Discrimination of
	this type is, of course, unlawful.

Contact details

Address, telephone including area code, mobile, e-mail. Say which is most convenient for potential employers to contact you on:

Work telephone (please use with caution)
Home telephone (with answerphone)
Mobile telephone (switched off during the day)
Home e-mail (the best way of reaching me)

Or even better, only list the number you want them to call you on.

Spell everything out in full and include area codes: Street, not St, and so on.

- If you have a little brother or permanently stoned flatmate who answers your home phone and mumbles or loses messages, only include your mobile number.
- If your e-mail is amusing or in any way inappropriate, change it to something more professional (*emma.woodhouse@* or *emma1982@* are fine, *slinkygirl82@* is not). If you're in a job elsewhere, make sure you use a personal e-mail address; it's very unprofessional to use your work e-mail to apply for a new job (and your work managers might read your e-mails, too).

- If you list your mobile, be prepared for calls at all times – when you're shopping, about to go into the movies or at your current job! Have a respectable voice-mail message; and carry a pen, paper and diary so you can set up interviews when you get that unexpected call.

Career summary/employment objective/career objective/ mission statement

These are all different, if only slightly, in function and purpose. Most people only have one of them and put them right at the top.

These serve two purposes, each with different emphasis:

- **Describing the role** you're looking for. You can get specific or reasonably general – not too general. Like this:

> Seeking a graduate position in marketing or sales
> Keen to secure a role as Publishing Assistant with XYZ Magazines

- **Describing yourself.** This is where things can go pear-shaped. Avoid HR jargon. Try this:

> Energetic Publishing Studies graduate
> Creative and confident marketing professional

- Use plain English: short, simple words

AVOID	USE
· Aspirational	· Astute
· Proactive	· Creative
· Engagement	· Determined
· Self-starter	· Articulate
	· Confident
	· Well presented
	· Ambitious
	· Keen to learn

Don't overdo it; one or two adjectives is much more powerful than three or four. 'Focused, motivated and conscientious' sounds over the top when you run them all together but any one of them would be OK.

I cannot stress enough that using the clichéd jargon found in certain business books and expounded by many careers advisors is a **mistake** in an industry that is powered by words and expression. They mean nothing and fool no-one. Be yourself and don't assume that you need to have a five-year personal plan to impress people. At the same time, it's best not to go for a job in the sales department and talk about how long you have dreamed of becoming an editor. Or about the manuscript you've been working on for the past ten years.

(JESSICA, AUSTRALIA)

Choose whether you want **career summary** or **career objectives**. (There is another option, the **mission statement**. We're against this, for reasons we discuss below.)

Career summary wraps up what you've been doing:

Career Summary:
- A keen and bright graduate looking for a career in publishing
- Experience in sales, marketing and customer service
- BA from Monash University; MA in Publishing and Communication, University of Melbourne

This can work really well if you've got a good range of relevant experience or skills for the role you're applying for. Note that as well as neatly summarising the candidate's background, this career summary also includes a short note on what they are looking for ('looking for a career in publishing').

Career objective/employment objective

Slightly different, in that it focuses on what job you're looking for rather than what you've been doing – though should still include elements of both:

> ## Career Objective:
> To pursue a career in publishing through a Sales and Marketing Assistant role in a major trade publishing company. To refine the skills I have acquired throughout my industry experience and studies, in a fast-paced, rewarding environment.

You could personalise this further with the name of the company where you're applying for your job.

Mission statement

We're against, since they usually end up as a bunch of meaningless adjectives in search of a job to do. Like this:

> Aspirational, proactive self-starter with successful work background; focused, motivated and conscientious team player seeks a substantial new challenge.

Who could be against any of that? And that's the point. This communicates nothing to someone reading your CV who has never met you, other than perhaps indicating that you take yourself a little too seriously. Much better to use your skills and background to explain what kind of person you are and where your strengths are. Try instead:

> Motivated, creative and conscientious team player
>
> An astute and successful Marketing Executive looking for a substantial new challenge
>
> A broadly skilled graduate with successful work experience in several sectors. Skilled in research, support and communication. Postgraduate and undergraduate degrees in literature, psychology and communication

Remember, you may need to talk about anything on your CV – including this section. What you write is an invitation to the interviewer to ask you to say more. After all, they have to ask something!

- If a recruiter rings your mobile when you're in the supermarket and asks you to **describe yourself**, what you've written in your career summary is roughly what you need to articulate
- If you're in an interview and they say, 'Your CV says you're creative. What are some examples of your creativity at work?' you need to have a **good answer**

Your career summary/mission statement should be about you, not about putting together a string of long words that you think will get you a job.

Employment

There are a couple of schools of thought about how to organise this bit.

Chronological is the old-fashioned way – what you've been doing and when:

- Company, job title, date
- Responsibilities
- Achievements

This goes in reverse chronological order (start at the most recent, and therefore most relevant, end and work backwards).

Chronological works well if you've had a logical career progression and growth in one industry or one type of job.

Skills-based talks about the skills and experience you've gained, rather than where you gained those skills. Somewhere at the back you list job titles and whom you worked for.

Play around with this format if you don't yet have too much work experience, you're looking to change your career or you've been having a break from work due to family/study etc.

> If someone is a new graduate and their only work experience is weekend work in a shop, for example, I have no problem with that – assuming it's an entry-level role they're applying for. I'd like them to say that from the start, though. What I don't like is getting a CV where they use the skills-based format to go on about how great they are at customer service, flexibility, problem-solving and so on – it feels like they're hiding the fact that they've never had a professional job. (SUSANNAH)

Mix it up: chronological and skills

This kind of CV is a good compromise. You might want to open with a career objective statement that includes a career summary, then list your fabulous and transferable skills and, finally, get into employment history.

As we said at the start, don't obsess over this. Just find a format you're happy with, focus on getting the content and details and language to be flawless, and you'll have a good CV.

Here are some sample **formats and layouts:**

Date, job title, company	July–Oct 2008: **Editorial Intern, *ABC Magazines***
Job title, company, date	**Editorial Intern, *ABC Magazines*** (July–October 2008)
Job title Company Date	**Editorial Intern** ***ABC Magazines*** July–October 2008

Play around with the formatting so that the important bits (job title, company) are highlighted. Then be consistent, or (a) the whole thing will look a mess and (b) your prospective employer will rightly suspect you're not consistent.

We prefer to include months you worked there – Jan 2005 to July 2007 gives a more accurate picture than simply 2005–2007. If there are large gaps in what you did, just list the years.

Next: it can work well to have a little brief on the company you worked for, especially if you're changing industries, to help recruiters visualise what sort of work you did and what size the company was.

July–Oct 2008: **Editorial Intern, *ABC Magazines***
ABC Magazines are a small publisher based in Brighton, specialising in colour monthly magazines such as *Gourmet Food* and *Travel in Style*. **www.abcmagazines.com**

Then you need to get into your role in the job:

Performed various editorial duties including sub-editing and compiling editorial, industry research. Developed a research project for academic and company assessment.

Again, bullet point style is fine.

Try splitting the job description into function and achievements, or function and skills acquired:

<u>June 2006 to December 2007: XYZ Publishers</u>
Section 1.01 Tertiary Representative: Southern Region
Role involved representing XYZ textbooks in universities; meet sales targets by retaining textbook adoptions and winning new sales; develop and maintain relationships with lecturers and booksellers.

Achievements:
- Secured 12% territory growth in 2006 and 14% in 2007, in a flat market
- Sales Representative of the Year Award 2007

Or

<u>June 2006 to December 2007: XYZ Publishers</u>
Section 1.02 Tertiary Representative: Southern Region
Role involved representing XYZ textbooks in universities; meet
sales targets by retaining textbook adoptions and winning new
sales; develop and maintain relationships with lecturers and booksellers. Secured double-digit growth two years running and won
Sales Representative of the Year Award 2007

Skills gained:
- Relationship building
- Acquiring new business and retaining and building on existing
  business
- Good information storage and database habits
- Presentation skills including small and large groups

As when you're doing any writing, especially about yourself, there are
tricks to making all this sound good.

1. Write it up first, **put it away** and return to it later; never send
   your first draft
2. Your work description should include an **outline of your role**,
   and more detail in the more challenging areas.
3. And stay on the **correct side of stretching the truth**. You *will* get
   found out!

So where a precisely honest record of your last job might read like
this:

<u>XYZ Publishers</u>
Section 1.03 Receptionist/Sales and Marketing Assistant
- Reception duties included answering phone, taking messages,
  greeting visitors, sorting mail, making tea and coffee for senior
  staff
- Sales assistant duties included photocopying, setting up

conference calls, making calls, keeping contact with territories for which there was currently no sales representative
- Marketing assistant duties included photocopying, distributing flyers, booking conferences and sending books, checking brochures for errors, answering author calls

What you'd actually prefer your new employer to be reading is probably:

<u>XYZ Publishers</u>
Section 1.04 Sales and Marketing Assistant
- Sales support included managing vacant sales representative territories through customer contact (numerous significant sales achieved)
- Marketing assistant duties included controlling events, creating brochures and promotional materials, managing author relationships
- Some receptionist duties

Good words here are 'achieved', 'controlling', 'creating' – they make your role sound stronger, and you more capable.

Ten Power Words

- Changing
- Directing
- Doing
- Improving
- Innovating

- Leading
- Making
- Managing
- Resolving
- Solving

If you've not got much formal work experience, think about your non-work experiences and how you can use them:

- Do you do **volunteer work** for a charity or not-for-profit?

- What have you **contributed** to? Sporting or debating clubs, political parties, church groups?
- Are you a **committee member** for any social groups?
- Have you **organised any significant events** – parties, games, days out?
- What **non-professional work** have you done – waitering, fast food, paper rounds, tidying up at the golf club?
- Have you **won awards** at school, university or in other avenues?

What level of responsibility/skills/experiences can you take from any of this?

Be careful, though – don't overstretch your babysitting experience into paragraphs of detail. Most recruiters would rather see an honest CV that indicates your level of experience and a handful of extra-curricular activities.

If you quite genuinely have never had an after-school or university job and never been involved in any social groups or volunteering, then your CV is going to look very bland indeed and we recommend that you try and get out a bit. See Chapter 8 for ideas on how to gain valuable work experience that can put you a nose ahead.

If you have a range of non-publishing/non-relevant experience, this is where focusing on skills and transferable experiences can work well.

Try picking out the most relevant skills for the kind of role you're applying for, and then in much less detail cover where those skills were gained.

Career Summary:
- Experienced marketing professional with skills in events, advertising and written communication, seeking a new challenge in book publishing marketing

Skills Summary
- **Event management:** Managed numerous small and large conferences and involvement at events; drove attendance and increased responses

- **Advertising:** Experienced at managing advertising contacts and database, selecting advertising targets, booking advertising for best effectiveness and budget; print and radio media
- **Communication:** Created advertising copy and draft designs, liaised with designers for ad creation and proofing, brochure creation, design and fulfilment

Employment:
Feb 2003 to current: Marketing Executive, ABC Bank
October 2001 to Jan 2003: Marketing Assistant, XYZ Insurance

Education
Graduates should add information on their studies:
    2005–2007 (part time): MA in Publishing Studies
      Kingston University
      - Modules included Publishing: the structure of an industry; Marketing; Creating a bestseller
    2001–2003: BA English (First Class)
      Oxford Brookes University
    2000: A Levels
      Stonnington Secondary College
      - English, French, German

There's no need to include school or even university marks, though an idea of what you studied can be good. If your marks have been exceptional, say 'Consistently awarded High Distinctions' or something similar, but keep this low-focus. A whacking great list of every grade you've got since you were 15 is definitely not called for.

School is really not relevant once you've completed tertiary studies. If your school has a very controversial reputation (deservedly or otherwise), leave out its name. (We said above you should **only include information you want to discuss**.)

Personal information

This is where you list stuff about you. You could put:

- **Professional associations**
- **Languages**
- **Skills**, especially technical skills such as computer literacy, specialised systems; the ability to drive and the state of your licence, if clean.
- **Community work** – shows what a rounded person you are.
- **Interests** – this is there to give recruiters a handle to chat to you – 'I see you like netball?' Three or four interests are fine. Don't assume you have to list a team sport to show you're a team player; only list things you can genuinely talk about. It is very awkward to be asked a 'soft' question like this and not be able to support what you've written.
- Professional **training**, such as computer or sales courses.

Referees

Referees help recruiters check up on you – to make sure that you've done what you say you've done, and find out what kind of employee you'd make. They are becoming increasingly important as job applicants produce better CVs – so a quick phone call to a contact listed can make a very positive impression. Also, since many referees are unwilling to put their references in writing (they may get sued by job applicants who feel it was the reference that lost them the job), they may prefer to discuss the applicant's merits on the phone. But however they are listed, assume they will get contacted, and think carefully about whom you ask.

Questions your prospective employer might ask your referees:

1. Check facts on your CV – are the job titles and time employed accurate?
2. How did they perform?

3. What were their strengths?
4. What were their weaknesses?
5. How did they get on with the team?
6. How would they perform in XXX type of role?
7. Were there performance or personal issues I should know about?
8. Would you employ them again?

Ideally, referees should be people you have worked for recently and are happy to tell recruiters how great you are. If you're currently working this may not be possible (as you probably don't want your manager to know you're job hunting), so think about

- **Work colleagues** who are more senior than you and will be discreet about your job hunting
- **Past managers** or work colleagues from your last place of work, or who have left your current work
- **Managers / senior staff** from temporary jobs/internships
- **University lecturers** who know you
- If you can't access any of the above, try **responsible/senior people** who can talk about you personally

There's a game going on here, and you need to know the rules. If it gets to the stage where your potential employer is chasing up your references, they are hoping for the right answer. So, find someone who thinks you're great and is happy to say so.

An important point: you *must* check with your referee to ask their permission first, and then again if you believe they're about to get a call. Not only is this plain good manners (and we talk elsewhere in this book about what a wickedly big advantage plain good manners can give your career), it also gives you the opportunity to refresh the memory of your referee and rebuild the rapport you had with them.

It's fine, by the way, to say 'Referees available on request,' as usually referees won't be required until you're in the interview process. In this case, have a version of your CV that you mail in to get the interview ('Referees available on request') and a version that you take to the interview that includes referee details.

However, if the job ad asks for referees, give them. Otherwise you're almost certainly condemning yourself to the 'Reject' pile, on the basis that you've blatantly ignored a clear instruction.

Lies, damn lies and salary expectations–ten things to leave off your CV:

1. **Date of birth**
2. **Marital status**
3. **Number of children**
4. **Photo**

   On all these above points, there is nothing to be gained, and the potential disadvantage of sparking off a recruiter's prejudice

5. **Excessive detail**
   - long lists of school results
   - every single thing you ever did in your last job

6. **Salary expectation**

   Definitely a no-no. If it coincides with what they're willing to pay, you haven't gained anything; if it doesn't, it flags a problem

7. **Photocopies of written references**

   Save it for the interview

8. **Stupid jobs**

   A newspaper round seven years ago impresses no-one

9. **Anything you don't want to be asked about**

   What you put on your CV is an invitation for a discussion: use it wisely

10. **Lies**

    Positive spin yes, out-and-out fibbing definitely not. We

promise this: you *will* get found out, you *will* lose your job and your reputation *will* suffer. Publishing is a very small world, and it'll be smaller by one more person if you tell porkies in your CV

By now you should have a powerful CV that makes its case well, doesn't irritate your future employer and gets you into the 'Yes' pile. But we haven't quite finished, because you've still got to create your covering letter – and it's more important than you might think. Now read on . . .

More reading

Bright, *Brilliant CV: What Employers Want to See and How to See It*, Prentice-Hall, 2005

Jackson, *The Perfect CV: Today's Ultimate Job Search Tool*, Piatkus Books, 2005

Chapter Twelve
How to put together a job application

This chapter takes you through putting together a great job application letter and personalising your application for a specific job. Read also Chapter 11 on how to write a generic CV as the basis for applying for jobs.

There are two parts to a job application:

1. **Your covering letter**
   Personalised, zippy and sharp. This is the bit recruiters read (or at least skim). Get it right and your CV gets honoured with a glance.
2. **Your CV**
   Suited to the specific job, area of publishing or company you're applying for.

Covering letter
Your covering letter is the first thing that hits a recruiter's desk. They have to get past it to look at your CV. So it must grab their attention and generate enough interest for them to want to find out more about you.

Your CV is a standard document, tailored to the jobs you are applying for. Your covering letter, on the other hand:

- Is **fully personalised** to the job and organisation
- Details **why** you want to work for them
- It's **short** (one page)
- Has all your **contact details**, and
- May summarise **key points from your CV**

Format: for consistency, this should be the same as your CV, on standard white A4 paper, in a clean, readable font.

Your cover letter must include:

Date of writing

1 November 2008 is standard. 1st November, 1/11/08 or other forms are less professional.

Your details

Include your name (right at the top), address, phone (landline and mobile, your accompanying CV should state which it is best to use) and e-mail.

Emma Woodhouse
2 Smith Street
Maidenhead SL6 2QL
t 020 8991 123
e emma@jobinpublishing.co.uk

- **Tel, e-mail** are fine as abbreviations
- **Spell out** Street/Road etc in full (not St or Rd)
- **Include a title** if you wish – certainly do so if your name doesn't make your gender clear ('Ms Alex Marshall'). For a woman, Miss, Mrs or Ms are all perfectly acceptable. As mentioned in the previous chapter, don't get overly formal here; no need to write

Miss Jacqueline Melissa Wise (Jackie)

Instead,

Jackie Wise

will do just fine.

Recipient details

It's amazing how many people stuff this up – usually by half-amending a saved standard letter and not proofing properly. Make sure all details are *exactly* as they are given in the job ad or on their website:

Human Resources Manager
The Big Book Publishing Company
12 Editorial Street
Maidenhead SL6 2QL
Dear Sir/Madam

Or

Ms Jane Manager
The Big Book Publishing Company
12 Editorial Street
Maidenhead SL6 2QL

Dear Ms Manager

Double and triple check the recipient name before you send. Even if you have been informed of the manager's first name, resist the temptation to use it and don't start your letter 'Dear Jane'. You have not been introduced. You wouldn't be offended, but (believe it or not) some older people may be. Why would you risk that for no gain?

> I once had a job application where I asked for responses to Susannah Bowen, and got one that said 'Susan Bowman' in the address detail and then 'Dear Mrs Brown' in the salutation. Three strikes in the first three lines. I didn't read the letter – it went straight in the 'no' pile – anyone with that level of sloppiness doesn't deserve a good job!   (SUSANNAH)

Template for letter

The first sentence of your letter should explain why you are writing; specifically that you are applying for a job and where you heard about it.

I wish to express interest in the Marketing Executive position advertised on **www.seek.com.au** on 9 June.

Next, say why you should be considered for the job. You might like to refer to your CV or key points from your CV, but don't repeat everything in your CV – remember this is a short letter. Pick out the two or three points from your CV most relevant to this particular role.

I am currently a marketing assistant in a large publishing house. My background and skills are well documented in the attached CV. However, the following points may be of interest, including:

- My wide range of experience, including communications, campaign development, and sales support
- Energy, enthusiasm, and excellent communication skills
- Achieved an MA in Publishing and Communications from The University of Melbourne

The points you pull out should be relevant to the role/company; having one of three or four highlighting something personal about you that demonstrates your drive can also work – if you've set up your own business, self-published a book, that kind of thing.

And then a wrap-up paragraph that highlights your interest in the particular role advertised or their company:

I am keen to progress my career with an independent publishing house such as XYZ Publishers.

And finally:

I hope to have the opportunity to discuss my application in more detail.

Yours sincerely

E. Woodhouse

Emma Woodhouse

And sign it with a confident signature in a decent pen – not the first blotchy ballpoint you find to hand. (Try out a few on a blank sheet of paper before attacking your application.)

Personalising your CV

When you're applying for a job, work though your generic CV and ensure lots of focus on the experience and skills relevant to the job you're applying for.

1. **Read the job ad carefully**, *out loud* (to be sure you're not missing anything) and note what they're asking for. Now, rewrite your CV and letter with this job ad fresh in your mind.

2. **Aim for phrases that hit the same notes** in a slightly different way – don't parrot the words they use. So if the job ad asks for a 'self-starter', think about what that means. Try peppering your letter and CV with things like 'Confident graduate with strong skills; quick learner' (at least, we think that's what 'self-starter' means).

3. **Now go through your CV** and draw out the bits most relevant to this job, from your work, study and personal experience. So if you've done internships in marketing and editorial, and you're applying for an assistant editor job, you know which one goes at the top of your CV and in the covering letter, right? Ditto if you're applying for a job in a non-profit organisation and you've done some good work as a student with Amnesty, Oxfam or anything else that shows your commitment to similar causes.

You'll probably end up with a variety of CVs saved for different types of job – **emmacv.doc**, **emmacvmarketing.doc**, **emmacveditorial.doc**, and so on. Even if this is the case, always double check your CV before sending it off to make sure you're making the most of your experience (and sending the one you meant to send!).

And here's a last golden rule for creating job applications:

Do *exactly* what they say in the job ad.

What if it's tedious and boring? Do *exactly* what they say in the job ad. What if you can't understand why they want it? Do *exactly* what they say in the job ad. So …

- If they ask for contact details for four referees? Include!
- If they want only a letter and no CV? Fine!
- If they want 1,000 words on contemporary magazine publishing? Put time into this and create the absolute best piece of writing you've ever generated. Make it *exactly* 1,000 words – not 1,001 or 999, but *exactly what they say in the job ad.*
- If they ask for salary expectations? Include yours! (This is, by the way, the only time which you should do this.) Give a range, from the lowest you might accept if it were the absolutely perfect job, to the highest you could reasonably aspire to (and don't think that by putting a stupidly high value on yourself you'll get paid that – it works the other way, you just won't get the job. Or the interview). See Chapter 16 on how to do a great job interview for more detail on how to handle this.
- If they want job applications only by fax/by e-mail/through their website/using their specific application form? *Do exactly what they say in the job ad.*

Never assume they don't really mean it. If it's in the job ad they honestly, honestly do – and it's probably a little test to sort out those who read instructions from those who do not. If you were in their shoes, and you had 500 applications to work your way through, and 480 of them had disobeyed your clear, explicit instruction on how to apply, you'd be very pleased, wouldn't you? You're already down to the last 20 …

Don't make the mistake of disqualifying yourself before the race has even started.

Getting it there
A printed CV and letter have most impact. Increasingly, applicants e-mail their CVs. We strongly recommend you **don't** do this (unless they specify that you should, of course), because you lose control – of the quality of print, paper, whether your letter and CV end up together, computer formats and so on. (Here's a single example:

varying ages of PCs means your prospective employers may be using a different version of Windows; they may be Mac users and your attachment might go all wrong with formats and fonts.) If you want this job, *print your CV and letter.*

We've also seen, more times than you'd believe, applicants take a huge amount of trouble over the CV and letter, then add a short, informal, misspelt cover e-mail, spoiling the entire effect. Ouch.

Still, if you must e-mail your CV – and we concede there is a case for both printing *and* e-mailing – here's how you do it:

- **Subject line**
  Should be something like 'Re: job application – Marketing Executive', so it can be forwarded to the right person without opening if required.

- **Keep it formal**
  Apply the same level of care and formality to your cover e-mail as to the CV and letter – addressing it to Ms Manager and not first name, and so on. There's something about e-mail that makes folk relax into informality, which is inappropriate for job ads. Resist.

- **Make it a simple covering e-mail**
  Include a full cover letter in a Word document, and your covering e-mail can simply say, 'Please find attached letter and CV regarding your Marketing Executive role advertised on **www.jobs.co.uk**' (remember they may have more than one job ad in the system and you've only seen one, so you need to say which job you're applying for). Don't put your entire cover letter into the body of the e-mail.

- **Save your CV with a sensible filename:**
  "emmawoodhousecv" not "mycvlatest"
  Here's how you get it there:

- **Print out your letter and CV**

  Use a good quality printer. If you don't have one, hike down to a nearby print shop and spend a small amount of money making sure your stuff looks professional.

- **Your envelope is your ambassador**

  It is the first thing that gets opened. So, use a good quality envelope – not one that will fall apart as it is subjected to the ravages of the postal service, and certainly not a pre-used one. Use an A4 envelope so nothing is folded (on the other hand if you are sending a single sheet, posting it in an A4 envelope will mean it probably arrives looking battered).

- **Stock up on attractive stamps**

  Make sure they're for the right amount. Stick them on straight.

- **Handwrite**

  Write the name and address with the same good pen you used to sign your accompanying letter (handwritten envelopes get opened first, because they look personal). Double-check the details again.

- **Throughout, take care**

  Get the presentation right. If *you* don't care, why should they?

Chapter Thirteen
How to get yourself out there

For many, the phrase 'job hunting' conjures up an image of the diligent would-be employee (that's you) sitting over the Saturday papers, red pen in hand, or setting up e-mail job alerts. But 75% to 90%[1] of job openings never get advertised. Instead, they are filled through:

- **Current staff** recommending friends (networking)
- **Managers** thinking of people they've met or heard of and calling them in (networking)
- **People sending in their CV** on the off-chance of a vacancy coming up (chasing jobs)
- **Internal promotions** (this is why internships are important)

If you're serious about getting a job in publishing (and we trust you are, otherwise you're in the middle of the wrong book), the activities we discuss in this chapter give you a much, much better chance of finding your job than if you simply spend your time answering job ads.

These ideas are not always easy, especially if you don't have a particularly outgoing personality. The good news is, surprisingly few job hunters actually do this stuff; so if you make the effort, you really do stand a much, much better chance than someone who doesn't.

Networking

Why would you deprive your friends of the opportunity to do you a favour? Tell them what you are trying to find/do/achieve and see what happens. Our bet is that, sooner or later, a friend will say some-

[1] *Data gathered from a very unscientific Internet search*

thing like, 'I was talking to someone I work with today and they told me they're looking for someone. I immediately thought of you, because I reckon you'd be great at that job'. Now if that's an outcome you'd be happy to have, then what's wrong with helping the process along a bit? But to get the process started, you have to be willing to tell your friends what you are looking for, and how much you want it. Without this information, you're not giving them much chance of helping you, are you?

One of the best things you can do to increase your chances of getting into publishing is to become a first-class networker. It's not as hard as you may think, and there's no question but that it pays off. This section is all about how to get to know the people who can help you, and how to get them to do so.

So, where do you begin? Here are ten basic tips:

1. **Decide you're going to do this**
   This whole thing doesn't come easily to many of us. But that doesn't mean you should not try. Deciding to do just that is an important start.

2. **Make a list of everyone you know who could possibly help**
   If you suspect they may be able to give you a hand at some stage, they're in – don't hold back. You could start with anyone you know, anyone at all, who has any connection, any connection at all, with publishing: authors, people already working in publishing, lecturers, friends, friends of friends, mums of friends, distant acquaintances of your cousin's sister-in-law, and so on.

3. **Keep track**
   For everyone you know who's on your 'hit list', try to remember everything you know about them: if they support a football team; if they have kids; if they have a partner; if they tell you where they're going on holiday. Very soon you'll have a surprisingly detailed portrait of their likes, dislikes and habits. And this is less spooky than it sounds – after all, your mum knows all this

information about a whole heap of people, it's just that she doesn't need to write it down because her brain is good at this stuff. Noting it down isn't cheating, it's just helping your memory a little – and giving you something to talk to them about.

4. **Mark birthdays and holidays with cards**

   Get over the 'yuk' factor (you're male, aren't you?), and send lots of Christmas cards with personal messages. Stay in touch with people.

5. **Remember names**

   Many people struggle with names, and assume that everyone else is really good at it. They're not; it's just that they work at it. There are many techniques, but the easiest is this: when someone tells you their name, repeat it, immediately, and use it, repeatedly. If you can, make an association (easy if you're talking to a fragrant Rose or a ferocious Leo) or try personal traits: Jackie likes jewellery (her name begins with J), Andrew wears Armani (and his with A). Like anything, the more you work at it, the better you get.

6. **Accept invitations**

   Just say yes. Just say yes, thanks, I'd love to. Go to lunches, coffees, dinners, breakfasts (prepare to eat and drink a lot). Always reply to every invitation you get (this is getting rare and will be appreciated and remembered). Attend as many as you can, and be the perfect guest. Dress up. Buy a good-quality present. Behave yourself. Don't get drunk. Be polite. Be charming. Be considerate. Send thank-you notes. Think of it this way: if you do all this, you're going to get great press.

   Go to any and all book events you can wangle an invitation to. If you're not currently in the industry, these might include:

   - **Book fairs** (there are usually public days) – advertised in publishing media. Introduce yourself to staff at publishers you'd like to work for. Ask who the right contact is in the area you want to work in, chat about what you're looking for, and hand over a CV.

- **Meetings** organised by those within the profession, such as the Society of Young Publishers and Women in Publishing. The dates and locations can be found in the trade press.
- **Book readings** and book launches – often advertised in book review pages and by independent/literary bookshops. Introduce yourself to the publishers (you'll see them setting things up and talking to the author).
- **Book and publishing awards** – same as above.

Browse the literary bits of the paper and try out different events. Hang about in the Publishing/Communication areas of your local universities; even if you don't intend to study there, you never know whom you might meet. Get your face known by industry people and hand your card and CV around. Publishing people will be impressed by your energy and initiative.

Make sure you're not being a pest, by the way; people are often really busy at events. Introduce yourself, explain you're looking for a career in publishing, ask for the right contact, ask for their card, which means they'll ask for yours in return; hand it over, with your CV, thank them and walk away. Afterwards is where you make the most impact; give them a call a couple of days later, thank them for their time, and ask for a follow up (a meeting with them/an introduction to the right person).

7. **Create invitations**

Once you've introduced yourself to someone you'd like to work for, ring to follow up. Ring people and take them out for coffee. (Ringing is better than e-mailing, by the way, because it's hard to say 'no' over the phone.) Offer to pay for the coffee, and when they decline, insist – it's startling the feel-good impact that spending a handful of coins on a cup of coffee can have. If there are no jobs on offer, ask for their advice and ideas and introductions to contacts in other companies (they all know each other).

8. **Have a business card – and carry it!**

   (You'd be amazed how many people don't, or only have battered ones with the shopping list on the back.) If you're not in current employment, or would rather not hand out your company business card, get a personal one made up – and not from those machines in shopping malls either – if you can afford it, get it professionally done. Remember mobile and e-mail details (and for this exercise, get a professional-sounding e-mail address – **andyw@**, not **mrlongshlong@** or **poochiecutie@**.

9. **Have a CV – and carry it!**

   > 'I'd love to come and work in your organisation, I love what you do.'
   >
   > 'Really? We're recruiting at the moment; have you got a CV, I'll pass it to the HR manager?'
   >
   > 'Um, maybe I can e-mail you . . .'

   That's so **not** what you want. Keep a clean copy of your CV[2] with you whenever you can in case of unexpected opportunities.

   The other clever thing about carrying a CV is that when you get an unexpected call on the mobile from someone who says, 'Tell me about your background' you can quickly remind yourself of the relevant points.

   Also always carry a pen and diary, so you can make interview times on the spot.

10. **Do what you say you're going to do and what you should do**

    You know when you're chatting to someone and one of you says, 'We must get together and . . .'? and when you meet someone who says, 'Send me your CV and I'll pass it on to . . .' Don't just think about it, do it!

---

[2] *Probably not at the beach, but definitely when networking and other semi-professional opportunities*

No, it's not insincere

Perhaps you're thinking, 'This is false', or 'This is insincere'. It's not, not really. You're paying respect to someone by showing a real, focused interest in them. You don't pick your friends because they can help you – but there's nothing wrong with getting a little help from your friends. After all, most of us choose our friends because we have things in common with them, so a shared interest in work matters isn't surprising. It would be a little bizarre to pick your friends only from among those you share no work interests with; and it would be bizarre, too, to get help only from people who aren't friends.

What should be obvious is that you may well be limiting yourself in this regard. With more focus and determination, you can almost certainly get more 'value' out of your social network than you do currently, just by focusing on what it can do for you.

Don't wait for *them* to call *you*

Something people usually only figure out when they have to do it themselves is that companies – all of them, everywhere – hate advertising for new staff.

Imagine this from the departmental manager's perspective.

Jackie has been promoted, and Melanie has resigned to go to a competitor, so now I have two vacancies at once. I need to find a new employee who will be happy to do this job for a few years, not need too much training, not have too much experience because they might get bored, be OK with the pittance salary I'm allowed to pay, and get on well with my other staff.

People internally are applying for this job; I don't think any of them are quite right, but I have to handle them gently.

I have to write a job ad and figure out where to place the ad. Advertising is incredibly expensive, and every time I advertise I get 100 or 200 CVs, which all have to be sorted through and responded to, and most of them are rubbish.

I might do some quick phone chats to decide who to bring in for interview, then first interview around eight people and second interview three or four. By the time I offer the best person a job they might have found something somewhere else or changed their mind about leaving their current job and then I have to do the whole thing again. Sometimes from those 200 CVs there actually isn't anyone quite right and I have to advertise again. If I'm lucky, I might be able to recruit someone in time to have a handover with the person who's leaving; doesn't usually happen though.

Meanwhile I'm covering for both the people who've left, while I wait for the new recruit to serve out notice with their old company. Once they get here I have to train them, mentor them and hope they fit in with my other staff and can do the job.

And I have my actual job to do as well! I'm tired just thinking about this.

Now imagine that manager, sitting and fretting about the long process. Just as they start to draft the job ad, the phone rings, and someone energetic, intelligent and just right for the job (you, of course) is on the line asking if there happen to be any opportunities.

Some publishing houses, in fact, *never* advertise, and instead rely entirely on applicants, internal promotion and networking.

This is why it's always a good idea to contact companies you'd like to work for, rather than waiting for them to advertise. You get in ahead of the hundreds of CVs that come in response to job ads; they know you've researched the company and like their product and you're actively keen on working for that company, rather than just applying for a job because it's been advertised.

I'm always delighted when people who are serious about the industry contact me and show genuine enthusiasm for what we do. I had an approach just recently from a junior designer simply looking for some advice on how to produce a strong design portfolio for interviews and who was looking to get into children's book publishing. I gave her some hints on presentation, and when she did send in her work, because it impressed

Of course, for every ten calls you make, you'll probably get nine *not right now thanks*; that's fine, because you expect that, it's part of the process, and every *not right now thanks* moves you a step closer to *actually yes, we are looking for someone*. Plus every *not right now thanks* is an opportunity for you to get your CV on file and make sure they give you a call when something does come up.

Try this:

1. **Figure out who you want to work for**
   (See Chapter 10.) Do a spot of Web research and talk to anyone you know who has a link to those companies.
2. Make sure you know why you want to work there and **prepare a little script** with a good opening line:

   > I'm a graduate looking for a publishing career. I like your innovative approach to marketing – that last ad campaign was fascinating – could I meet with you to talk about job opportunities?

   Or

   > Your product development process is the best around

   And

   > I hear it's a great place to work

   And NOT

   > I'm sick of my current job, so I'm calling all the competitors

Whatever you say, keep it basically true; it comes across as more believable. Write it down as well, otherwise you risk getting to the person you're targeting and ending up having a horrible stammering attack. Even if you go off-script, you have it there to fall back on.

> I once hired someone who phoned in and said 'I've just moved to the area and thought it would be great to work for the local publishers rather than travelling to London every day'. That sounds all wrong, but actually it hit exactly the right note; the office was in a small town, quite hard to get to, and I kept losing staff because the commute was just too hard, so finding someone local worked well. Also I wouldn't have believed a caller who spun me a line about always wanting to work with our books, because the product line was academic social science books – interesting to work with, but not sexy. So I brought the caller in for a chat and she was excellent. She turned out to be hard working, intelligent and loyal – a dream employee (hi, Malie!).
> (SUSANNAH)

3. In some companies the **HR manager** looks after recruitment; in others it's the **head of each department**. The department head is probably the right place to start, and then if there's nothing available at present, call again for the HR department and get your CV on file.

To find out who to speak to, ring the switchboard and ask for the name of the marketing manager/sales manager etc; then thank them and hang up. Here's why: now you can ring back a few hours later or the next day and ask confidently for 'Adrian Jones, please'. This ringing back helps to avoid the receptionists/personal assistants, also known as gatekeepers – they block calls from people who aren't already known to the manager you're chasing.

Remember your aim here is to have a conversation with the manager, so they can find out that you're great and they should hire you. E-mailing a CV won't cut it; it's a chat you want.

If you do get a gatekeeper, don't get stressed: it's their job to screen calls and not personal, so try not to feel rebuffed:

- If asked for your name, give it.
- If asked for your company, try 'Emma Smith Associates' (where Emma Smith is your name), tell them it's a personal call, or if you're feeling cheeky just make something up – try 'Brinley Patch' or 'Miles Davis Limited'.
- If asked what it's regarding, hopefully you can say something like, 'Fred Lim asked me to call Adrian' (that's the advantage of networking!). If you're cold-calling, don't share your life story with the gatekeeper; they don't know that the sales manager actually is looking for new reps, and they certainly don't know how utterly fabulous you are, so they'll mistakenly think they're doing the right thing by keeping you out. Instead try, 'It's regarding a meeting date – if Adrian isn't available can I just leave a number?' (Subtly implying they're holding you up; going on the attack can work well!) If all that doesn't work, get an e-mail address, and send a note introducing yourself on the themes below; don't send your CV in though; it's way too early.

4. When you get to your target, **start on your script**

> I'm a graduate looking for a publishing career. I like your innovative approach to marketing – that last ad campaign was fascinating – could I meet with you to talk about job opportunities?

You might well need a script Part 2 that sums you up in a couple of sentences:

> I've just completed the Publishing and Communications MA at University of Melbourne, and I have worked through projects with ABC and XYZ publishers in this area. I'd love to come and work for you; could we have a coffee to chat?

Having got a phone conversation, your aim now is to get a meeting. Asking for a coffee date can work; it keeps the meeting informal and quick. Let them choose the date, time and location.

If there is really nothing going on and they don't want to meet you, ensure you lodge your CV, and call back every two months or so to check if anything has come up and remind them how fab you are.

Two Top Tips

- **Do not** rely on their having your CV on file
  They may forget they have it, lose it, assume you're working somewhere else by now, the manager might change . . . always phone back again.
- **Do not** rely on e-mail for this
  Phone, phone, phone! Much more personal and some people are rubbish at replying to e-mails or only read the ones sent by people they know.

Treat an informal chat as an interview

A quick coffee with the departmental manager is basically a **mini-job interview** (even if there's nothing available at present). So treat it like one. Read the interview section of this book (Chapter 16) and practise with friends. Take the opportunity as seriously as you would a formal job interview. Take your CV. Dress professionally. Give the impression you're ready to walk right into their office and start work and they're more likely to visualise you there! If you feel silly getting dressed up for a coffee meeting, pretend to yourself (and them, if you like) that you have an interview or business appointment that afternoon.

If you're meeting at a café, e-mail them a photo or carry one of their recent publications so they know who you are. Drink the same beverage as them (that's the rapport thing), unless it'll make you throw up. Don't eat a snack unless they do – and if they do, don't make them eat alone.

Unlike an interview where they've advertised and there's an opportunity, you've asked for this meeting; so you now have a great chance to set the tone of the discussion.

You might want to try something like:

> Thanks for meeting with me. As I said on the phone, I'm looking for a publishing career and I'd love to come and work for you.

(There are books that advise you to spend several meetings getting to know your target, courting them gently rather than being this outspoken. Try the direct approach, we say. Senior people are very, very busy, and will be puzzled and impatient with someone hanging about and not saying what they actually want. Cut to the chase, in the politest way possible of course, and you won't waste their time or yours.)

If they indicate on the phone that there are no current opportunities, but are still happy to meet with you, well done – you must be good! Try something like:

> Thanks for meeting with me. As I mentioned on the phone, Belinda Harris suggested I meet with you. I'm keen on a career in publishing, and I'm hoping you can give me some tips and ideas.

From here on, follow their lead. Think of this as a mini job interview, an opportunity to show off your skills, talents and confidence.

Chapter Fourteen
How to find advertised jobs

I was told that publishing jobs aren't advertised in the newspapers, so I never bothered to look there. One day my dad comes in with the employment pages and says, 'What about this job for a publishing assistant with a scholarly publisher?' I thought he was teasing, but it was real – and I got the job!

(SHARON MULLINS, EDITOR, MELBOURNE, AUSTRALIA)

We flagged back in Chapter 13 that only a small proportion of jobs is advertised. It's a small proportion, but it's a vital one. This is where you find publishers who are looking for staff: ready, willing and eager to hire you. Here is what to do about it.

Spend time on job websites

Browse relevant websites for jobs. If you don't have decent Web access from home, your local public library or any institution you belong to (university, work and so on) can help out. (And if you're not Web-savvy, you need to sort that out before you go looking for a job in the media.)

Various places on the Web carry job ads (see p. 184):

- **Newspaper websites**
- **Agency websites**
- **Job-specific websites**
- **Company websites**

Look for a heading that says something like 'career opportunities' (most common in larger companies which have the resources to do this). If you have a particular employer in mind, keep checking their website for information on what has cropped up.

Good search terms for job websites include:			
• Copy editor	• Editorial	• Media	• Sales
• Creative	• Journalist	• Publisher	• Staff writer
• Editor	• Marketing	• Publishing	• Writer

(If you're Web-savvy you can skip this paragraph.) You can usually do a quick search and trawl through lots of results, or an advanced search that refines things down. Where possible, set up a regular automated search using categories and sub-categories. Once you've registered your interest, the website e-mails you jobs weekly or even daily. While job search e-mails can be frustrating in pulling out a thousand jobs that aren't right for you, it's better to have a wider search and skim though a long list, than a narrow search that misses something. It's also useful to see who is recruiting, even if not for any job you might be interested in, and how long jobs are advertised for (or re-advertised). You will pick up an idea of which firms lose most staff/have most new vacancies and are therefore likely to be difficult places to work or expanding quickly.

Think laterally: check job function websites and journals as well as publishing-specific sites. For example, if you're interested in Marketing, try marketing organisations such as the Direct Marketing Association near you. Many of these jobs may be in industries you don't want to work in, but some will be in publishing or related careers.

We also recommend you Google and read industry magazines and newsletters to find the latest sites and job advertisers.

Read job ads in newspapers, magazines and journals

Read the papers. Do this *as well as* using the job websites – ads get categorised in different ways and you can't afford to miss something. Not every printed job ad makes it to the websites (and vice versa).

Remember:

- **Don't just turn to P for publishing, E for editing or M for Marketing**
  Skim though the *entire* job section. Non-publishing companies

might have a job for you, and employers categorise jobs differently from how you do.

- **Read national and local papers** – you never know.
- Look at the **job ads in the general news section** as well as the job ads section.

Read widely and be constantly on the lookout. Don't forget that non-publishing companies have publishing jobs, too.

Who do you want to work for?

As well as the companies you know, do some research on publishing companies you don't know:

- Check out **books and magazines** in shops – publisher details will appear in the first few pages, including address details, and, in magazines, contact names.
- Check resources that have **lists of publishers**. If you can't afford to buy them, your local library will stock them.

Then look at company profiles and check their websites – would you want to work there? If so, bookmark their sites, and as well as contacting them (see Chapter 13), check company websites regularly – often jobs go up on their site well before being advertised, so you can get in early. And when you reply, make it clear you saw the job on their website rather than in the paper – it shows keenness, which can't hurt.

In the corporate world, direct mail, newsletters, brochures, press releases and other material (referred to as 'collateral') are now all big business.

> You wouldn't necessarily imagine that law firms and accountancy practices had publishing opportunities – yet someone has to put together all that marketing collateral. In fact, there's a whole industry of publishing, much of it online, that goes on in the professional world which we consumers never see. (STEVE)

So, as well as traditional book and magazine publishers, think about:

- **Professional services firms such as accountants and lawyers**
  They publish a great deal of marketing material.

- **Community groups** and what used to be called charities (they now prefer 'not for profit organisations')
  The big ones have publishing and communications departments, and some do lots of direct mail with catalogues; and you get the warm fuzzy of working for a Good Cause. They pay well, too.

- **Banks**
  In fact, virtually every big company – no feel-good factor about good causes here, but the career prospects are terrific.

- **Universities** and large non-government schools
  These usually have good job sections on their websites and they don't necessarily run the job ads in the paper. Universities have publishing divisions, for internal communications and sometimes for books and journals.

- **Government and the public services**
  Local, national, international – of all sizes – create reams of printed and Web-based publications.

Not only is working in corporate communications a great way to build up your publishing experience, it also exposes you to a level of commercial-mindedness that many traditional publishers, frankly, cannot match. In fact, you may find you end up as a highly-sought after expert in this area . . . and perhaps, like many people we know, you'll find your home there, and never move into 'traditional' publishing after all.

Many smaller publishers and organisations don't have websites, or not websites that are updated regularly with job ads. If that's where your interest lies, you'll need to look out for their ads in the papers, or better yet, get in contact with the best of them and let them know you're interested, and get your CV into their system.

More reading

In the UK
- www.thebookseller.com/jobs
- www.publishingnews.co.uk/pn/pnc
- **www.bookcareers.com** – a career development advice bureau which runs a CV – clearing house, where you can register that you are looking for a job within the industry
- *Guardian* (*MediaGuardian* – Tuesdays in print)
- *Guardian* **http://jobs.guardian.co.uk/browse/media/index.jsp**
- CV Clearing House **http://www.bookcareers.com/cvonline/intro.htm** is a great place to browse publishing jobs and post your own CV
- Regionally based papers (*Birmingham Post, Western Daily Press, Liverpool Echo*)
- The Institute of Direct Marketing (IDM) **www.theidm.com**

In Australia
- *The Australian* (Thursdays and Saturdays)
- State based papers (*Sydney Morning Herald, The Age, Courier Mail* etc) – Saturdays
- SEEK **www.seek.com.au**
- **mycareer.com.au** – these are the job ads from *The Age* (Melbourne) and *Sydney Morning Herald*, and other Fairfax publications
- **www.careerone.com.au**
- **www.meapcareers.com.au** – job search service for the media, entertainment, arts, public relations and publishing industries in Australia and New Zealand
- *Weekly Book Newsletter* (generally known as Blue Newsletter or Blue News) – THE place for book publishing jobs. This e-mailed newsletter isn't cheap to subscribe to, but you can get a free 30-day trial to start with and then subscribe for a month at a time until you get your job
- Australian Direct Marketing Association (ADMA) **www.adma.com.au**

Chapter Fifteen
How to use a recruitment agency

So, how does the idea of trawling through a ton of different ads and websites in search of a job sound? It is effective, we can vouch for that. But there's no doubt it *is* time-consuming. That's where the idea of using a specialist recruitment agency comes in.

Besides the advantage of saving you time, a good agency will give you an interview before agreeing to take you on, and this itself can be a great way to find out more about publishing, and to explore career options you may not even have thought of so far. And most staff there will have worked within the industry themselves, and so be well placed to identify what you have to offer the market – and what the market has to offer you.

What's more, a good agency will also help you sharpen your CV so that it presents you to your best advantage. Here's some great advice:

Most applicants don't think through how to sell themselves in enough detail. For example, they put on their CV that they've spent time 'working in a catering firm' during a holiday job, but looking closer we discover they did some marketing and also got involved in the management of the database.

These are transferable skills and it's vital the publishing houses you apply to know how much experience and initiative you actually have. We will not write their CV for them (there is no point – we don't want them to look identical) but we can show candidates how to present themselves advantageously, and of course that is free guidance they can benefit from, whether or not we find them a job.

(MARGARET MILLS, MANAGING DIRECTOR OF JUDY FISHER ASSOCIATES, UK)

There's an old saying that if you want to catch a fish you have to think like a fish, so it's worth thinking about why a publishing house might use an agency to find staff.

A well-known publishing house may not need to advertise starter jobs; they can rely on CVs submitted from those who write in hoping for a vacancy. But for more senior positions, or posts they find hard to fill, they may use the services of an agency. Some publishing houses use recruitment agencies for all their positions, as a standard process, and it's worth thinking about why they find it helpful. Christie Davies, Senior HR Officer at Walker Books, uses agencies – sometimes:

> The HR culture at Walker used to be one where an ad in the trade press was deemed all you needed to do to find staff – and yet the costs of the ad were not good value if we received only a handful of CVs as a result. We continue to advertise, but I also like to use agencies when the need arises. I have a strong relationship with several, and know they will be good sources of high-quality people for jobs that are perhaps tricky to fill or where a specific type of person, or skill set, is required.
>
> The agencies I like to use are publishing specialists, and are very well networked. They have excellent connections within the industry and can find me the kind of person I know will fit in.
>
> (CHRISTIE DAVIES, SENIOR HR OFFICER, WALKER BOOKS, UK)

The publisher saves both time and money by using an agency. A popular firm can attract hundreds of CVs for each vacancy they advertise, and trawling through them all looking for the right aptitudes is very time-consuming. Secondly, advertising is hideously expensive (the cost of the ad space, the time involved, the temporary loss of the job function . . .) and the more smoothly this is managed the better.

A recruitment agency handles all aspects of recruitment: advertising, sifting, interviewing and providing a shortlist, and for this publishing houses pay for the agency's services, usually 17.5% of the starting salary. So, if you get a job and are paid the price of a new car a year, your company is paying around the price of a motor scooter for the pleasure of your company on top of what they actually pay you. This may not sound a lot (considering the high costs of space advertising in particular) but an agency may be able to shortcut some of the costs of recruitment. Advertising online costs less than advertising in print – and sometimes may not be needed at all. A good agency can offer suitable candidates from their existing resources, high-quality candidates whom they already represent, and whose CVs are on file, and ready to go – which means that if you're on their books they may be able to match you straight away, without going through a long application process.

Using an agent to find you a job sounds enticingly simple: on the one hand, they have vacancies to find candidates for; on the other, you are willing to offer your services. But hang on a second: it's not quite as easy as all that. Here are three words of warning before you pick up the phone.

Working with recruitment agencies
He who pays the piper . . .
Agencies are paid by the firm doing the recruiting, not by the people they place. In fact, they're not allowed by law to accept fees from job hunters. Of course, it's in an agency's own best interest long term to deal fairly with those they offer as potential employees, since, if well advised, you may return to them in the future, perhaps first for a more senior job, and later as a client. And placing people where they don't fit just to fill the spot doesn't build an agency a great reputation. Even so, never forget they are there first and foremost to serve their *clients:* they're not there to get *you* a job.

Still, that's not all bad. Because they're working for lots of different employers all the time, they will definitely know of more vacancies than you, so while you may approach them for one position, they'll know other firms looking for an employee with a similar skill set – and which may not have been advertised, or leastways not yet. So you're actually beating the crowd. And it's quite a crowd you're beating, too: the advertising manager of the UK *Bookseller* magazine, Natalie Daniels-Browne, estimates that 80% of those using the magazine's website consult the careers section, and there are 7,500 subscribers to the job e-bulletin every week. Do the maths and you'll soon see that you're up against . . . *(you didn't do the maths, did you? It's OK, we did it for you)* another 5,999 other keen job hunters. It's the same in Australia:

> The jobs section is by far the most popular section on the BOOKSELLER+PUBLISHER website. We don't create a special job bulletin, so job ads are included in our Weekly Book Newsletter e-mail, which reaches pretty much the entire book industry in Australia, and readers in about 40 other countries, including the UK, USA and New Zealand. The e-newsletter drives job searchers onto our website. Job searchers account for just under 30% of all traffic generated on our website by the roughly 5,000 individuals who visit the site each month.
>
> (ANDREW WILKINS, PUBLISHER & DEPUTY GENERAL MANAGER, THORPE-BOWKER, AUSTRALIA)

Get yourself in with an agency and you cut the odds dramatically.

Don't relax just yet

Warning: you're about to be lectured. It's for your own good, so just put up with it for a moment. Normal service will be resumed shortly.

> So never come to me again, if you can't show that you've been working with your own heads, instead of thinking you can pay mine to work for you. (SCHOOLMASTER BARTLE MASSEY, FROM *ADAM BEDE* BY GEORGE ELIOT)

We've just said that the agency's primary responsibility is to the employer, who's paying them, rather than to you. So, please, *do not* make the mistake of relaxing and expecting your agency to do all the running for you. They expect you to put every bit as much effort into thinking about what skills you have to offer as if you were targeting the firms yourself. They expect you to show an understanding of the industry you seek to be part of. They expect you to research your potential employer.

In short, the best way to use an agency is *in addition* to your own efforts – not as a substitute for them. End of lecture.

Agencies target the employed, not just the restless or unemployed

It's common for a publishing firm to use an agency to find those who are *not* looking for a job, and hadn't even thought about moving. Organisations want team players, and many of these may be happy, satisfied and fully busy doing a really good job for their current employer, rather than actively looking for another job. Negativity is seldom as appealing, so while telling an agency how much you loathe and detest the firm where you did work experience, or your current boss, or where you're sure you would *absolutely not* fit in, is always an option, bear in mind the kind of impact you're likely to make. (If you look carefully, even upside-down you can see the interviewer writing *'Whinger'* on your CV.)

Beware of the sharks

Some agencies are great. But there are sharks out there, so if you find yourself on the receiving end of any of the following, take our advice: start swimming and *don't look back.*

1. **No interest in you**

   Is the firm showing heaps of enthusiasm to get you onto their books – and absolutely no interest in what you have to offer the publishing world? *Start swimming.*
2. **Offers you interviews as 'practice'**

   What *can* they mean? What they actually mean, of course, is that you're wrong for the job and they know it, and/or the job's wrong for you and they know it, and you're about to waste your own time and/or that of the interviewer – and they know it.

Trouble is, some agencies rather stupidly insist on presenting a range of candidates for the would-be employer to consider, even if half the candidates really aren't right for the job. They think it makes them look as if they're working hard. Actually, any decent agency cares about quality, not quantity, and won't put you through the agony of going to interviews just to make up numbers. If you get a sense you're being offered up as interview bait, *start swimming*.

Here's what a *good* agency's approach sounds like on this subject:

> There is no point in sending candidates along for an interview they are not interested in. I've sometimes pushed candidates to consider a vacancy that they would not otherwise have thought of, if my knowledge of the organisation interviewing, and their specific skills, led me to spot a strong overlap. But otherwise no. What's the point? We are looking at careers, not just filling jobs, and we want both employees and organisations to come back to us in future as people they like to work with and trust.
>
> (MARGARET MILLS, BOSS OF JUDY FISHER ASSOCIATES, UK)

3. **Agents who spend too much time finding out what else you've gone for**

You're not the only fish in the sea, you know. The agency's busy looking for jobs for other people on their books beside you. So if you tell them where else you have applied, and tell them of the job vacancies on offer, you might just be inviting them to submit some of their candidates to those very vacancies. That doesn't do your chances any good, to put it mildly. Of course, we're not saying that any casual enquiry about what other things you've been considering is a sign of sharky tendencies, but if they're rather insistent on this, and you just get the feeling they're not looking out for your best interests, *start swimming*.

Of course, we must make it absolutely clear – and not just because our lawyers told us to, but because we really believe it to be true (they told us to say that bit, too) – that the great majority of recruitment agencies specialising in publishing are, like the majority of recruitment agencies in general, good, decent, honest people working hard to do the very best they can for their candidates as well as their clients. The word quickly gets out, particularly about bad experiences, and since they live and die by their reputations, with any luck those doing the wrong thing will soon be looking for agencies to find them work themselves.

All we're saying is that there is the very occasional shark, is all. If you find one, just very politely let them know you're no longer in the market thank you very much, strike them off your Christmas card list . . . *and tell everyone you meet.*

Chapter Sixteen
How to do a great interview

Always remember that it's just as important for you to like the interviewer as it is for them to like you.

(SUZIE DOORÉ, SENIOR EDITOR, HODDER & STOUGHTON, UK)

I've had bad interviewers rather than bad interviews. The key thing is to make personal contact with the interviewer while you are working out what it is they really want: then, if you want it too, show them how much you want it, otherwise bail out.   (ANTHONY FORBES WATSON, PUBLISHER, UK)

Only apply for the jobs you really want! I can't tell you how many times I've interviewed people for entry-level sales and marketing positions only to find covert editorial assistants who really don't care about the marketing and selling of books! Not only is it difficult to make the leap from one departmental camp to the other, but it is also wasting a position that someone else might really love.

(NATASHA BESLIEV, SENIOR PRODUCT MANAGER, HARDIE GRANT EGMONT, AUSTRALIA)

If you've made the interview, then technically they like you. Don't overwhelm the interviewer with more detail stuff. Let them get to know you.

(TRAVIS GODFREDSON, RESEARCH MANAGER, AUSTRALIAN CONSOLIDATED PRESS)

Just turn up and entertain the interviewer.

(RICHARD CHARKIN, BLOOMSBURY PUBLISHING)

Well, your persistent phone calls and spectacular CV have done their job, and your toe is firmly wedged in the door: you've been invited in for an interview. Now for the rest of you to follow … This chapter is all about that all-important job interview, and how to present yourself in the best possible light.

By the way, if you're not yet quite at this nerve-wracking stage, and you're still at the nerve-wracking stage before that, of awaiting the phone call to invite you in for an interview, here are a couple of thoughts. Your call to interview will almost certainly come via a phone call to the number on your CV. As we've said before, you should carry a pen and diary with you at all times while you are job hunting; then when the phone call comes you can be ready to book in an appointment time. In fact, you should have some available times ready to hand that suit you, so if they do offer you some leeway you're ready.

If you're currently working and don't want your employers to know you're job hunting, try for a start of day or end of day interview time, and most prospective employers will do their best to arrange that – if they won't at least make the effort, you probably don't want to work for them. Even so, it's not always possible, so you may need to kill a grandmother to get to the interview. Note by the way that you should tick off your elderly relatives as you kill them, because even the most benign employer may get suspicious if you're heading off to a fifth grandmother's funeral.

There's no need to ask questions about the job during the 'come for interview' phone call – unless there genuinely are burning queries you want answered before you get all frocked up and troop in for your interview. But do check and double-check the time and date *and location,* since some companies have numerous offices, and you really want to make sure you're going to the right one.

Ready ... steady ... dazzle!
Remember, you only get one chance to make a first impression. Don't waste it. Here's how:

1. Be really clear about what the interview is for: which job, which stage, which organisation

Be very clear what the job you are going for entails and also what it is you're actually being interviewed for. One of my first interviews was very convivial and chatty, and I mistakenly thought I'd been offered a job, instead of a second interview. Not only did I feel a total dork, but my chances of actually getting the job disappeared very quickly!

(JULIA MOFFATT, FREELANCE EDITOR AND WRITER, UK)

There was this awful misunderstanding during the meeting for my first job in publishing, as a writer for an international dental publication based in London. I had applied, completed various subsequent writing tasks that they'd requested, and was then invited for what I thought was an interview. In fact I had got the job and they were inviting me to meet the team and tell me the good news. So I was there, confident but anxious and on best behaviour and couldn't understand why they were being so amazingly friendly and welcoming. Subsequently I learnt that they couldn't quite understand why I wasn't more excited about getting the job. Oh how we laughed! Publishing, you see, it's all about good communication.

(STEPHEN HANCOCKS, EDITOR-IN-CHIEF, *BRITISH DENTAL JOURNAL*)

2. Practise, practise, practise

A quick flick on any decent recruitment agency or job search site will find you a ton of typical interview questions (and, even better, suggested answers) – such as 'Why are you considering leaving your current position?' or 'How do you handle pressure?' or 'What do you consider your greatest achievement?' Make a list, then come up with a good answer … and then practise. In fact, there's no reason why you should have to answer a question you haven't already prepared for.

Here are a few typical questions, and suggested responses:

Five sample questions and answers

They say ...	You say ...	But don't say ...
1. 'Why do you want to leave your current role?'	'I really enjoy my job. After two years I feel I've learned a lot, and I'd like to move on in a different direction/stretch myself in the area of XXX'	'My boss is really weird and they don't pay enough' Or Bridget Jones-like: 'I shagged my boss' **Because:** *Makes you sound negative/unhinged*
2. 'Tell me about your university studies'	'I loved university! I really enjoyed my studies in the area of XXX – and now I'm looking forward to trying out what I've learned'	'I loved university! Sleep all day and drinking competitions. Beats working, that's for sure!' **Because:** *Makes you sound lazy and uncommitted*
3. 'How long do you see yourself in this role?'	'At least a few years – so I can learn the position thoroughly. I'd hope to have additional responsibilities when you felt I was ready to'	'About six months, I'm just saving up to move overseas with my boyfriend' **Because:** *Makes it clear you're not committed*
4. 'Where do you see yourself in five years?'	'I'm committed to a career in publishing and I'd love that to be with a company like this where I can forge a long-term career'	'In your job! Hahahaha!' **Because:** *They've heard this one before. Lots of times*
5. 'Why should we hire you?'	'Well, as we've discussed, I've shown I can do X, Y and Z. I'd love to work for you, and I know I'll do a fabulous job'	'Search me!' *or* 'I need to work to pay the rent' *or* 'Um ... er ... I erm ...' **Because:** *You really haven't thought this through, have you?*

3. Research, research, research

The more you know about a company, the more it will show and the more convincing you will be when you say 'I really want this job!' (as you should). Hop on the company website as a starting point. You probably did this before applying for the job anyway; now's the time to get serious. Get familiar with the company structure, divisions and business units, office locations, recent publications and bestsellers.

Do your research. If you're applying for a job on a newspaper make sure you read it from cover to cover both in the weeks leading up to your interview and on the day itself. If you're going to a publishing house read some of the books they publish. It's essential to be able to talk intelligently and fluently about the publishing enterprise you've applied to work for. Publishers want people with lively, original and workable ideas – they're always searching for the 'next big thing'.

(EMMA LEE-POTTER, JOURNALIST, NOVELIST AND FORMER PUBLISHER, UK)

I'd say always make sure you know exactly what the job entails. I was applying for anything that said 'Editorial Assistant' and so ended up in an interview for a magazine – unnamed in the advert – which turned out to be *Air Ambulance Monthly*. Try feigning an interest in emergency transportation with 5 minutes' notice! I'd also say that you should always try to stay composed and confident even if you think the interview started badly, or you think you're underqualified. In my BCA interview I made the mistake of reading (upside down) the note scribbled on my CV by one of the interviewers beforehand. It said 'Worth a look??', which didn't exactly fill me with confidence. But I got the job.

(SUZIE DOORÉ, SENIOR EDITOR, HODDER & STOUGHTON, UK)

Browse a few big bookshops/newsagents to see which books/magazines from this company are on shelf. If you're interviewing for a job in marketing, look at their promotional displays. If you're into design, look at the covers.

Check out **competitor websites** (anyone publishing magazines or books similar to your potential employer's).

Ask friends in the industry what they think of the company; trawl industry magazines (*The Bookseller, Bookseller+Publisher, Media Week* and so on) for gossip and news about the company. Don't repeat anything bad or derogatory in the interview, of course. Be aware of your prospective employer's reputation and be able to ask relevant questions: 'I noticed your managing director joined the group six months ago. What sort of changes has she brought to the company?' will make a seriously good impression.

4. Dress to impress

First impressions count. A lot. That initial greeting will get you halfway to the job if you look right. This is important not just for front office or sales roles, where you'll be very visible, but for all jobs. Even for editorial/production jobs that are mostly internal, the interviewer still has to like the look of you and be able to imagine seeing your face every morning. Basically, by looking professional and well groomed, you're decreasing your chances of someone objecting to something about you, and increasing your chances of getting the job. In fact, when it comes to personal appearance, you're not so much trying to make an impression at all as trying to avoid making a bad one.

The best tip I'd give anyone going for any job is just be yourself. People like to like people and the best way to get them to like you is to be you. It

seems ludicrous advice until you try it. Be brave. Oh yes, and smile a lot
and smell nice. (STEPHEN HANCOCKS, EDITOR-IN-CHIEF, *BRITISH DENTAL JOURNAL*)

Top Rules for Interview Accessorising

Dress the part

If you look professional and right for the job, it's much easier for
the interviewer to visualise you at that desk. As a rule of thumb,
interview wear is a little more formal then what people actually wear
in the office. Publishing is a creative industry – that does *not* mean
you can show up in your slick Saturday night gear and expect to get
the gig.

Staff wear business casual (trousers, and shirts)?
You: *wear a suit.*
Staff wear suits?
You: definitely *wear a suit.*
Staff wear casual gear (jeans and t-shirt)?
You: *think trousers and a shirt. If in doubt: wear a suit.*
**Job is sales, front-desk or anything else where you are
representing the company?**
You: *pull out (yep) that suit.*
Your interview is on a Friday and they do 'casual Fridays'?
You: *don't.*

'Suit' means **tailored jacket and trousers** or a skirt for girls, and **full
suit and tie** for guys, from a decent quality shop – Selfridges, Jigsaw
in the UK, Witchery, David Jones in Australia if you can manage it.
If you're broke, it's worth saving to get a really good interview outfit
you feel happy in. If you really can't manage it, borrow from a
friend or try vintage shops, or the conservative end of the less
expensive high street stores. If you feel overdressed or it's a hot day,
start in your jacket and take it off when you're in.

Suit colour should be conservative – beige, dark blue, browns
all good. Grey is less severe than black. Add a splash of colour

with jewellery, a scarf, tie or handbag to lift the look and show your style.

It's far, far **better to overdress** and have the mickey gently taken out of you – 'You didn't have to dress up for little old us!' – than to sit there feeling like you've arrived in your pyjamas.

The easiest way to do this is to have an interview outfit that's appropriate and helps you feel confident, and dust it off for interviews. You'll want to vary the shirt/accessories between first and second interviews.

Shoes should be clean and polished and not show toes (especially for guys).

Hide **tattoos**, tone down out-there **haircuts**. You want interviewers remembering your snappy answers, not your **outrageous frock**.

I sometimes get asked to be part of an interview panel within publishing; firms often like an external, and objective, viewpoint. I remember once interviewing candidates for a senior job as commissioning editor, a job that would require extensive liaison with academics and professional information managers. The person who turned out to be the runner-up candidate turned up in a low-slung pair of trousers, a decorated belly button and a crop top which showed a large expanse of her midriff. We like to think we chose solely on the quality of the application, but frankly the surrounding presentation did not feel appropriate to the position for which she was interviewing.

(ALISON)

For women, **hair and accessories** should be simple and stylish. Hair should be well groomed; make-up simple and low key – today is not the day for bright purple lipstick with a sparkle. Nothing should dangle, including **earrings. Low heels** are professional. Take it easy with the **perfume**.

For men, **clean-shaven** is better, or neatly trimmed if you usually wear facial hair (though in current style, goatees can look studenty and beards hippy, so best to remove if you can bear it. Ditto **jewellery** other than a simple ring). Gentle on the **aftershave**.

Sorry if this sounds boring. You can probably relax these guidelines a little if you are a designer, though not too much: your interviewers may be senior managers used to people in suits. By all means add a touch of your own flair and personality – a quirky ring, a bracelet, deep red lipstick, a stylish scarf or tie. Quiet sophistication and style can be shown in your accessories. Which brings us on to …

Accessories

Carry a professional briefcase, shoulder bag or handbag, big enough to fit a folder or papers. Women can be tempted to take a handbag and separate folder, but this can lead to fumbling. Men should keep keys, wallet and other stuff in a briefcase to avoid Lumpy Pocket Syndrome. Quality accessories show your quality: metal pen, leather bag.

The successful interview for my first job? I'd broken my arm two weeks earlier playing football, so looked like a real idiot suited up and looking professional but for my arm in a sling. To my amazement, the then Marketing Manager at Lothian, Liz Foley, came out to interview me with her arm in a sling, the result of a skiing incident. Consequently we talked broken arms for a good ten minutes, so by the time the interview actually started I was feeling very comfortable and confident. This was clearly the best way to break into publishing!

(KEIRAN ROGERS, MARKETING MANAGER, HARDIE GRANT, AUSTRALIA)

More accessories

- Two **clean copies of your CV** – one for you and one for them
- **Samples of past work**/references can be good – mention them, and you can pull them out if they are requested, and not if not
- **Pen and notebook** for writing notes, to remind you of questions to ask, etc

> I once interviewed a nice chap who showed all other signs of interest in the role, but didn't carry anything – not a copy of his CV, not a notepad and pen. Eventually I offered him a pen and paper and he said no thanks. I figured he wasn't that interested in the job if he couldn't be bothered making notes.
>
> (SUSANNAH)

5. 20 questions to ask

Picture this. Your interview is going swimmingly; you are knowledgeable, self-deprecating and witty, and getting on like old mates with the interviewer (though actually, being too matey in an interview can backfire – see below).

At the end the recruiter says, 'Right, that's me done; what would you like to know?'

You: 'Umm … nothing, thanks.'

You walk out, thinking *I'm in there;* the interviewer makes a note on your CV: *No questions, no imagination, no job.*

Questions show that you were listening, thinking critically, have something to say and are interested.

Here are 20 questions you could start with. Don't use them all, and do bear in mind that we are giving you a list of 20 suggestions, not 20 short scripts; each will have to be customised to the situation. So just taking our first example, instead of bluntly saying: 'What's the interview process?' you might be better asking: 'Can you tell me how the interview process works?'

1. What's the **interview process**? How many people are you shortlisting, and what happens now? *(This could be a second interview, psychological testing, project, reference checking … or a decision.)*
2. What's the **company culture** like?
3. Where is your group/division/company **going**?
4. What are the **key issues** you face?
5. What are some recent **successes** of your group/division/company?

6. What are some of the **challenges** your group/division/company faces?

7. Who are your main competitors?

8. 'I notice you **publish a lot** in the social sciences. Do you have plans to move into humanities as well?' 'Several of your non-fiction scholarly titles have performed very well. Is there a market trend here that you're responding to?' – *that kind of thing. Show off your familiarity with the company and their product. This where your research pays off.*

9. **Why** is the position vacant?

10. **What** happened to the person who's been doing this role until you advertised it?

11. Would I be **reporting to you**? *(Try and sound thrilled if the answer's yes and disappointed if the answer's no.)*

12. **How long** have you been with this company?

13. What's the **best thing** about working here?

14. Tell me about the **prospects for promotion**/career prospects?

15. Will there be opportunities for **travel**?

16. Does your company support **independent study**?

17. Does your company support **training** for employees?

18. If I get this job, **what are my workmates like**? How big is the team? What is their mix of experience like?

19. If I'm successful, **when would you want me to start**?

20. **Can I have the job please?** *Seriously, if you strike up a good relationship with the interviewer you can make it very clear you really want the job. Don't risk leaving him or her in any doubt!*

6. Getting there

Plan your travel route. Give yourself **heaps of time** to get there, especially if you don't know the area. If this means you arrive way too early, find a café for a coffee. Make the coffee a small one so you don't need to use the loo halfway through the interview, and now is not the time to visit your fave burger joint – smells get into your clothes and ruin that good impression. Arrive in the office **around**

10 minutes before your start time, neither less nor more. But aim to arrive within striking distance much longer than this. There is nothing worse than arriving all sweaty and flustered. If you're driving, have a **pile of coins** for the meter. Have an umbrella in the car.

Make sure you've had something to eat beforehand, even if you feel too nervous to eat – you don't want your stomach rumbling or to feel faint if the interview takes longer than you expect. Visit the loo for the same reason.

> I once went for an interview at the BBC. Preparing to alight from the bus at Oxford Circus I stumbled over the foot of another passenger who was getting out of his seat. I apologised but he looked very grumpy about it and I made a quick exit. About twenty minutes later we faced each other across the interview table. I am sure it was for that reason that I didn't get the job. (STEPHEN HANCOCKS, EDITOR-IN-CHIEF, *BRITISH DENTAL JOURNAL*)

7. Getting going

For everything up to this point – job hunting, writing your CV and sending it off, figuring out what to wear – you can rely on your Honest Friend, your mum, and above all, of course, this very book. From here on, you're on your own. But if you've done all the right preparation as discussed above and in previous chapters, you can be confident you'll do a good job.

Here are four things to check off your mental list and get you into the interview proper in good shape:

* **Show interest**

> Be seen reading your future employer's books they have on display in the foyer while you're waiting for the interview. (PAUL WATT, EDITOR, AUSTRALIA)

* **Smile, shake hands**
  Practise handshakes with your Honest Friend beforehand. You're aiming for firm and friendly – a wet limp lettuce or a cold wet fish

is *very* off-putting, and happens right at the very start of the interview

- **Make small talk**

  As they walk you upstairs or into the interview room, talk about the weather, the traffic, the view from the office building. Doesn't matter if it's banal, it's better than a silent walk, and shows you have social skills

- **Copy them**

  If they offer you refreshments (coffee, tea, water), there are two, and only two, correct responses –

  1. *'Yes please, only if you're having one'*
  or
  2. *'Yes please, a glass of water would be great, thanks'*

  Oddly, 'Nothing for me, thanks' is strangely off-putting. Somehow it suggests that you're too good for your host. Bizarre, but true. So use (1) or (2) above. It's much more important that you do that, even if you don't actually drink anything when it arrives.

  To push the rapport, literally have whatever they're having – if they have coffee with two sugars, guess what? Ditto anything else they offer – windows open, sit in the big chair – say yes. It builds that rapport, and it works. You're copying them so that you're like them. If you're like them, they're more likely to like you. This may sound very corny, or even insincere. But it's proven to work, so if you've gone to all this trouble, the competition is fierce and you really want the job, you may as well do these little extra things.

> Once the interview proper starts, get out that notebook and pen and make notes of what they say – not everything, but definitely key points. This makes them feel like you value what they're saying, as well as giving you the real benefit of being able to remember what they said!

(On the other hand, don't make too many notes. While you're doing so you're not maintaining eye contact and you're not in rapport.)

(SUSANNAH)

8. How to charm an interviewer

There are as many ways to conduct an interview as there are to conduct a conversation. Here's the three you're most likely to encounter:

- **Standard Q&A**
  Usually you and one or two of them sitting around a table – perhaps an HR manager or junior manager who will be your direct boss

- **Panel of junior and senior managers and HR**
  All sitting in a row looking scary

- **Second interview**
  Usually you and one or two of them, might be the senior manager of the department, the person whom your direct boss reports to

Here are some strategies for making a fantastic impression at interview:

- **Listen. Listen, listen, listen**
  Get the idea? This is hard to do well, which is one reason why doing it is such a good idea. Naturally you'll want to have your next question lined up and ready to go, but if you concentrate on it you may find that your attention has drifted, and a good interviewer will notice. Certainly you should listen attentively – look at them, nod from time to time at appropriate points, smile at their hilarious comments.

Listening is good, on both sides. My best interviews were ones where I did a lot of research first, and then bought a new outfit on my credit card, and went in feeling positive and ready.

(LIZ SMALL, PUBLISHING SERVICES AND MARKETING, PUBLISHING SCOTLAND)

I was very nervous for my first interview. The interviewer asked me about my work experience with Marks & Spencer and how long I had been there. I looked up at the clock and said 'about twenty minutes'. We both laughed and the interview carried on with a greater ease on both sides. And I got the job.

(ALISON)

At junior levels there are usually a number of applicants who are capable of doing the job being advertised, publishing being a popular choice and attracting high-calibre people. So personality, compatibility and ambitions become decisive factors. No-one expects you to be an expert in publishing when you go for a first interview. But you would be surprised at how many people I have interviewed who were unable to remember the title of the last book that they had read – even when 'reading' was on the CV as an interest.

(CHARLES NETTLETON, MANAGING DIRECTOR, WORKING PARTNERS TWO, UK)

- **Follow their lead**
  The interviewer is always right, even when they're wrong. If they want to show you the red caterpillars coming up the woodwork, fine. (Though that may give you a tip that this is not the right workplace for you.) Laugh at their jokes. Avoid saying, 'Yes, that's a good one – I've heard it before' or 'Ah, an oldie but a goody'. Show amazement when they say things they think are amazing. If they want the interview to be straightforward, professional and serious, that's what you do. If their tone is more friendly chit-chat, you should respond.

- **Be positive about yourself**
  Your experience, your schooling, and why you want this job, why you're leaving your current job. Never ever criticise – your current

boss, your university, your ex-boyfriend. Find the positive in any experience.

> Regarding interviews, I offer the same advice I give anyone applying for a job in any industry: sell yourself – no-one else will; never point out your weaknesses, focus on your strengths; don't indulge in gossip or be indiscreet about former employers during interviews. Learn something about the company before you attend the interview. Pay attention to your appearance. You'd be surprised how much your presentation can affect interviewers. How you are dressed says a lot about your personality, your attention to detail and your work attitude.
>
> (AVERILL CHASE, DIRECTOR, THE AUTHORS' AGENT, AUSTRALIA)

- **Keep it professional**

Show your personality off – just a bit with a little humour and smile. But don't overdo it – and stay on message, about the job, the company, and why you're the best person for both. Definitely don't get overly matey – this is almost worse than being frozen stiff. It looks unprofessional and can backfire. Don't get into things that just aren't that relevant either.

> Be very clear about your areas of expertise, and also be honest about what you don't know. You'll soon get found out if you can't do something. It is difficult when you are starting out, as of course you have no experience, but enthusiasm, a keenness to learn, and an ability to accept advice will stand you in very good stead.
>
> (JULIA MOFFATT, FREELANCE EDITOR AND WRITER)

> I once interviewed a girl who spent half an hour talking about her struggles with anorexia and how really she wanted to work in the caring industries, helping other people with similar problems. I was sympathetic but it was obvious she wasn't very committed to publishing or the job I was actually interviewing for.
>
> (SUSANNAH)

- **When it goes wrong**

  If you feel like you've got off on the wrong foot and everything you're saying is all wrong, don't panic or point it out – they probably haven't noticed. Just carry on and do a better job from that point.

If they say something you take moral exception to, you have to make a decision on the spot: could I *really* see myself working with someone who, for example, clearly doesn't like black or gay people. If the answer's no, we recommend simply getting through the rest of the interview with the maximum grace you can muster. We don't recommend you getting into a heated debate, even if you don't want the job, for two reasons: first, on the whole, people don't change their mind as the result of an argument, even if and perhaps particularly if they don't have logic or reason on their side; second, the interview is a very one-sided affair. They hold all the aces, and even if you do make it clear to them they're a blithering idiot (which they are), they'll just turf you out anyway.

9. Show me the money

If they ask what salary you're looking for, don't tell them. Or rather, instead of naming a figure, ask what their range is. An offer will probably be made somewhere within that range, depending on your experience/skills.

If forced to respond, give a range: 'I'm looking for something between X and Y, which seems about right for my experience,' is the best way to handle this.

Don't be tempted to exaggerate what you're earning/looking for in the hope of getting a higher offer, or making yourself look hot. This rarely works in publishing, and is more likely to make the interviewer think you don't know what you're talking about (they know what the market rates are, remember). Besides, if you do convince them that's what you're earning/after, they may well decide they can't afford you so they should hire someone else.

If you don't know what you're worth (and there's no reason why you should), do some research. Do one or more of these four things:

- **Ask friends** in similar roles or working for similar companies
- **Ask your university lecturers** or previous employers
- **Get on the net.** There are freely available salary surveys for most job functions that will give you a guideline
- If what you're earning seems fair, look for about **4–6% increase for each year of experience** in that role, and larger jumps for changing to more advanced roles

Don't be surprised if book publishing pays badly at junior levels; don't be surprised if magazine publishing pays well.

And if you genuinely can't figure it out – if you've not worked before, or don't know anyone in the industry, or are moving countries and you don't know what you're worth, say so! Most employers will pay you what you're worth, not try and take advantage of you.

If coming from a better-paid industry, you might even find yourself saying things like this: 'Well currently I'm on X, but I realise that to move into the right kind of role a slight pay cut may be necessary.' This has the advantage of making it clear you're genuinely committed to publishing. It has the disadvantage that you end up making less money.

10. Finishing up

When they're done, they'll ask you for questions *(see earlier)* and then wrap up the meeting.

By this point you should have asked enough questions to make sure you have a grip on the job and the company and to show that you care. Make sure you understand what the interview process is too – when you can expect to hear, if they'll call you back for second interview or straight out offer you the job.

Follow their lead, remember to thank them for the opportunity, and it wouldn't do any harm at this point to underline how much you like the idea of the job and how much you would love to have it.

Now all you have to do is make your way out of the office without falling over, standing on your interviewer's toes or otherwise embarrassing yourself. And then the waiting begins ...

This is one of the things every book about interviewing says to do, yet no-one ever does it.

Two or three days after the interview, send a card, an e-mail or, even better, a letter to thank them again for the interview, and perhaps pick out something specific to say that shows you were listening.

> I was very impressed by the new catalogues you have put together and would love the opportunity to work with your team in this area.

Interviewees very rarely do this, yet it can make you really stand out ahead of the pack. It's unlikely to do harm, at least.

Second interviews

The same guidelines apply for second interviews as the first time around. You may find the interviewers change and the questions are the same, or the same interviewers and different questions; either way, follow their lead and be courteous, professional and on the ball.

Always think of some new questions for the second interview, ideally based on things they've told you at first interview that you'd like them to clarify or to enlarge on.

> You mentioned your company has a commitment to training. Can you tell me more about that?

That kind of thing.

Then, same again: same clarification of the process now, thanks at the end, and polite thank-you e-mail a few days later.

Tests and tasks

Don't be surprised if you get asked to do a little test or fulfil a task to demonstrate your stuff. This might include:

- **Written exercise in the interview**

  This is pretty much standard for a copy editing role, and sometimes also used in marketing and assistant editor jobs. This should be related to the job you're applying for. It's often given in a tight time frame to see how you react under pressure (the meanies).

  Don't freak out; remember you've done a zillion exams at school and university and you did OK there. This is stuff you can do (otherwise you shouldn't be going for the job), and the recruiters make allowances for your nerves. Everyone else doing the test is operating under the same conditions, so they're comparing how you perform in your stressed-out test with other people's stressed-out tests.

> I give Marketing Executive applicants a book and 20 minutes to write me a promotional piece (postcard or brochure) for it. It's cruel, but you really see who can be calm, imaginative and accurate under pressure – all traits I like.
>
> (SUSANNAH)

- **Job-related field exercise**

  Used most often for sales rep jobs, where you might be required to research a market by chatting to prospective clients (booksellers, lecturers and so on). Put some time into this, as if they ask you to do this you're probably down to the final one or two candidates, and what you produce can well decide whether you get the job. Make sure you ask lots of questions so you're clear what they're expecting from you, and then follow guidelines exactly. If you need to hand in a written report, go over it with the same level of care you did your CV, including having your Honest Friend proof it, and ensure your presentation is attractive, error-free and professional.

- **Written or oral 'personality' test at one of your interviews**
  Very hip a few years ago but perhaps seem to have gone out of
  fashion now. They're designed to see what kind of person you are
  and if you'd fit their team/culture.

- **Drug test**
  Big in the USA but yet to really catch on in Europe or Australia.
  Some drugs can be detected in your system a month after you use
  them. Some of these tests have been reported to have common
  false-positive so if you're not a drug user and you get a positive, be
  sure to push for a re-test.

- **A test that doesn't look like a test**

  Publishing is a hothouse and there will always be what appears to be an
  unreasonable aspect to the interviewing. As an editor or producer, you
  want someone who fits into the team, and the judgement is a mix of gut
  feeling, business, and personal dynamics. On one mag I ran, we started
  the interview for would-be journos in the office to check them out in
  daylight, then we took them down to the ineptly-named Golden Age pub
  (where it was always twilight) for the post-deadline lunch. If they mixed
  well with the small editorial and ad sales team, had a spark of writing
  talent, but also knew when to shut up, they had a chance.

  (GUY ALLEN, PUBLISHER OF GUIDOMEDIA.COM, AUSTRALIA)

  I have been on the board of The Artists Information Company (www.
  an.co.uk) for about ten years now, and as part of the personnel
  subcommittee, I help interview staff. For key positions we have
  developed a routine that has proved very successful:

  We organise a two-day interview, and this includes a presentation from
  each candidate and some on-the-spot exercises – team tasks and
  workshop, and joint problem-solving within team delivery. But the key

factor has become the dinner for all staff that we organise on the night between the interview days. We arrange a table in a local restaurant and move the candidates around every so often so that all have the chance to talk to them. We are a small team and so getting the right staff mix is vital.

Staff feedback the next day is always significant, and often reveals things that did not come out during the formal interview process. We are interested in their body language and how colleagues relate to each other, who was a good listener – and who seemed to want to talk only to those interviewing. And by involving all staff we feel this encourages inclusion and team-building. (ALISON)

A good recruitment process should as far as possible replicate the work environment. Most applicants do seem to like our interview process, and say they feel it is thorough and fair – although some say they find it odd that they meet all the other candidates! The recruitment process we use means you have also started the induction process for the successful candidate. Staff turnover is not high.

(SU JONES, PUBLISHER, THE ARTISTS INFORMATION COMPANY)

Other types of interviews

If you are interviewed by a **recruitment agent** rather than directly by the publisher, you can be certain there'll be a multi-stage process – you'll go though to the publisher for at least one more interview. Recruitment company interviews tend to be a bit less specific – partly because they don't know the job as well as the employer, so are homing in more on whether you'll fit in the company culture – and partly because they probably want to check you out for other roles in other companies too. They are also more likely to get technical with formal personality testing and the like. For more on their processes, see Chapter 15 on using recruitment agents.

After you've sent off job applications you may well get an **unexpected phone interview**. This usually happens when you're in

Woolworths buying birthday cards while babysitting your ten-year-old nephew, or in the middle of a chat with your current boss. Employers do this if they're a little bit interested in you and aren't quite sure whether to spend the time on bringing you in for interview. For them it's a quick way of narrowing down a long shortlist, or checking something on your CV. For you it's an opportunity to get in the door for an interview. Here's how to handle it:

- There's nothing wrong with explaining that **you can't talk**, and making a time to call them back. This gives you an hour or a day to get your head together, to read the job ad again, to remember which version of your CV you sent in and feel in control.
- **Give the conversation your full attention**; look away from what is currently on screen or has just arrived in your inbox. Stand up (it helps your voice, as well as your concentration).
- **Always carry a pen and paper** so you can scribble down phone numbers and names. Have your diary with you so you can check interview times.
- **Make sure you get their name and position** – again, this helps you feel more in control, and reminds you of which job you applied for.
- Answer their questions **precisely and succinctly**. If the discussion gets too long, or they ask for more detail, it might be an opportunity to say, 'That one's a long story – maybe we should discuss it face to face. Would I be able to come in for a meeting?'
- **Finish with a query** or two about the role, a request for a meeting, or ask what the process is from here. If you get a chance, mention how keen you are to work for their company and always thank them for calling. Ask them for an interview – they might say they'll call you back when they've decided who they will be interviewing, but it's good to show initiative. This phone call shows they're interested in you – don't let them get away.

- And finally, **don't beat yourself up** if you think you screwed it up – you probably didn't, and even if you did, it gives you a reminder to be better prepared next time.

If this idea of a phone call out of the blue freaks you out, we suggest you a) practise with friends beforehand, b) always, always offer to call back at a better time, or c) don't put your mobile number on your CV.

What if you don't get the job?

You may write it down to experience, but if it was one you really wanted, it's not a bad idea to write back thanking them for interviewing you, saying that you are disappointed and hope they will keep in touch should events not work out as expected. If it doesn't work out with their first choice, they may come back to you; or they may pass your CV on internally and you get a second bite (perhaps even for a job role that might suit you better than the one you applied for in the first place).

My first job in publishing was as Rights and International Sales Exec for McGraw-Hill Education. I was referred on having applied for another position, in the Marketing department; however senior management felt that my experience and interests were better suited to the Rights and International sales role.

(AMY BLOWER, RIGHTS SALES MANAGER, PEARSON EDUCATION, UK)

My first job was for a Marketing Co-ordinator at Pergamon Press, which became Maxwell Macmillan Publishing within weeks of starting there. It was in response to an advertisement placed in the *Sydney Morning Herald* and while I had a wonderful interview with the Sales Manager, I didn't get the job. The universe aligned three months later when the show-pony they hired went globetrotting. Thankfully, the Sales Manager had kept my details on file, asked if I was still interested, and I started a few weeks later. I worked with him for four years and still speak of him as my finest industry mentor. (RACHAEL MCDIARMID, JAMES BENNETT, AUSTRALIA)

But don't keep reminding them how sad you are not to have got the job – you could start to sound like you are stalking them:

> Do follow up the interview if you're really interested in the position. By follow-up, a quick e-mail is sufficient but not weeks of e-mail, phone and mail correspondence – I once received weekly motivational business cards from one applicant even after he was advised he was unsuccessful. Disturbing.
> (RACHAEL MCDIARMID, JAMES BENNETT, AUSTRALIA)

More reading

Lees, *Job Interviews: Top Answers to Tough Questions*, McGraw-Hill, 2003

Amos, *Handling Tough Job Interviews: Be Prepared, Perform Well, Get the Job*, How To Books Ltd, 2004

Jay, *Brilliant Interview: What Employers Want to Hear and How to Say It*, Prentice-Hall, 2005

www.job-interview.net

www.jobinterviewquestions.org

Chapter Seventeen
How to handle a job offer

You've given a great interview, because you followed all the advice in the previous chapter. Or perhaps for whatever reason it didn't work out quite so well – maybe because the interviewer was even more nervous than you were, or maybe because they just weren't very experienced or very good at it. However the interview has gone, there will now be an awkward pause of anything up to a week or more while you wait, quite possibly in agony (depending on your circumstances) for the interviewer to let you know whether they want to hear from you again.

Meanwhile, as discussed before, *do* send a card or a letter or an e-mail to thank them for the interview and refer to something that was said during the interview. Beyond that, we recommend that you try and put this whole thing to the back of your mind and get on with further job applications. Don't put all your eggs in one proverbial. Not only will you avoid losing a whole week, you'll also find something to do with all that nervous energy, and distract yourself from just wondering, wondering, wondering ...

And now, perhaps when you least expect it (see previous chapter: always have a pen and paper with you!), you get the call for a second interview. As we said earlier, there's no need to vary the routine: be polite, be interested, listen hard, don't bump into the furniture, don't beg but don't overstate your value either.

Once again there's no other option but to wait (and send a thank you). Eventually it comes: The Letter. Your fingers may shake a little as you slit it open to reveal the job offer!

Fan-bloody-tastic! You absolute legend. All your hard work and all that research and shoe-polishing has paid off. Now what? You should of course celebrate the moment, in however extravagant and debauched a fashion as feels excessive and disproportionate. Whatever happens from this point on, it's always far better to have options than not.

Still, there's actually a little thinking to do before you rock up to the office on a Monday morning at an impressively early time. The most important, and really in one sense the only question, to ask yourself is this:

Do you want this job?

Don't be silly – of course you do! That's why you applied in the first place. Hang on a second, though. If you're in any way typical you'll have applied for plenty of jobs, some of which you know you didn't really want. Question is, is this one of them?

How do you tell? Elsewhere we talked about the less-than-perfect job, which you take because it helps you on your way to your goal, even if it doesn't directly take you to it. So the first thing to do is to think hard about all the pluses and negatives of this role, by which we mean:

1. What's the role like?
How well do you fit what they're after? More importantly, how well does it fit what *you're* after? Go back to Chapter 10 for further thoughts on this.

2. What's the company culture like?
Will you enjoy working with this mob? Is it somewhere you can get to? Anything much more than an hour each way is going to kill you, or at least kill your enthusiasm, pretty quick. Be honest with yourself about all the positives and negatives, because it is an awful feeling to realise only months or even weeks into your new job that you've made a horrible mistake that you could have avoided if only you'd given it more thought.

3. What's your new boss like?
Tough one – the question, we mean, not the boss (we hope). Presumably you've met them at least once, so at a bare minimum you'll

know what they look like and how they talk to you. But remember the interview is a very artificial environment, for both of you. What were the subtle or not-so-subtle clues you picked up? Did they spend too much time talking and not enough time listening? Did they really listen to your answers? Did they, as someone who once interviewed Steve did, show all the signs of being massively overworked, stressed-out and clinically depressed?

4. What's the pay like?

Publishing doesn't pay very well, especially at the starter's end. Can you survive on this? It might seem like a lot of money if you say it quickly, but take out the tax (actually you can rely on the government to do that for you), the rent, the food, the transport to get to work, the cost of some decent clothes to wear once you get there and suddenly it doesn't look like such a huge stash.

5. What else is on offer?

If you're seriously job hunting, you'll almost certainly have a few irons in the fire at any one time – including this job, which you may or may not want, and a couple of other jobs which you definitely don't want, and another job which you like the sound of but you've only done one interview, and your absolute dream job which has only just been advertised and you've sent in your CV but not heard anything yet … you get the picture.

So how to balance up a firm job offer with a job that's OK, say, with a potential job offer sometime in the future with your dream job?

If you've been job hunting for months, and this is your first firm offer, and you're basically happy with what's on offer, you'd probably be best advised to take this job. On the other hand if you've only just started job hunting, this is the first offer through your door and you're basically not that keen, think seriously before leaping into it – you don't want to make a false start if you can help it or to get stuck for ages in a job you don't like.

Four key points here:

- You're better off considering the job offer in hand without thinking about prospective other jobs that you might or might not get.
- There is nothing wrong with asking for 48 hours to think over the offer. This gives you some breathing space to chat to people whose opinions you care about and hopefully make the right decision.

If you're quite far down the track (completed second interviews, say, and waiting for news) with another job that you think you'd like more, definitely give that company a call. 'I wanted to let you know that I've received a job offer with another company. I would really prefer to work with you – as I mentioned when we met, your job sounds perfect for me – but I need to let this other company know in the next 24 hours, so I am hoping you can tell me how your decision-making process is going.' This is fine, though don't mention the name of the company who has offered a job, or what the position is.

- Finally, never ever accept a job and keep job hunting with the idea of not taking up Job 1 if you get a better offer in the next few weeks. This is a horrible thing to do to the Job 1 people and will get you a terrible reputation in the publishing industry – and it's a very small and insular industry, so you really don't want to do that.

OK, let's assume that your new job gets a tick on all these issues. That leaves the issue of money and other conditions – and the possibility of negotiating.

Negotiation to get a better deal for you

What happens now, whether you like it or not, is now a process of negotiation. You've had a job *offer*, remember, and if you accept it as it is, then that's how you've chosen to play your side of the negotiation. In effect, your employer has said that they'd like to employ you, and that they propose to pay you X, have you start on Y date, and offer you Z conditions. How do you feel about that? Are you happy to accept? But saying a straight-out 'Yes' is not your only option – and we're not talking about just saying 'No', either.

If there is *anything at all* that you'd like to improve about the job and conditions, now is the time to bring it up. They think you're the best person for the job, and they've offered you the job with their standard conditions; in most cases, if there's something you'd like a bit different, it won't be a big deal for them to tweak the contract for you, so don't agonise over it – just ask.

Think about:

- **Salary** – base and package (bonuses): see below.

- **Length of probation period,** if any: they want you to be on six months' probation, you think three months sounds better.

- **Job title**: they want you to be Marketing Assistant, you prefer the sound of Marketing Executive.

- **Start date**: most places won't have a problem with you starting a week or two after they'd hoped – though if there's a conference or other fixed-date event that you're needed for, you may have to be flexible. We strongly advise taking at least a week between the end of your old job and the start of the new to clear your head, by the way.

- **Holidays and leave for study**: it's unlikely you'll get more holiday than is standard, though if you've got a trip to Italy booked for summer, you should be able to get enough holiday time advanced to cover yourself. Most employers won't have any problems with you using your holiday time in dribs and drabs to support your study, and some will have programmes to give you time off for professional advancement without dipping into your holiday time – and may even help you pay for it.

- **Flexible hours**: unless your new employer has a stated commitment to having staff work flexibly, you may well have more success at this once you've been in the job a year or two and proven yourself. Always worth asking though and as with any negotiation, if you can offer them some benefit it will go down better: working 8.15am to 4.30pm instead of 9am to 5pm, for example, actually nets them more work time from you, and helps you avoid the worst of the traffic.

In this discussion on **how to negotiate**, we'll use the example of salary negotiation, which lots of people find very hard to do but can really pay off in the long run! The same basic principles apply for any offer negotiation prior to your accepting the job.

I would encourage people to have the courage to negotiate a good salary. If an employer thinks you're the right person for the job, they'll be willing to consider giving you more than just award rates. Having said that, be wary of those who do not receive your attempts to negotiate a better pay deal very well. Consider if this means they will appreciate you in the job. Remember that a job interview is a two-way street; treat it as an opportunity for you to work out if the company/job is right for you.
(RUTH JELLEY, COMMUNICATIONS OFFICER, SWINBURNE INTERNATIONAL, AUSTRALIA)

Here's how to negotiate for better pay or conditions. Certainly if it's a sales position, it's hard to see how you *wouldn't* negotiate for better pay. Would you want someone working for you in a sales position who didn't push for more? Of course, that's not to say you'll *get* better pay – but if you don't ask, you won't get (and if you do ask, you still may not get).

Before we get into that, though, here's one very, very good reason why you should go to a lot of trouble about this now: most of the things you can improve a bit, even slightly, will have a big impact over the course of your time with this company. If it's flexible working hours, for example, the hours you choose will make you happier and enjoy your job more and be a better employee. If you improve your salary, it's not as small an amount of money as it looks. After all, the salary you earn at this company for as long as you're there will be determined largely by two things, your performance (which will be brilliant), and your starting salary (which probably won't). Next year's salary will be this year's, plus any increase and/or bonus you get. And when you get promoted, the increase will again largely be determined by the starting point – which is what you're fighting for.

And here's how you get your better conditions, using salary negotiation as the example:

Negotiation: Part I

Ask for it. Yes, it really is as simple as that – though in fact there's a little game of skill involved. Firstly, call the person who's made the job offer, thank them very much and ask to see them. Don't say why, and if they ask if you'd like to accept the job, you can say, *'I'd love to accept the job* [which is true – if they up the salary!], *but I do need to see you for just a few minutes at a time of your convenience if that's possible.'*

By not specifying why you want to see them, you're keeping your cards close to your chest. It's always much easier to negotiate in person – and much harder to say 'No' in person (which is in your favour). How can they not see you? It may well be another issue altogether for all they know.

Now, when you're sitting down with them, tell them how excited and grateful you are to be offered the position, and pick out a couple of things about the role that you're particularly keen on – perhaps like this:

'Thanks, Anne, for offering me this role. As you know I'm really committed to working in publishing, so this is a great opportunity for me. I love the way the department works and the way you've set it up.'

Then, if you're able, leave it at that. There now ensues a slight pause, which invites Anne, of course, to make the response, perhaps with a slightly raised eyebrow:

'But … ?'

To which your response might go something like this:

'Yes, but … [A tiny sigh would come in handy here.] There is a little problem, which I'm sure between us we can overcome, and it's this. You did make it clear at the interview that the salary range on offer was X to Y, and to be honest I was rather expecting to see an offer closer to Y than to X –'

and this is the key bit. You can't just say you were hoping for more. Well, you can, but good luck to you in getting it. The really critical thing is having the reason, right up front, and a damned good one, too …

'… expecting to see an offer closer to Y than to X, because of my experience. I do have a postgraduate degree in publishing, and as you know I have done a very relevant internship with a highly regarded publisher, so as I say I was thrilled to get the job offer and just a little disappointed the salary wasn't a little more.'

If you think this sounds as if you're putting the entire job offer at risk, think again. For one thing, Anne's already decided that you are the very best person for the job – not the cheapest, but the best. She wants to see you in that chair, performing that role, and she's convinced herself that you're the best person for the job. She's a woman of fine judgement and discernment. She must be: she picked you.

For another thing, she may well have some room to play with here. In many organisations she can always find a bit more cash – perhaps even a lot more cash. She's not going to just spray it about, but if you make a good case and make it clear that you are serious about it and not just trying it on, she's got to balance the risk that she's going to lose you for the sake of what in the bigger scheme of things is not a whole heap of money.

For a third and final thing, she'll admire you for it. It proves you know your worth, and it makes it very clear that you're not going to get rolled.

Now, her response is likely to be more or less standard, whatever the true situation. Even if she's fully intending to give you more just for asking, she's unlikely to tell you that straight up. In all probability, you'll hear something very much like this:

> 'Hmm ... I do take your point, and of course I was very impressed with your CV and your performance at the interview(s) – otherwise we wouldn't have offered you the job. However, the offer we made was one we thought about very seriously, and we think it's a fair reflection of your experience. After all, this is your first job and you don't have a great deal of directly relevant experience, unlike some of the other candidates.'

She said that last bit, of course, just to remind you in a subtle way that you're not the only fish in the sea, and that there were other good candidates. OK, so this is absolutely standard. Veiled threats and a blank refusal even to consider what you're saying. So you just give up right now, yes? Actually, no.

Notice that what she *hasn't* said is that there is definitely no more money and that under no circumstances will the offer be increased, over her dead body and may God strike her dead. If she *does* explicitly say that, then perhaps it may be time to move on to the second part of this discussion. You need to use your own judgement here, and try and work out whether she's just giving you a bit of resistance for form's sake (which is what it sounds like to us), or to make sure when she does offer you more you don't keep pushing, or to make it clear who's boss, or because she honestly and truly isn't going to go any further.

So, having decided that you haven't yet hit the wall, you could come back like this:

> 'I do see your point [don't call it an argument, or you'll turn it into one]. That said, I really, really do want to work for you, and I'm assuming that you've offered me the job because you want me to work for you, and that in fact I'm the best candidate for the job. Would you be able to increase the offer at all?'

And here's a big secret that even she may not know: *you want her to name the figure.* The reason is, research in negotiations of every kind over the past 30 years has shown that the person who first names the figure tends to lose. No, we don't know why, and nor does anyone else. But it's true. So if you can get her to come up with even a nominal increase of just a few hundred or perhaps a thousand, then immediately you're on the way. You've now established the principle that she'll pay more for you than she originally said she would: it's now just a case of how much more. And even if you don't go any further than this, you've still got some free money, which can't be bad. So, get her to suggest something if you can. If she absolutely won't name a figure (perhaps she's read this book), then you'll have to, of course. But if you're going to, make it worth your while. Go big, and then she'll take advantage of the fact that you've named the price and pin you back.

From here it's just a case of haggling. She's named a price, ideally; so you suggest she double it. She refuses, so between the two of you, you end up with something more than her original revised offer, and less than the ridiculous figure you knew you were never going to get anyway.

However, it doesn't stop there, because there's a second part.

Negotiation: Part 2

You've done beautifully. You've got yourself some extra free money, which will be paid you not just this year but every year you're at the company, and you've actually increased your future employer's respect for you even before you started working for her. Hurrah for you.

Now on to the soft benefits. Soft benefits are everything that isn't cold, hard, guaranteed cash. It might be sales commission or performance bonus, it might be terms and conditions such as annual leave loading, annual leave, the date of your next (first) salary review, or anything else at all that you know the company uses as incentives for its staff. And one way to bridge from the first part to the second is like this:

> 'I see you're a great negotiator. I did have my heart set on Y salary, but I can tell I'm not going to win that one. Ah well, at least you can say I tried ...'

Flattery will get you everywhere, with luck. It's a fact of human nature that however outrageously we're flattered, we very rarely pick up on it. We almost always assume that the other person is wise and observant. (Observe someone telling your mum that you must be her younger sister and see what we mean.)

> 'There was just one more thing I wanted to ask about, and that was the performance bonus/annual leave package you mentioned at the interview. I note that it only kicks in after six months' service, and I was a little disappointed by that. I do understand that of course there's a need for a probationary period, but I'd have thought that three months might be fairer, and I wondered if you had any thoughts on that?'

Or perhaps it's the first salary review, promised after a year, which you can ask to be after six months (she'll agree to this, because it costs her nothing and she's getting tired, and at the same time make a mental note to herself not to increase your salary at that point. But that's another negotiation, and at least you've brought forward the discussion).

By now you should get the picture. Be polite but firm, know your own worth, keep your head, make her name the price first and be a little brave (but know when to fold).

We've spent a fair bit of time on this, largely because it's not often you get the opportunity to start a new job and ask for what you want, and also because hardly anyone does it early in their career, and everyone always does later on (and gets away with it). After all, we do speak as publishing folk who have between us employed well over a hundred people. Please note there is a big fat gamble in here. We are fairly sure that you won't upset your employer or lose the job offer, provided you negotiate respectfully and with a playful smile playing about your lips; in almost every case, the worst that can happen is they'll say 'no'. But there is an ever-so-slight chance that this might go horribly wrong. So tread carefully, and if you're thrilled with what's on offer consider simply accepting happily.

Responding to the job offer

Whether you negotiate for better salary or conditions or not, you'll eventually have to respond to the job offer itself, and the tip here is to respond in as close to the fashion the job is offered as you can. If they're happy to offer it to you by e-mail, then an e-mail response is fine (be sure to request their confirmation that your acceptance has been received). If they write to you on company letterhead, with a formal contract attached requesting your signature, then naturally you'll fill it out, make a photocopy and return it, attached to a covering letter. Again, ask for confirmation that they've received it.

Then, polish up your shoes and dust off your work clothes (and get some in, if all you have is one set of interview gear): you're on your way!

Chapter Eighteen
How to get an international job in publishing

Publishing is an international industry, and what is more, publishers worldwide share the same characteristics and look for the same skills, talents and personality styles. It follows that if you like the kind of people who inhabit your local industry, you are likely to feel welcome and fit in wherever you decide to work.

If you long to work overseas, there are several main options.

1. Work for an international company and apply for jobs overseas

Get your start at a company that has offices overseas, prove yourself over a few years here in your home town/country, and then apply for a promotion or job swap to an overseas office.

This is different from getting a transfer (see below) in that you're doing the work on it – applying for jobs overseas, probably going through an interview process and if you get the job, you may well be covering your own moving costs and figuring out your own accommodation and visas.

This works best as a long-term plan – you need to prove yourself first by building a good reputation, and that usually means at least a few years with an organisation. If you start as a sales assistant and two weeks later request a job in the Hawaii office you will get laughed at. If you want to move this along quickly, you'd be better placed to go for option 3 – job hunting overseas.

As a young rep in Melbourne I knew I'd love to work overseas at some point in my career. When I was promoted to Marketing Manager based in Sydney I started being sent to company conferences in the USA, which helped me meet the managers from the UK – and not just meet them but get to know them! By the time I was ready to move overseas I was offered a fun-sounding job in New York at the same time as I was interviewing for positions in the UK. The USA immigration laws meant the company could have got me a visa but my husband wouldn't have been able to work there – so that didn't get very far – but we both had UK residency so that made things much easier, and I ended up working with a wonderful bunch of people at McGraw-Hill UK.   (SUSANNAH)

2. Get a transfer

This is the easiest option if you can manage it – get a job at a publisher that operates in a number of countries, including where you'd like to go, and angle your way into an overseas posting.

If the publisher where you work decides to send you overseas, you're getting a transfer – often a promotion (going into a smaller market but with larger responsibilities), and they'll sort out moving costs and help you with accommodation and visas and life in a different part of the world.

Indeed, sometimes large firms try out new recruits with a spell overseas as a key method of finding out what they are made of:

I got my first job in publishing by applying to the Macmillan Graduate Training Scheme. The job was as trainee Marketing Executive and six months later I went to Australia to look after the marketing of the UK books there.   (MARTIN NEILD, MANAGING DIRECTOR, HODDER HEADLINE, UK)

My first job in publishing was as a European Sales Rep for Oxford University Press, which involved travelling for up to six months p.a. explaining in German how it was that the orders I had taken from them on my previous visit four months before had still not emerged from the industrial relations carwreck that was OUP's Neasden distribution centre in the late 1970s. From my short time at OUP I met most of the brightest and most independent-minded people I've met in 30 years in publishing.

(ANTHONY FORBES WATSON, PUBLISHER, UK)

When you are in a relatively junior position, early in your career, getting a transfer is more likely to work from the UK, where many publishing companies run European operations from the UK office. It's less likely to work from a country like Australia where if you work for any of the big internationals you are essentially starting out in a branch office, with the head offices in UK or USA.

3. Move overseas and look for a job when you get there

If you have relatives or friends you can stay with while you get yourself sorted, this can work well. You get to pick the place you want to live in (as opposed to an international transfer where you may end up in a city you weren't that keen on) and it can happen right now – rather than investing the years it might take to find the right organisation and get a good name for yourself.

This can work particularly well if you are starting your publishing career. If you need to find yourself that starting job, why not do it in the place you actually want to be living?

Be aware that you'll have to work that much harder to get your job in the first place – you'll be up against local candidates who know the neighbourhood and the publishing scene, so make sure you double your research efforts so that you can fit in.

As well as publishing companies, consider organisations that operate internationally and have publishing divisions, such as international government and government support groups with positions in Geneva, New York and other cosmopolitan cities, universities, big professional groups, and other workplaces mentioned in Chapters 10 and 14.

Ten Key Tips for Working Overseas

1. **There's novelty in being a foreigner**

   Lots of people like foreign accents and to hear about how you got here, and to have a representative on hand to tease about sporting triumphs. Play up to this (it will happen anyway so you might as well use it to your advantage).

2. The weather is better

If you're in the UK, the weather everywhere else is better. And if winter makes you sad and unhappy, that on its own can be worth moving for.

After a decade away from the UK, I still feel as if I'm living on holiday – with work thrown in. (STEVE)

3. 70% of international placements fail

Meaning that they last less than 12 months before the person packs up and goes home. As well as settling into your work life, make the effort to enjoy living where you've moved. It will be different from what you're expecting and it's easy to get disheartened when you're far from your normal family and friendship networks. So, holiday in places you wouldn't normally be able to get to, go to local theatre, join local sporting groups or whatever makes you enjoy your weekends.

4. Spend (some) time with other expats

Your fellow exiles are going through similar issues – it gives you a great base for friendship when you can moan about the locals together! But you should also …

5. Spend time with locals

Whether it's through work or other avenues, make an effort to get to know the locals. For a start you don't want live overseas and only associate with people you could have hung out with at home – what's the point of that? And for a second, expats tend to go home, as you probably will sooner or later, and if your only networks are expats and they all go home you will feel very lonely indeed.

6. Partners can get unhappy

In fact, that's the main reason international placements fail. In almost every couple we know who have moved overseas, one partner loves it and the other is chafing at the bit to get home again. So invest in making your partner feel comfortable, help them build up networks and recognise that your happiness depends on theirs.

I could have stayed in London forever – I was living where I'd always wanted to, in my dream job, seeing Europe, and we'd made good friends. My husband Adrian found it hard work, though. Coming from Sydney, he really missed the good weather and outdoor lifestyle. His career was stalling and he was spending hours on the tube every week commuting. He used to wake up and say, 'Look at those clouds. Another grey day', every single morning for three-and-a-half years. Finally I cracked and we moved back to Australia. He was thrilled.   (SUSANNAH)

7. **Don't underestimate how different another culture can feel**
If you have not had this experience before, you can find it more alienating than you expect. And you suddenly realise how much you value the support you've previously taken for granted. In addition to finding a job, you have to find somewhere to live, and find substitutes for all the other support mechanisms you have depended upon at home.

When I started at McGraw-Hill UK there were two other recent international arrivals – a guy from Spain and a woman from New York. They brought in a chap to give us all a day of cultural training about living in the UK and dealing with being away from home. We thought it was a bit of a laugh at the time but it really made me think about the challenges ahead. And guess what – 18 months later both of the others had moved back to their home countries.   (SUSANNAH)

8. **You *will* miss your family and friends**
It *will* be hard. You *will* spend a lot of time on the phone and e-mail and you *will* be tempted to spend all your holiday time flying home to see people.

9. **Working overseas is a great way to see the world**
   Especially compared to backpacking and working in bars!
   You're building up professional experience in other markets,
   you've got money to live decently on, and if you're lucky your
   job will cover a wide territory and you'll get to travel in style
   you couldn't possibly afford.

   When I was in the UK my job responsibilities covered all of Western
   Europe – so I travelled a lot through Scandinavia and continental
   Europe as well as the UK. This is much less glamorous than it sounds
   – mostly I was seeing airports, hotels, bookshops, universities – but I
   always tried to see something of every city I was in, and quite often I'd
   do a trip on a Weds-Thurs-Fri and stay on for the weekend.

   (SUSANNAH)

10. **Visas are vital**
    Check them out *before* you construct a five-year career plan all
    around working in Turkey/Sydney/Edinburgh/Boston. If you
    don't have a visa, will your company be able to sponsor you?
    Often this only happens at very senior levels. More than that,
    even if you have one, will your partner be able to live with you
    and work too?

And something you won't care about now, but you will in the
future:

Coming home is very, very hard

Just about everyone suffers horrible culture shock when they move
back from living overseas. (That's if you do come home, of course,
and most people do.) Everything seems different/far away/provin-
cial/isolated/too full on. You lose the glam factor of saying to your
friends, 'I've just flown in from New York' or 'I've been sunbathing at
Bondi Beach' because once you move home you probably won't be
doing that any more. If you've been working in a bigger economy,

your pay and benefits were probably substantial over there, and you're suddenly getting paid about half of what you were before. That's if you can get a job at the seniority level you were working at before, as once you are away, it's hard to hear of opportunities and you are no longer on the spot to follow them up. Or your experience may be on a more international scale than you can use back in your home city. You feel like an alien in your own land and it can take years to wear off.

> After working in Japan for years, on returning to my home city I felt changed but as if the city and people hadn't moved on. I'd grown but I felt pulled back to who I was before I left. It was like I'd become more worldly but it was going to be stomped out of me. They say it takes as long as you've been away to readjust. Now I feel like this is my home and I wouldn't want to live anywhere else – but it took quite a while.
>
> (LOUISE, AUSTRALIA)

How to internationalise your CV

To prepare for your move you need a CV, and crucially you need to adapt it for the market you are approaching. Don't assume recipients know what you are describing or will take the trouble to find out.

The most important consideration is that you don't want to put any obstacle in the way of a company thinking about employing you. It's vital therefore that you provide a smooth path to them drooling over your relevant qualifications, terrific experience and undoubtedly sunny personality – rather than wondering what on earth a TAFE[1] college is.

---

[1] *Technical and Further Education colleges in Australia, offering more practical courses than universities – the equivalent of what used to be polytechnics in the UK*

Here are ten tips on how not to appear parochial:

1. **Add international dialling codes**
   If you are applying from your home country, add international dialling codes to the phone numbers you quote and the difference in time from the time at your home:

   (001) 212 274 1160 GMT – five hours behind you

   And if the time differences are too hard, nominate e-mail as a starting point for conversations, and then you can negotiate a phone meeting at a mutually convenient time.

2. **Make it clear, if it is not obvious, how your name is pronounced**
   If your name is 'Ruarig', explain that it is pronounced Rory.

3. **Get rid of local terms which may be unclear**
   So for example if you originally wrote in your (Australian) résumé:

   Attended Holmesglen TAFE: Certificate IV Marketing

   Then you might amend it to read:

   Holmesglen Further Education College: Certificate in Marketing

   State the age at which educational qualifications were taken in case the recipient is not familiar with the name, and put in the local equivalent:

   GCSE (age 16, year 11)
   A level (age 18, year 13)

   Note that in Australia, undergraduate degrees are achieved with or without Honours, and usually without other delineation, whereas in the UK degrees are classified in First Class (First or 1st), Upper Second (2.1), Lower Second (2.2), etc. Unify your CV so it's easy to read for someone from your target country, not full of mystifying abbreviations and terminology. The best way to do this is to …

4. **Rope in a friend**

   If you possibly can, make sure you're getting this stuff right by having a friendly local go through and help you 'de-foreign' it.

5. **Highlight your ability with languages**

   Do not lie or talk up your basic skills – you may find yourself being interviewed by a fluent speaker!

6. **Underline travel you've undertaken**

   State where you've been – or if you've lived overseas previously, of course. Emphasise your ability to cope with change. Stress occupations (vacation employment can be particularly handy), and what you have learnt from them, that draw attention to your flexibility:

   > Have lived in UK, Australia and New Zealand previously.

   But don't overdo this – your aim is to sound like an interesting person who can thrive away from their roots and bring a valuable external perspective to the host organisation, not to sound like you are in a permanent state of restlessness.

   > At one interview I was told that the fact that I had taken time to travel after university definitely disqualified me from being a serious applicant; later in my career the fact that I had travelled alone around India proved to be the thing that tipped the balance in my favour against a more experienced candidate.
   >
   > (HELEN FRASER, MANAGING DIRECTOR, PENGUIN UK)

7. **Highlight your familiarity with the country where you want the job**

   A potential employer may be more interested if they sense your ambitions are based on realism. Mention that you are committed to a long-term (three or more years) stay in the country.

8. **Highlight your availability for interview**

   You want to make this easy for the employer! Offer yourself for phone or Internet (Skype etc) interview.

9. **Stress the benefits of employing you**
   Such benefits might include your flexibility, objectivity, your new perspectives and fresh insights.

Working overseas is a wonderful experience in many ways, and incredibly hard in others. Consider the long-term consequences before you leap in.

More reading

Reuvid, *Working Abroad: The Complete Guide to Overseas Employment*, Kogan Page, 2007

Hampshire, *Living and Working in Australia*, Survival Books, 2007

Dunman, *Living and Working in Australia: A City by City Guide*, How To Books, 2006

Collins and Barclay, *Living and Working in the United Kingdom*, How To Books, 2006

Hampshire, *Living and Working in Britain*, Condé Nast, 2005

Laredo, *Living and Working in London*, Survival Books, 2004

Hampshire, *Living and Working in America*, Survival Books, 2006

Liebman, *The Immigration Guide to the USA*, How To Books, 2005

Chapter Nineteen
Your first job in publishing and your future in publishing

This last chapter is partially a summary of what's gone before. It's also a way for you to plan your progress, and measure how you're doing.

It starts with **five things we really wish we'd known**, and then talks about one of them: **making a career plan**. Next are a few thoughts about **what to do when things *don't* work out** the way you'd planned. Finally, we encourage you to look to the future – your future – and encourage you to **take yourself seriously** (but not too seriously, obviously).

Five things we really wish we'd known ...
Here are five things we wish we could go back in time and tell ourselves. The next best thing is to tell you, and then perhaps you can avoid making the same mistakes that we did. (Of course, that simply means you'll have to find some new ones to make instead ...)

1. Yes, you can do it
Too many people spend too much time telling you that you *can't* do this thing and could *never* do that thing. It starts sometimes with a careers counsellor who thinks that if they can talk you out of something then clearly you're not serious about it. Or maybe a parent or sibling tells you not to aim so high – perhaps for the best of intentions, because they don't want to see you disappointed and hurt.

Well, never mind all that. *Someone* has to do it, so why shouldn't it be you? Aim high, have a bash at it and you'll almost certainly not regret it. Regret more often comes from things not done, rather than things attempted.

2. Find your mentor

If you have someone you respect and whom you can turn to for advice and help in your career, you're very lucky. Make the most of that person.

If you don't, find one. A good boss, perhaps, or someone who takes an interest in your career.

You'll find them invaluable as a sounding board – and a good mentor often does nothing more than nod sympathetically and murmur the occasional 'Hmm …', which can mean almost anything, from 'Tell me more' to 'That's interesting, what do you think that means?' to 'Are you sure you've not got that back to front?'

What you really *don't* want is someone who takes you literally and gives you advice when you ask for it. You're actually not after advice at all, though that may be what you ask for. Instead, you're after someone who can give you just enough of a response so that you know they're actually listening and haven't nodded off. Almost always you'll end up talking yourself into the advice you need, at which point you can thank your mentor profusely and praise them for their incredible wisdom.

3. Make friends and build your network

It's a fact that some of the people you work with now you'll continue to bump into, and may work with again, for years and even decades to come.

So be nice to them, (a) because you never know when you'll find yourself needing them to be nice to you, (b) because they'll be nice to you back, (c) because you should be nice to people, and (d) because publishing is a notoriously small business, and while people may job-hop they seldom industry-hop, and an argument with a key person could haunt you for ever.

You don't have to be friends with everyone, though you will in fact make friends now you'll keep forever. Mutual respect is quite sufficient. So get networking (see Chapter 13 for more on this).

Believe us, in 20 years' time you'll be doing this almost constantly. Better if you take our advice and start now – you'll have a massive head start on everyone else!

4. Read (and stick to) *The Rules of Work*

We like Richard Templar's book very much.[1] These rules are about how those who always seem to get on, avoiding the backstabbing and the nonsense and succeeding at work, actually manage it. If you like, it's a codification of what they're doing. It saves you having to do it the hard way, making mistakes and learning the lessons (which is how we did it).

Some of it sounds too obvious to be worth saying – dress smart, don't sleep with the boss – but in fact if you follow this book and observe the rules, you're virtually guaranteed success.

(We like it too because it reminds you that doing the right thing, such as telling the truth and not bitching, is good not only for your moral bank balance but your real one, too. Tell the truth and you don't have remember your lies; don't bitch and you won't get known as a bitch – that kind of thing.)

5. Have a plan

If you were going to tackle Mount Everest or run a four-minute mile, you'd probably want some sort of a plan before you started, wouldn't you? Sounds sensible. Yet many, and perhaps even most, of us don't really bother building a plan for our own careers. This needn't be anything too elaborate, but a clear, written statement of perhaps just a couple of pages, stating what you're aiming to achieve and how you plan to achieve it. The writing down means you take it seriously, reviewing it regularly ensures you think about what you are trying to do. Now read our box on 'How to Make A Plan in Four Easy Steps'.

---

[1] *Pearson Education, 2002*

How to Make a Plan in Four Easy Steps

Why don't they teach you some really useful stuff at school, like how to make a career plan? Here's what you should have been learning, when you were actually doing algebra or some other such nonsense.

1. **Plan to plan**

   The world is divided into two kinds of people: those who divide the world into two kinds of people, and those who don't. We're in the former group, and we reckon there are two kinds of people in the world: those who plan, and those who don't. Guess which mob are more likely to hit their goals? Yes, that's right: those who have them in the first place, and make a plan to get there.

2. **Make a plan**

   If you're in London and you want to get to Birmingham, then you'd make a plan on how to do that. Admittedly you mightn't recognise it as a plan exactly, since the elements are so obvious, but it is definitely a plan. It's worth thinking for a second about what you'd do. You'd consider:

   - Resources – in this case, what mode of transport you'd take (car, train, hitch-hike etc)
   - Budget – not just money, but time. If you have lots of money and no time, then your method of getting there will be different from someone with loads of time and no money (or 'student' as they are sometimes referred to)
   - Practicality – cycling is good for your health, but if you have a heap of luggage it's not really on
   - Time frame – you have a fair idea it'll take a couple of hours. You won't be there in the next minute, but neither should it take all weekend …

   … and so on, and so on. Now, let's apply that same very obvious logic to your career plan. Ask yourself a few simple questions and see where they take you:

a) What is truly important to me?

Career, cash, satisfaction and the pleasure of a job well done, helping others, keeping busy ... there are many reasons people do what they do. Be clear about what you want and you're closer to getting it.

b) What is my goal?

Be honest about this and say out loud and very clearly what exactly you want. If you really, really want to be a copy editor, then say so. If you actually want to run a multinational publishing company and make squillions, then say that instead. In the first instance, becoming a copy editor is the goal; in the second, it may well be a means to an end. (That reminds us that the man who founded and built up the magazine publishing business Haymarket, Michael Heseltine, was always doing so with an ulterior ambition on his mind, to become prime minister of the UK, something he'd dreamt of since he was very young. He didn't quite make it, but he did make Haymarket, and millions, in the process. For him, however, the aim was always to get to Number Ten. Most of the rest of us would be happy just to have the millions.)

c) What do I need to get there?

To become a copy editor you need a terrific eye for detail, a high degree of literacy and the ability to live very frugally. If you can't organise the proverbial in a brewery, you can't spell to save your life and you spend money before you've earned it, then the gap between where you are and where you want to get is fairly wide. Either you start bridging that gap – take training on time management, copy out entries from the dictionary every night and buy a piggybank – or you accept that your goal is unrealistic, in which case you need to revisit it and create a goal that is both aspirational *and* achievable instead.

d) What's the first step?

Confucius's statement that a journey of a thousand miles begins with a single step has become a cliché – but only because it's true. If you want to get into publishing, think about what you can do right now to start you off. If you're at school or university, contribute to every publication you can, get as heavily involved in student media as you can and suck up to everyone who can help you. Choose subjects to study that are publishing/media/words relevant. Work on your writing. Find out everything you can about the publishing industry.

The great thing about this is you can start right away. In fact, there's a school of thought that getting your stuff published early is by far and away the best thing you can do – more effective, even, than getting a postgraduate degree in publishing or journalism:

Like Nike, my message is Just Do It. Any journo who is after a job needs to show me a portfolio of work that they've had published (paid or unpaid), or bring me ideas and people they have teed up for interviews. Rather than turn up with qualifications and expect to be given work, they need to bring something to the party – which is vigour and pragmatism, rather than ideals. The quicker they get that, the quicker they'll get their foot in the door.

(ROB PEGLEY, EDITOR, *ALPHA MAGAZINE*, AUSTRALIA)

Get some work experience as I'm more interested in your common sense than whether you have a PhD in English Lit.

(ANDY JONES, DIRECTOR, FEEDBACK MEDIA & PR, UK)

Main tip is: just get published. School mags, student mags, freelance stuff, hole-in-the-wall budget-of-thruppence mags – just get published. It shows a determination, an interest, a desire to communicate.

(GREG INGHAM, CHIEF EXECUTIVE, MEDIACLASH AND FORMER CHIEF EXECUTIVE OF FUTURE PLC, AUSTRALIA)

3. Visualise your goal

It gives great power to your plan to make it as real and tangible as you possibly can. Rather than vague, abstract, airy-fairy goals (like 'get into publishing'), set yourself as specific a set of targets as you possibly can – such as 'Become a full-time employee in an editorial position working for a company, the main business of which is publishing, within two years.' Now you know *exactly* what you're trying to achieve. You also have something clear and uncompromising that you can work your way backwards from, and for which you can develop some short-term goals along the way.

4. Revisit your plan

It's harder than it sounds to keep a plan alive. The temptation is to work on it till it gleams, then lay it to one side in your bottom drawer and never take it out again.

Don't worry; you're not the only one. We all do it.

So, part of your plan should include specific review dates – perhaps every three months. Then you can check on your progress.

And every significant step on the way should include a date by which you're aiming to complete it. That helps keep you on track.

When things go wrong

Forgive us if we've sounded a little too gung-ho throughout this book, making it all sound as if everything is fun and easy. We know it's not, and we know that sometimes things can go badly wrong. If that's what's happening for you right now, then this is for you ...

1. Sick with nerves?

You're nervous, perhaps sick with nerves. *Whose stupid idea was this in the first place? I can't go through with this. Why did I ever think I could? I'm a fraud, they'll see through me and they'll laugh and point ...*

Calm down. Every person you meet today was once experiencing exactly the same feelings. In fact, as hard as it may be to believe, some of them may be experiencing the same feelings this very day, too. Think about it this way: how would you regard a new person, if you were in their shoes? Of course, you'd be patient and understand their nervousness. You would expect them to get things wrong and muck up. Well, guess what? That's just how all these strange new people *do* think about you.

OK, so let's be honest about it for a moment. There *are* people out there, in senior positions and positions of power, who've lost touch with their own humanity, and in fact don't show much sign they ever had any to start with. But fortunately, in publishing they're rare and, in truth, rather sad. They lead unhappy, self-centred lives and no-one likes them.

2. Undervalued, underpaid, under stress?

You're doing the work of three people. *No-one here understands what I do. I don't get paid to put up with this crap. Less talented people are being promoted and I'm getting left behind …*

Stop. Stop it. This is not going to help. What will help is taking control of the situation, doing one of two things and doing it well: stay and sort it out, or leave. Because if you don't do one of those two things and just sit there suffering, it's only going to get worse.

Instead, analyse the situation and then make your decision. Listen to yourself a little:

'*No-one here understands what I do.*' OK, so if that's true, then what can you do to change that? After all, it's unlikely your boss is going to wake up tomorrow morning or any time soon, slap their forehead and exclaim, 'My God, I've been so blind! What a brilliant job X is doing!' At least, that won't happen without a bit of help. From you.

Be positive. Be cheerful. Volunteer. Work hard. Smile. Dig in.

'*I don't get paid to put up with this crap.*' Er, excuse us, but that's *exactly* what you get paid to put up with. Unless what you're talking about is bad behaviour, such as bullying or sexual harassment for example – in which case you need to speak to your manager or HR director immediately, document everything and do not permit the perpetrator to be alone with you in work or out of it – then doing stuff you don't like doing is why they're paying you, rather than you paying them. For the great majority of the world's population, enjoying what they're being paid to do is an impossible dream.

Do you have a job/position description? No? Well, why not? Because you *haven't been given one?* Listen to yourself, and get a grip. Sit yourself down and draft one and ask your boss if they agree with it, and if not can they help you improve it. See? There's something you can do, rather than waiting for someone else to provide the solution to what is after all *your* problem.

'Less talented people are getting promoted and I'm getting left behind …' Hmm. When you say *less talented*, perhaps what you mean is *less talented than I am at slaving away in the dark and getting no thanks for it.* You obviously don't mean, for example, *less talented than I am at being promoted.* Well, perhaps you can learn from their skills in this area. Are they sucking up to the boss, by any chance? Good at getting the credit? Always getting mentioned in despatches? If they are, perhaps this explains why they're getting promoted? After all, if their talent isn't the reason, there must be *some* explanation that's currently eluding you.

Big businesses aren't always the best place to be for shrinking violets. Look at how your business itself behaves. Does that tell you anything about what works in the market? And your boss, are they a quiet achiever who never takes credit for anyone else's work and always takes the blame when they screw up? (If they are, can we come and work for them, please?)

So, as we say, decide whether you're going to stay here, play the game and play it better than anyone else – or get the hell out of there. (Incidentally, your three authors all decided to do just that: get out and work for themselves rather than put up with the crap. It's an option.)

Of course there's still no guarantee you'll find yourself somewhere where talent is all and self-promotion is useless as a technique for getting noticed ...

3. Miserable?
You hate your job. *'It's not what I thought it was. It's a boring grind. I hate Mondays – and Tuesdays, Wednesdays, Thursdays and Fridays aren't much cop either ...'*

Oops. Honey, I Took The Wrong Career Path? Or perhaps just: Honey, I Took The Wrong Job? The distinction is important, because while you may have discovered that in fact you're not a sales rep at heart, or an editorial assistant, you may simply have found a horrible job/boss/company. Every job/boss/company is different, and what is basically the same job can be a whole lot of fun if you're working with good people, have a half-decent boss and are employed by a human company.

Transport the same tasks and responsibilities to somewhere where you're surrounded by zombies, report to the boss from hell and work for a rubbish company and it's no wonder you're climbing up the walls.

If that's the situation, you'll leave eventually, so you may as well get on with it and leave now. (Better if you can to line something up, not just because your landlord is curiously fond of getting paid rent, but also because employers tend to be suspicious of applicants not already working.) In six months' time you'll wonder how you put up with it so long.

But be sure first that it really *is* that bad. See if you have someone whose advice you trust and who's a good listener, and describe the worst thing that's happened to you recently. If they sit there at the end still waiting for the bad bit to come, then it's just possible (though by no means certain) that you've developed some unhealthy expectations of what work ought to be like and how bosses behave in the real world.

4. Close to someone you HATE?

Just as, with any luck, you'll find someone you can turn to and lean on, so at some stage it's highly likely you'll find someone who just rubs you up the wrong way, big time. Whether it's an incompetent boss, a glory-hogging co-worker, a neurotic colleague whom you are forced to share an office with, or just someone who has the ability to make you seriously unhappy, they have the capacity to spoil things for you. If it's making you miserable, it's time to face facts.

Here's the bad news: it usually doesn't get better by itself. Here's the good news: you can move. It's a healthy job market, there are lots of opportunities and you're a highly skilled, attractive asset that any business should be eager to snap up. The best revenge, as they say, is to live well. Go, and don't look back. You won't regret it. No amount of money can compensate for being unhappy.

(Note, though, that we're talking about real, heavyweight, first-class misery here, not just mild irritation. If you up sticks every time you come into contact with someone who's a pain, you'll be moving every week. You need to know the difference.)

5. Trapped?

You can't see where your next job is coming from. '*I've been here forever, or so it seems. What's next? I want my boss's job but she's superglued to her seat and looks like being here forever.*'

Buy a book – we reckon *How to Get a Job in Publishing* is pretty terrific. Sign up to the online jobsites. Polish up your CV. Ask friends about other possible job vacancies (quietly). Ask for a pay rise and see how it goes. Make triple sure your manager, and their manager, and their manager, all know that you're energetic and capable and keen to move on and up – don't take it for granted that they will see you beavering away and know what you're thinking.

If it really isn't going to work out, there's no solution to this one, other than moving or perhaps arsenic, which is illegal. Publishing is a limited market, and there aren't always too many options for internal promotion. (That's why your boss is stuck – for the same reason you are.)

Conclusion: have the time of your life

Fortunately things are rarely as bad as all that. And when they are, there are things you can do about it. The first thing to do is to decide that **it's up to you**, not anyone else, to change your situation – to get that first job, or your next job, in publishing. And, after all these pages, we could actually have told you just to read this last bit (except you probably wouldn't have bought a book with only one page in it). Here, then, is what we really, really think about How to Get a Job in Publishing ...

For most of us, most of the time, work is just ... well, it's just work. Life is what happens when you're busy making other plans. You get up, you go to work, you do what you're told, you go home. A little bit ho, but mostly hum.

But it doesn't have to be like that, you know. It really doesn't. Look around your circle of friends and family and you'll almost certainly know someone who seems to be more alive and alert than the rest of us, and having an absolute blast – the time of their life, quite literally. Take a look at what they do and you'll see why. Try their approach for a bit and see what happens. What do you see?

You'll see someone who **takes control** – because if you don't, no-one else will. It's your life, so own it. There are plenty of rules we live by that aren't rules at all, they're just habits or tradition or customs. If humanity had behaved like that we'd still be living in trees. Someone took it upon themselves to say, 'I've had enough of this; let's try it down there. It could work!'

You'll see someone who's **better at learning from mistakes than at not making them**. Wisdom comes from experience, and experience comes from bad decisions. If you don't take a risk you won't do anything.

You'll see someone who **knows their own worth** – because if you don't believe, and really believe, that you're valuable then it's virtually certain that no-one else will. It's an odd thing, but true: people tend to take you at your own valuation.

You'll see someone who **plans to be somewhere** and is in a hurry to get there – because the faster you go, the further you get. And since you're going to get there anyway (yes, you are), you might as well get there as quick as you can.

You'll see someone who **goes the extra mile:** remember how our mate Stuart Jones in Melbourne put it: 'It's less crowded there.'

You'll see someone who's **loving what they're doing** and doing what they're loving – because that's what they've decided is important to them. That bit is much more certain than whether they're earning a ton of money or not. They might be (and it's surprising how much money you can make when you're doing what you're passionate about, just because of the energy it brings you). But some of the happiest people we know (ourselves included) aren't particularly well off. And some of the most miserable sods around are loaded. That tells you something. It doesn't mean you can't be rich and happy, and it certainly doesn't mean you can't be poor and miserable. All it means is that if you're miserable, being rich won't take the pain away.

Right then, that's pretty much it. As you can tell, you've come to the end of this book, and it's time for us to part ways. We hope you've enjoyed it as much as we've enjoyed spending the money we earned writing it (though since you've been paying attention you'll have realised that it wasn't really all that much). By the way, you didn't think we really meant all that stuff about how publishing isn't glamorous and sexy and warm and moist and gorgeous, did you? We keep on trying to be all grown-up and serious and tell ourselves it's a business and it's all about the money. It isn't, of course. It's the best flippin' career and the best industry going, is what it is. Just don't say that in your job interview. After all, if it were only about the money we'd all go off and be lawyers, and then where would we be? Doesn't bear thinking about.

> Remember to enjoy yourself. Publishing is one of the entertainment industries, and if you enjoy yourself, you'll love what you do.
>
> (STARR JAMIESON, SALES COORDINATOR, WALKER BOOKS AUSTRALIA)

One last thing before we knock off – and then we really do have to be going. You'll have noticed that we quote lots of friends and colleagues and their wisdom along the way, and we thank them very much for it. Now we'd love to hear *your* story, and even more so if it's about your first or next job in publishing, how you got it and what advice you'd give others. Then perhaps in the next edition you'll find your own words of wisdom quoted. Do drop us a line, please. We'd really love to hear from you.

- Alison: a.baverstock@kingston.ac.uk
- Susannah: susannah@bloompartners.com.au
- Steve: steve@bloompartners.com.au

More reading

Richard Templar, *The Rules of Work – A Definitive Guide to Personal Success*, Pearson Education, 2002

Appendix 1
Glossary of publishing terms

There's a whole language people in publishing use – try and find out as much as possible before you start about the publishing process and the language that accompanies it! I was initially baffled by terms like rights, permissions, pub date, binding, jacket . . .

(AMY BLOWER, RIGHTS SALES MANAGER, PEARSON EDUCATION, UK)

When you head off to a job interview, it's a great idea to know what publishing terms mean, and particularly the marketing jargon commonly used. Reading this glossary, based on the one in Alison's *How to Market Books* (Kogan Page, 4th edition, 2008; reproduced by kind permission of the publisher), will help.

above and below the line The traditional distinction between different sorts of advertising. 'Above the line' is paid for (eg space advertisements taken in newspapers or magazines). 'Below the line' marketing involves no invoice; it is normally negotiated in a mutually beneficial arrangement between two or more organisations. The usual result is an augmented offer to the consumer (more than just the product being sold), often with a time limit. The distinction between 'above' and 'below the line' is blurring as techniques get used in combination; some marketing agencies are now offering 'through the line' services. The origin of the term is the line at the bottom of the invoice that separates what has been done from what is owing as a result.

advance notice (or **advance information sheet, AI)** A single sheet giving brief advance details of a forthcoming publication. Usually circulated six to nine months before publication, it is sent to anyone who needs the information – bookstores, reps etc.

advertorial Advertising copy that masquerades as an editorial feature.

affinity marketing Marketing based on choices made by the consumer that indicate that they like/are likely to be attracted to products and services related to those for which plans are being made. Penguin's promotion of fiction titles on the back of Galaxy chocolate bars is an example of affinity marketing in that both products (a good read and a bar of chocolate) are assumed to appeal to the same person. The proposal becomes particularly effective if the two products can be enjoyed together (read while you eat chocolate).

answers Shorthand used on a publisher's or distributor's invoice to show the status of particular titles ordered by a bookseller and not immediately available. The most common abbreviations are:

nyp	not yet published
nk	not known
oo	on order
op	out of print; no plans to reprint
os	out of stock (reprint under consideration)
rp Jan	reprinting, will be available again in January

artwork Typesetting and illustrations were conventionally pasted on to board to form artwork which could then be photographed to make printing plates. Today most artwork is produced on computer and despatched online.

backlist Older titles on a publisher's list that are still in print.

barcode A machine-readable unique product code. The barcode usually appears on the front cover of a magazine and the back cover of a book, and is used for stock control and sales.

benefits In a marketing context, benefits are the advantages that come to the user/purchaser from a product or service's features (see 'features'). Too much publishing copy is feature- rather than benefit-orientated, but the market is far more interested in what the product will do for them than in how the publisher has set up its specifications. For example, product features of a guidebook might be lavish illustrations or high paper quality. The benefits to the reader, however, might be that it provides a lasting souvenir of the holiday, really gives a flavour of the place to be visited before they get there, or stands up well to use throughout the trip because it is well made. Similarly a picture book for very young children may offer attractive illustrations by a well-known artist, but be appreciated by a grandparent because it makes a welcome present that they can enjoy reading together.

binding How the pages of a book are held together and presented: paperback, hardback etc.

blad Originally this meant a section of a book printed early to help in the promotion, and shown as a sample. Today blads can consist of marketing information about, a random assortment of pages from, or a synopsis of a forthcoming publication, and do not necessarily constitute a distinct section.

bleed Printed matter that extends over the trimmed edge of the paper; it 'bleeds' off the edge. To obtain a bleed in a magazine ad, you have to book a full-page space.

blog A blog is a user-generated website where entries are made in journal style and displayed in reverse chronological order. The term blog is derived from 'Web log', but the word also gets used as a verb, meaning to run, maintain or add content to a blog.

blurb A short sales message for use in leaflets or jackets.

body copy The bulk of the advertising text; usually follows the headline.

boss The person paying (or approving) your wages. Never forget this.

bottom line Financial slang referring to the figure at the foot of a balance sheet indicating net profit or loss. Has come to mean the overall profitability, for example: 'How does that affect the bottom line?'

brand A product (or service) with a set of distinct characteristics that make it different from other products on the market.

break-even The point at which you start making money. In a publishing context reaching break-even means that sufficient copies of a publication have been sold to recover the origination costs. The break-even point in a mailing is reached when enough copies have been sold to recoup the costs of the promotion.

bromide A type of photographic paper. Producing a bromide is a one-stage photographic process on to sensitised paper or film which is then developed. PMTs (see p. 269) are routinely produced on bromide paper but alternatives now include acetate or self-adhesive paper.

budget A plan of activities expressed in monetary terms.

bullet point A heavy dot or other eye-catching feature to attract attention to a short sales point. A series of bullet points is often used in advertisement copy both to vary pace and to engage the reader's attention:

- good for **attracting attention**
- uneven sentences and surrounding spaces **draw in the reader**
- bullet points enable you to **re-state the main selling points** without appearing over-repetitious

---

buyer The person within a retail or wholesaling firm responsible for selecting/ordering stock. Large shops will have a different buyer for each department.

b/w Abbreviation for black and white.

card deck (also called business reply card mailing or cardex mailing) A collection of business reply cards, each offering a separate sales message to which the recipient can respond by returning the card concerned. Handily, recipients often tend to pass on individual cards to others they know may be interested. Often used for selling technical, business and professional titles.

cased edition A book with a hard cover, as opposed to limp or paperback.

centred type A line or lines of type individually centred on the width of the text below.

Type on a title page can also be centred on the page width.

character 1. An individual letter, space, symbol or punctuation mark. 2. A person with poor social skills.

Cheshire labels Old-fashioned format for labels. Cheshire labels are presented as a continuous roll of paper which is cut up and pasted on to envelopes by a Cheshire machine. Still sometimes used for the despatch of items bought on subscription, ie where customer loyalty is established.

closed market Closed markets are created when local selling rights are sold to a particular agent. Booksellers in an area that is part of a closed market must obtain stock of titles from the local agent rather than direct from the original publisher. This arrangement is under threat from the Internet, which knows no geographical boundaries.

coated paper Paper that has received a coating on one or both sides, eg art paper.

colour separations The process of separating the colours of a full-colour picture into four printing colours (Cyan, Magenta, Yellow and Black – abbreviated to CMYK and not CMYB), done either with a camera or electronic scanning machine. The separated film may then be used to make printing plates.

competitive differentials What a company is good or bad at; the things that set it apart from its competitors.

controlled circulation A publication circulated free or mainly free to individuals within a particular industry, advertising sales paying for circulation and production costs. Much used in medicine and business.

cooperative mailing (or **shared mailing**) A mailing to a specialised market containing material from several advertisers who share the costs between them.

copy Words that make up the message, often used of material prepared for advertising or newspaper features.

cover The difference between success and failure.

cromalin proofs *See* **digital proofs**.

cut-out An irregularly shaped illustration which requires handwork at the repro stage of printing.

data *See* **media**.

---

database marketing Building up increasingly complex information about your customers in order to serve their needs more precisely and sell more to them in the future. The long-term aim of direct marketing.

database publishing Publishing from information stored on a database. Can be a fast method of producing complex material or material which dates quickly.

die-cutting A specialised cutting process used whenever the requirement for a cut is other than a straight line or right angle (ie when a guillotine cannot be used). A metal knife held in wood is punched down on to the item to be cut. Many old letterpress machines have been adapted to form die-cutting equipment.

digital proofs Digital proofs are of two broad sorts – high-res (short for resolution) or low-res. High-res proofs are made from the final printing files, normally PDFs. There are a number of quality levels. At one extreme, they may be little more than the sort of colour prints you would get from an office laserjet printer; and though they may look fine, they won't necessarily represent the printed product very faithfully because they are produced in a fundamentally different way. To get closer to this ideal, most printers use special laser printers which are calibrated to the platesetter (the device that exposes the printing plate) in a very direct manner. Digital cromalins are this sort of proof; high-res, calibrated proofs which can be used to check for colour before the item is printed. Low-res proofs, by contrast, are for position and content only, and are made using standard office equipment.

direct costs Costs attributable to a specific project, as opposed to general overheads or indirect costs. For example, the printing bill for producing a particular title is a direct cost; the photocopier used to copy proofs that are circulated is an indirect one.

direct marketing The selling of services directly to the end consumer – including e-mail, direct mail, telemarketing and house-to-house calling.

direct response advertising Advertising designed to produce a measurable response, whether through e-mail, mail, telemarketing, space advertisements etc. This compares with direct promotion, where material is sent directly to the market, which may, or may not, produce a direct response back.

disintermediarisation An interruption in the former process of doing things. For example, authors who offer their content direct to users, by self-publishing or publishing through their websites, are changing the usual sequence of intermediaries (publishers, distributors and booksellers); this is a process of disintermediarisation.

display type Large type for headlines, usually 14 points or more. (Sales people are usually the display type.)

distributor In magazine publishing, the company blamed by the publisher for not getting the magazines to the right place at the right time, and blamed by the newsagent who didn't order them in the first place.

dues (also called **arrears**) Orders for a new (or reprinting) publication before it is released. Publishers record the dues and fulfil orders as soon as stock is available. Checking the dues of forthcoming titles is a good way of finding out how well the reps are subscribing particular titles in bookshops, and hence of estimating sales.

dumpbin Container to hold, display and stock in retail outlets; usually supplied by the manufacturer to encourage the retailer to take more stock than might otherwise be the case. Most are made from cardboard, to be assembled in the shop. Supplied free but on condition that a stock order to fill it is received, too.

duotone A half-tone shot printed in two colours. This is a more expensive way of printing a photograph than simply using a single printing colour, but can add depth and quality to the image presented. It is usually printed in black plus a chosen second colour. An alternative effect can be produced by using a tint of the second colour behind a black and white half-tone.

ELT English language teaching.

embargo A date before which information may not be released; often used on press releases to ensure that no one paper scoops the rest. Often regarded by the media as applying to everyone else.

EPOS Electronic point of sale. Machine-readable code that can be read by a terminal at a shop checkout to establish price, register any appropriate discounts and reorder stock.

extent Length of text. For example, for a magazine or book, extent: 192pp (192 pages); for a leaflet, extent: 4pp A4 (four sides of A4 paper).

features The specifics of a product or service that distinguish it from other products and services produced (eg extent, illustrations, level of content). What a sales person who does not hit targets sells with. *See also* **benefits**.

firm sale The orders placed by a bookstore from which the publishers expect no returns. In practice, most publishers have to be flexible and allow at least a credit for unsold titles, to ensure goodwill and the stocking of their titles in the future. The approach used by a sales person who won't take no for an answer.

flush left (or **justified left)** Type set so that the left-hand margin is vertically aligned, the right-hand margin finishing raggedly wherever the last word ends.

flush right (or **justified right)** Type set so that the right-hand margin only is aligned vertically.

flyer A cheaply produced leaflet, normally a single sheet for use as a hand-out.

font The range of characters for one size and style of type. This book is set in New Baskerville.

format The size of a book or page. In the UK and Australia this is usually expressed as height x width, in the US and most of Europe as width x height.

gsm (or **g/m2)** The measure by which paper is sold: grams per square metre.

half-life The point at which the eventual outcome of an experiment can be predicted. A description of a career or job you're not enjoying.

half-tone An illustration that reproduces the continuous tone of a photograph. This is achieved by screening the image to break it up into dots. Light areas of the resulting illustration have smaller dots and more surrounding white space to simulate the effect of the original. A squared-up half-tone is an image in the form of a box (any shape), as opposed to a cut-out image.

hard copy Copy on printed paper as opposed to copy on computer or other retrieval system (which is soft copy).

hb Short for hardback, the binding of a book.

hc Short for hardcover, the binding of a book.

HE Higher education. Study at university level and above.

headline The eye-catching message at the top of a magazine article, an advertisement or leaflet, usually followed by the body copy. The difference between someone reading what you've written and not.

Honest Friend An honest friend. Someone who, when asked, will tell you what they really think. Invaluable for many things, but in the context of this book for compiling CVs and helping prepare you for interviews.

house ad An advertisement which appears in one of the advertiser's own publications or promotions. In magazine publishing, often evidence that the space hasn't been sold – hence the pronunciation: 'how sad'.

house style The typographic and linguistic standards of a particular publishing house. For example, there may be a standard way of laying out advertisements, standard typefaces that are always used and standard rules for spelling and the use of capital letters. Smart publishing houses provide their authors with a sheet of instructions on the house style.

hype Short for hyperbole, it literally means exaggerated copy not to be taken seriously. It has come to mean over-praising, and is part of the generation of interest in titles that appeal to the mass media.

impression All copies of a publication printed at one time without changing the printing plates. Several impressions may go into the making of a single edition.

imprint The name of the publisher or the advertiser which appears on the title page of a book, or at the foot of an advertisement. One publishing house may have several imprints, eg Grafton is an imprint of HarperCollins, Puffin of Penguin.

indent 1. To leave space at the beginning of a line or paragraph; often used for subheadings and quotations. 2. To order on account; to 'indent for'.

in-house and **out-of-house work** Jobs that are carried out using either the staff and resources within the firm or those of external companies or freelancers.

in print Currently available. Telephone enquirers will often ask if a particular title is still 'in print'.

insert Paper or card inserted in a magazine, book, journal or brochure. A 'loose insert' is not secured in any way; a 'bound insert' is stitched into the spine of the magazine or book in question.

inspection copy Copy of a particular title (usually a school text or other educational book) supplied for full examination by a teacher in the hope that a class set will be bought or the title will be recommended as essential on the course reading list. If the title is adopted and a certain number purchased, the recipient may usually keep the inspection copy. Books for which a multiple sale is unlikely are generally available 'on approval'; after inspection they must either be returned or paid for.

ISBN International standard book number; a system of providing each edition of a book with an individual identifying number. The appropriate ISBN should appear on any piece of information to do with the book: it is essential for bookshop and library ordering, stock control, despatch and more.

ISDN International standard data number, use of a telephone line for the exchange of data between computers.

ISSN International standard serial number, a similar system to ISBN for identifying serial publications. The number allocated refers to the serial in question for as long as it remains in publication. It should appear on the cover of any periodical and in any promotion material. Libraries catalogue and order titles by ISSN.

jacket The cover of a book. Originally this term referred to the loose, wraparound cover on a hardback title, but now is often used to refer simply to the cover, whether on a paperback or hardback.

jacket rough A design for a book jacket prepared for the approval of author, editor and marketing department. The kind of clothing worn by a 'character' (*see* **character**).

justified type Type set so that both left- and right-hand margins are aligned vertically – as in newspaper columns.

lamination A thin film available in matt or gloss applied to a printed surface; often used for book jackets, glossy brochures or the covers of catalogues which can expect a lot of use. Varnishing has a similar effect and is becoming less expensive; it adds less to the bulk than lamination, but is not as durable.

landscape A horizontal oblong format, ie wider than it is deep (as opposed to **portrait**).

letterpress A printing process whereby ink is transferred from raised metal type or plates directly on to paper. All newspapers used to be printed by this method.

limp (or **C format**) A format midway between hardback and perfect bound paperback; the spine is usually sewn but encased in card covers rather than boards.

line work Illustrations such as drawings that consist of line only rather than the graduated tones of photographs. The cheapest kind of illustration to reproduce.

list All the publications a particular publisher has for sale. Also used for a group of new publications, eg spring list.

litho Short for lithographic. A printing process which works on the principle of greasy ink not sticking to those parts of the wet plate which are not to be printed. Most usually ink is transferred (offset) from a printing plate on to an intermediary surface ('blanket') and then on to the paper. How most marketing materials are printed.

logo Short for logotype. An identifying symbol or trademark.

magazine publisher The main reason why a newsagent's life is so hard. *See* **newsagent**.

MarComms Short for Marketing Communications.

mark up 1. To prepare a manuscript for the typesetter by adding the instructions needed such as type specification, width of setting, indentations, space between paragraphs and so on. 2. To increase the price of a particular title above that shown in the list price. Examples of use include when individual copies – rather than class sets – of school books are ordered (this is also called double pricing) or when selling expenses are likely to be high, perhaps due to exporting.

measure The width of text setting, usually measured in pica 'ems' (the m is chosen because it is the widest letter for setting).

media 'The media,' like 'data', should be plural, with 'medium' the singular. (The singular of data is, of course, anecdote.) However, if the person interviewing you for a job says 'the media is . . .' we don't recommend correcting them.

merchandise Branded goods.

merchandising In a publishing context, this means persuading retail outlets and those who supply them to stock branded goods related to a key title, for example a stationery range that relates to a key children's title. Merchandising is a key function of the reps in bookshops, now that so much buying is done centrally.

monograph A single subject study by an author or group of authors, usually of a scholarly nature.

negative option A practice often used by book clubs whereby, unless a member responds to say a particular title is not required, it will be sent – eg the 'book of the month' is often a negative option. The process will have been part of the terms and conditions of membership.

net The final total. In the case of a price or sum to be paid, the net price means that no further discount or allowances are to be made; 'net profit' is the surplus remaining after all costs, direct and indirect, have been deducted, as opposed to 'gross profit', which is the total receipts, only allowing for the deduction of direct costs. For a mailer, asking for a list of *net names* means that several lists are run against each other to eliminate duplicates so the final mailing list, while containing names from several sources, will only include each individual once.

newsagent According to magazine publishers, the main reason why they, the magazine publishers, don't make more money. *See* **magazine publisher**.

nix (-ies) Addresses on a mailing list which are undeliverable by the carrier. If these amount to more than a certain percentage of the total list supplied, a reputable list owner or broker will provide a refund or credit.

online Connected to a telecommunications system. More and more publishers' products are available this way, with customers gaining access through a telecommunications link to the continuously updated publishing information database.

over-run 1. Type matter which does not fit the design and must either be cut or the letter and word spacing reduced in size until it fits. 2. Extra copies printed, over and above the quantity ordered from the printer (*see* **overs**). 3. An invitation to make a remark about cricket.

overs 1. Short for over-run. The practice of printing a slightly larger quantity than ordered to make up for copies spoilt during either printing or binding. It is commercially acceptable for the printer to allow 5% over or under the quantity ordered unless otherwise specified. You will be charged for the overs. 2. An invitation to make another remark about cricket.

ozalid A contact paper proof made from the film and usually used as a last-minute check on positioning on more complex jobs. A final check before printing, unless a printed proof is requested.

pb Short for paperback.

perfect binding 1. In book publishing, the most common binding for paperbacks. The different sections of the book are trimmed flush and the pages glued to the inside of the cover. This is more expensive than **saddle stitching** but cheaper than **sewing**. 2. In magazine publishing, a more expensive and therefore upmarket binding than **saddle stitching.** Sometimes called 'square binding' (for the effect it has on the spine).

permissions The right (requested and approved) to reproduce quotations and extracts from other people's work in new publications. Usually arranged (the jargon is 'clearing permissions') by the author, but sometimes handled by the publishing house, if time or authorial inclination are short.

PMT Short for photo mechanical transfer. The production of a PMT is a two-stage process: the creation of a photosensitive negative which is then developed with a chemically sensitive carrier. The line image produced provides artwork.

podcast A podcast is a series of electronic media files, such as audio or video, that are distributed over the Internet by means of a Web feed, for playback on portable media players and personal computers, at a time that suits the listener. The word podcast is often used to mean either the content itself, or the method by which it is made available (although this is also referred to as podcasting).

point of sale Eye-catching promotional material to be displayed with the product where purchases are made. For example, publishers produce showcards, posters, bookmarks, balloons, single copy holders, dump bins and counter packs for display by the till.

point system 1. A typographic standard measure based on the pica, eg 12 pt. 2. The arrangement for identifying characters (*see* **character**).

portrait An upright oblong format, ie taller than it is wide (*see* **landscape**).

pos 1. Abbreviation for positive, eg pos film. 2. Point of sale.

print on demand As printing technology becomes cheaper and specialist publishers increasingly target highly niche markets, it may be cost-effective to print only the number of copies you have actual orders for. This can work particularly well for a high-price product relevant to a very small market, for example a market research report. Don't forget, however, that before any printing on demand can begin the origination costs must be covered. It follows that this is not as cheap an alternative to conventional production as is often imagined!

positioning A marketing term for how you want your designated customer to feel about the product or service you are offering; the emotional relationship you want them to have with it.

print run The number of copies ordered from a printer (*see* **overs**).

pro forma invoice One that must be settled before goods are despatched, often used for export orders or where no account exists.

progressive proofs A set of printed proofs showing each colour individually and then in combination.

promotions This originally referred to mutually beneficial arrangements between non-competing organisations approaching the same target market (now often referred to as 'affinity marketing'); today the term is used more generally, to refer to general pushing or promoting of titles to a wider prominence.

proofreading Reading typeset copy for errors. There is a standard series of proofreader's marks, which should be made both by the mistake and in the margin. Typesetter's mistakes should be noted in red, and author's and publisher's in black or blue.

pub 1. Where long Friday lunches are spent. 2. Short for 'publication' – as in 'pub plan', 'pub date' and so on.

publication date 1. The date before which stock may not be sold, to ensure no one seller saturates the market before all have the same opportunity. Sometimes ignored to secure a competitive advantage. (*See* **release date**.) 2. In magazine publishing, the publication date is frequently one and sometimes even two months before the date on the cover of the magazine. Given the choice between two magazines, one the August edition and the other the September, consumers usually choose the latter.

reading copies Copies of a forthcoming title distributed before publication date to key people in the trade (notably booksellers and wholesalers) to create enthusiasm and promote by word of mouth. Done on the grounds that those who sell books are more likely to enthuse to customers about titles they have themselves read and enjoyed.

recto The right-hand page of a double page spread (with an odd page number). The opposite of **verso**.

register Trim marks that appear on the artwork supplied to a printer, should reappear on the plates made, and need to be matched up when printing to ensure the whole job will be in focus or register. If the plates have not been aligned according to the register marks, or the marks placed incorrectly, the job is said to be 'out of register'.

release date Date on which stock is released from the publisher's warehouse for delivery to booksellers in anticipation of the publication date. Some booksellers complain release dates are far too early and they end up warehousing the books instead of the publisher. This can fuel the temptation to sell early.

remainder To sell off unsold stock at a cheaper price, often to 'remainder shops' such as discount book stores.

repro Short for reproduction; the conversion of typeset copy and photographs into final film and printing plates.

response device How the order or response comes back to the mailer, for example a link to the website to place an order, or a reply card or envelope.

retouching Adapting artwork or film to make corrections or alter tonal values.

returns Unsold stock of particular titles that may be returned to the publisher by the newsagent or bookseller with prior agreement. In magazine publishing, newsagents hate handling returns almost as much as publishers hate newsagents. In book publishing, reps often use the authorisation of returns as a bargaining point in persuading booksellers to take new titles.

reverse out To produce text as white or a pale colour 'reversed out' on a darker background colour, as opposed to the more usual practice of printing in dark ink on a pale background. This technique is used by designers to win awards and persuade readers to stop reading.

review copy You will hear this term used widely to mean 'free copy', and probably receive many calls and e-mails requesting one. In precise terms, a review copy is a title sent to a potential reviewer (or review editor) in the hope that they will feature it in the media. Early copies released this way end up for sale in second-hand bookshops and through online bookselling mechanisms, often before publication, and this practice is an ongoing source of tension between publishers and the media.

review slip 1. The enclosure in a book when it is sent out for review by a publisher. It should include details of title, author, ISBN, price and publication date, as well as a request for a copy of any review that appears. 2. A sentence written by a critic that reveals they have not, in fact, actually read the book in question.

rights The legal entitlement to publish a particular work. Permission is given by the copyright holder (usually the author or editor) to reproduce the work in one particular format. Subsidiary rights (for other formats, such as paperback and online as well as film, merchandising deals and so on) are then sold by either the firm's rights manager or the author's agent. The major occasion for selling rights is the annual Frankfurt Book Fair.

roman Upright type (not bold), as opposed to italic.

royalty The percentage of list price or net receipt paid on each copy sold to the copyright holder, usually the author. There are regional variations in how long the royalties must be paid for. In the UK, royalties are paid to the author's estate for 70 years after his or her death; the manuscript is then out of copyright and may be reproduced by anyone without paying royalties.

rrp Short for recommended retail price. Usually set by the manufacturer, this is the basis for calculating the discount given to the retailer. The actual selling price is decided by the retailer, who may choose to lower prices and take a reduced profit margin in the hope of selling a greater quantity.

run of paper Refers to the position of an advertisement that will appear in a particular journal or paper wherever there is room, at the editor's or designer's discretion. This is usually cheaper than specifying a particular (or preferred) position.

saddle stitching A method of binding magazines, pamphlets or small books (48–64 pages is probably the limit for saddle stitching successfully). Wire staples or thread are used to stitch along the line of the fold. Also called 'wire stitching'.

salary In publishing, usually an unfunny joke.

sale or return Newsagents, bookstores or wholesalers take titles 'on sale or return' on the understanding that if they have not been sold after a specified period (usually by the time the next edition comes out for magazines, or 6–12 months after ordering for books), and provided the titles are still in print, they may be returned for a credit. This leaves the long-term financial risk with the publisher. The opposite of firm sale.

school supplier (also called educational contractor) A firm which seeks to supply both schools and local education authorities with books and other educational products.

screen 1. The process used to convert continuous tone photographs into patterns of dots, in order to reproduce the effect of the original when printed (*see* **half-tone**). A coarse screen is used in the preparation of illustrations for newsprint and other less demanding jobs. 2. Short for silk-screen printing.

see safe Bookstores or wholesalers usually take books on a 'see safe' basis. They are invoiced immediately for the total taken; those they do not sell may be returned for a credit or exchange. While the immediate financial outlay is thus with the shop, they are protected by the practice of sale or return.

self mailer A direct mail piece without an envelope or outer wrapping. Often used to refer to all-in-one leaflets, which combine sales message and response device. Space for copy is limited so this format works best when the recipient already knows of the product being advertised.

serif; sans serif A 'serif' typeface has 'handles' on the letters, like the typeface used in this book; sans serif is the opposite.

showthrough How much ink on one side of a printed sheet of paper can be seen through on the other side. The type of clothing that may be worn by a 'character' (*see* **character**).

spam unsolicited or unwanted electronic advertising messages sent in bulk and received as e-mails.

specs 1. Short for type specifications. Designers may refer to 'doing the spec' by which they mean laying down the parameters of text design – choosing a typeface and size. 2. The specifications for printing a job are all the production details (format, extent, illustrations, print run etc) sent to printers for a quote.

spine What a book has that your boss doesn't.

subscribe 1. In magazine terminology, to buy a series of magazines in advance. Publishers love it because it means a guaranteed sale (you only print one copy to sell one copy), with cash up front. Newsagents are not so keen, since it takes them out of the loop. 2. In book publishing terminology, to secure orders from bookshops and wholesalers before publication date, either by phone or through a rep visiting. The results are recorded by the publishing house as **dues**.

tag line (or **strap line**) A line of copy that sums up the product or the general philosophy of the company. Often displayed on the front cover of magazines or books.

telemarketing (or **teleselling**) Using the telephone to sell. Often thought of as referring to the making of calls to promote products, effective telemarketing also means considering the way incoming calls are handled as well as the way outgoing calls are made.

terms The discount and credit conditions on which a publisher supplies stock to a bookseller or wholesaler. Terms will vary according to the amount of stock taken, the status under which it is accepted, what the competition are doing and how much the customers want the book. (*See* **see safe**, **firm sale** *and* **sale or return**.)

they, them In this book we use 'them' as a non-gender-specific singular. If someone tells you that's wrong, ask them [ahem] what you should say instead. Saying 'he stroke she' is ridiculous, not to mention potentially suggestive.

tint A pattern of dots that when printed reproduces as a tone. Using tints is a good way to get value from your printing inks. For example, even if you have only one printing colour, try putting the text in solid, and using a 10% tint of the same colour to fill in and highlight certain boxes around copy. Further variations can be achieved if you are using more printed colours.

trade discount The discount given by publishers to booksellers and wholesalers on the price at which they will subsequently sell. The amount of discount given usually varies according to the amount of stock taken or the amount of promotion promised. 'Short discounts' are low-scale discounts on products that are either very expensive (often those that are extensively promoted by the publisher directly to the end-user) or those that are sold in sets (eg school textbooks).

trim Short for 'trimmed size' of a printed piece of paper, ie its final or guillotined size.

turnover The total of invoice value over a specified period for a particular company's sales.

type area The area of the final page size that will be occupied by type and illustrations, allowing for the blank border that will normally surround text.

typeface The style of type, eg Garamond, **Helvetica**.

typescript The hard copy (usually a printout) of the manuscript or copy to be reproduced and printed.

typo Short for typographical error, a mistake in the setting introduced by the typesetter. Authors do not make mistakes.

unjustified type 1. Lines of type set so that the right-hand margin does not align vertically and thus appears ragged. This can also be described as 'ranged left' or 'ragged right'. 2. Text that has not been approved by the company lawyer.

upper and lower case Upper case characters are CAPITALS, as opposed to lower case.

verso The left-hand side of a double page spread (even page numbers). The opposite of **recto**.

viral marketing and **viral advertising** Marketing techniques which use social networks that already exist to produce an increase in awareness. Because they use pre-existing (and usually online) social networks, and encourage the spread of word of mouth as a personal communication, they can be a very useful and effective means of reaching a large number of people quickly.

visual (or **mock-up** or **rough layout)** A layout of planned printed work showing the position of all the key elements: headlines, illustrations, bullet points, body copy and so on. Blank 'dummy' books (and, less commonly, magazines) are created for promotional photographs before finished copies are available.

website A **website** (or **web site**) is a collection of Web pages, videos and other digital assets and hosted on a particular domain or subdomain on the World Wide Web. A Web page is a document, typically written in HTML, that is almost always accessible via HTTP, a protocol that transfers information from the website's server to display in the user's Web browser. All publicly accessible websites are seen collectively as constituting the 'World Wide Web' (*see* **www**).

weight of paper Paper is sold in varying weights defined in gsm or g/m2: grams per square metre. Printers can offer you samples of various papers in different weights.

wholesaler An organisation that stores books in bulk, in order to supply other retail outlets quickly and efficiently, often securing higher than usual discounts in return for the large quantities taken. The national bookshop chains, and outlets with large designated markets (eg library suppliers and school suppliers) will similarly demand substantial discounts from the publisher for large quantities of stock taken.

www An abbreviation that takes longer to say than the thing for which it is an abbreviation.

Index